PRESSURE

WITHOUT SANCTIONS

Other books by CHARLES S. LIEBMAN:

Suburban Differences and Metropolitan Policies
The Ambivalent American Jew: Politics, Religion, and Family in American Jewish Life
Aspects of the Religious Behavior of American Jews

PRESSURE
WITHOUT SANCTIONS

The Influence of World Jewry
on Israeli Policy

CHARLES S. LIEBMAN

Rutherford • Madison • Teaneck
Fairleigh Dickinson University Press

London: Associated University Presses

DS
132
L5

Associated University Presses, Inc.
Cranbury, New Jersey 08512

Associated University Presses
Magdalen House
136–148 Tooley Street
London SE1 2TT, England

Library of Congress Cataloging in Publication Data

Liebman, Charles S
Pressure without sanctions.

Bibliography: p.
Includes index.
1.   Israel and the Diaspora.   2.   Israel—Politics and
government.   3.   Religion and state—Israel.   4.   Jews
in the United States—Attitudes toward Israel.
5.   United States—Politics and government—1945–

I.   Title
DS132.L5   327–5694   75–18242
ISBN 0–8386–1791–3

To:
RIVKAH
AARON HILLEL
AVIGAYIL LIBBY

Contents

7

Preface

I began the research for this study convinced that Diaspora Jewry exercised no influence over Israeli public policy. It occurred to me that it would be interesting and important to explore why this is so, given the vast political resources that Diaspora Jewry commands. This question seemed to me an important aspect of Israeli-Diaspora relations and might serve as a useful handle in the exploration of a whole gamut of questions involving Israel and the Diaspora. My central purpose, however, was to focus on the political dimensions of Israeli-Diaspora relations—a dimension that has, heretofore, received virtually no attention.

Part One consists of two chapters that set out the context for the study of the political relations between Israel and the Diaspora in general and the efforts of Diaspora Jewry to influence Israel in particular. The following four chapters constitute Part Two. They focus on various aspects of Israeli public policy and institutions in which and through which Diaspora Jewry attempted or might have attempted to influence policy—religious policy, other domestic policy, foreign policy, and the reconstituted Jewish Agency. I found more attempts that had met with greater success than I had anticipated. But my basic expectation—that Diaspora influence is disproportionately small compared to the political resources it possesses—was fulfilled. Part Three, consisting of three chapters, is both a summary and ex-

planation of Part Two. Chapters 7 and 8 explain the conclusions
at the ideological and sociopsychological, as well as the political
level. The final chapter is an expression of my own conclusions
about the kinds of political relationships that ought to exist
between Israel and the Diaspora.

The choice of the topic stems from my own involvement, personal as well as professional in Israel-Diaspora relationships. I
am a Diaspora Jew who lives in Israel. I first came to Israel in
my teens. At that time I thought that nothing could be more
insulting than to describe another person as a Diaspora Jew
(*Yehudi galuti*—literally a "Jew of the exile"). When I returned
to the United States after finishing high school in Israel, I tried
to fool myself for a while into believing that I was an Israeli
living in America. Now, having lived in Israel again for the past
six years, I have a better idea about myself. I am a Diaspora
Jew. This, I believe, makes me no less proud of Israel or less
committed to her survival. But it does make me different from
many other Israelis. It permits me a sense of wonder at Israel's
very existence, but makes me a little less confident of her future.
I think that in general it makes me a little less provincial than
most Israelis, and a little less self-confident. It makes me a little
less dependent on power and authority as instruments of legitimacy, a little more sensitive to whether my side is the side of
"justice." I think this is true in the context of interpersonal relations as well as in public policy. Perhaps this dichotomy of
Diaspora Jew and Israeli is unfair. Perhaps I am being too self-
righteous. Perhaps I am rationalizing my increasing sense of un-
easiness with the Israeli mentality and personality. Perhaps I am
romanticizing a Diaspora from which I fled in 1969 because of
my conviction that there was little hope for Jewish survival
there. I hardly need add, however, that I find many other Israelis
who are basically Diaspora Jews.

Whether I am being fair or unfair, accurate or inaccurate,
this is my perception of Israel and of myself. I am therefore not
at all unhappy that I am a Diaspora Jew. Consequently, it is
only fitting that I dedicate this book to my children, Rivkah,

Aaron, and Avigayil. They bear my personal vision—to raise a generation of Diaspora Jews in Israel.

The manuscript was completed a few days before the Yom Kippur War of 1973. In preparation for publication I have re-read the manuscript and find no need to revise my conclusions which, if anything, have been strengthened by the Yom Kippur War and subsequent events. No doubt the book would have been enriched by reporting these events in detail, but a book must end somewhere.

Acknowledgments

My research on this manuscript began in 1970. It has been supported by grants from Bar-Ilan's Research Committee. I wish to thank the Research Committee for their generous support. This support made it possible for me to employ Mrs. Mala Tabory as a research assistant. Methodical, meticulous, yet imaginative and critical—I cannot imagine a more competent research assistant than Mala. I am deeply grateful to her. I am also grateful for the assistance I received from the Center for Jewish Community Studies and my colleague in the Political Studies Department of Bar-Ilan University, Eliezer Don-Yichye, who was most helpful in preparation of the chapter on religious policy.

I am also grateful to the following publishers for permission to quote from copyrighted material:

Forum for permission to reprint a revised version of my article "Does the Diaspora Influence Israel? The Case of the Reconstituted Jewish Agency," from the Spring 1975 issue (no. 23), pp. 18-30.

Jewish Social Studies for permission to reprint "Diaspora Influence On Israel: The Ben-Gurion Blaustein 'Exchange' and Its Aftermath," from the July-October 1974 issue (vol. 36), pp. 278-80.

PRESSURE

WITHOUT SANCTIONS

PART 1

The Context for Israel-Diaspora Political Relations

1

Israel and the Diaspora: The Political Dimension

This study is concerned with the extent to which Diaspora Jewry exerts an influence over Israel's public policy. But the question is really a part of a far broader problem, the political relationship between Israel and the Diaspora. The purpose of this chapter is to set the topic in the context of the broader problem that this and, hopefully, future studies will inform: What are, and what ought to be the political relationships between Israel and the Diaspora? Let us begin with a definition of the terms *Israel, Diaspora,* and *political relationships.*

Israel in this study will refer to the State of Israel as distinct from the Land of Israel (Eretz Yisrael) and the people of Israel. There are special sentiments that Jews have about, and attachments to the Land of Israel quite apart from whatever associations they may feel toward the State of Israel. The sentiment that world Jewry holds toward Israel stems in part from the fact that two-and-one-half million Jews live in the country, in part from their sense of pride over the attributes of statehood that Israel possesses, in part from the accomplishments of the people of Israel, but not least because Israel is the Jewish State in the territory of Eretz Yisrael. One cannot always distinguish between ties or relationships of Jews to the State of Israel and to the Land of Israel. Conceptually, however, such distinctions can be made and in many instances, particularly when one comes to evaluate the relationships between Orthodox Jews and Israel, the distinction between Eretz Yisrael and the State of Israel carry important consequences.

Jews outside Israel also relate to the people of Israel on an individual and even an organizational basis. These relationships are interesting and important, but they do not concern us here except insofar as they affect the relationships between the State of Israel and the Jews who live outside the state.

The *Diaspora* (from the Greek word for "dispersion") has sometimes been used to distinguish between communities whose Jewish inhabitants voluntarily lived outside Israel and those communities or epochs referred to in Hebrew as the *Galut* ("exile"), where or when Jews were prevented from settling in the Land of Israel. During the 1940s and 1950s the terms carried heavy ideological overtones. Western, but especially American Jews, including most Zionists, insisted that they lived in the Diaspora. When Israelis referred to them as living in *Galut*, or failed to distinguish between Diaspora communities and *Galut* communities, they sensed unfavorable connotations about their countries of domicile, the nature of their loyalties toward their own countries and the likelihood of their continued security. Things have changed. Neither Israelis nor Diaspora Jews, even non-Zionist Americans, are so sensitive about Jewish loyalties to, say, America; about Jewish security in the United States; or about *aliya* (immigration to Israel). Each side not only understands the position of the other side much better, but has in fact come closer to adopting its position. For example, Israelis understand and to some extent have even learned to appreciate American Jewish loyalty to the United States; they do not believe that the security of American Jews is in imminent jeopardy; and they do not, for the most part, anticipate widescale *aliya* from the United States. American Jews on the other hand, are not the superpatriots they or their parents and grandparents once were; they are no longer outraged by those who question the prospects of their long-term security in the United States; and they do not object to a serious consideration of *aliya* or to raising the question of a Jew's obligation to live in Israel. This is not to suggest that vast differences do not continue to separate the two sides. But the fact is that Israeli and American Jews are closer together today than they were twenty years ago. Indeed, one suspects that Israelis on the one hand, and leaders of such non-Zionist organizations as the American Jewish Committee on the other, share more of a common language on these issues than was true of Israeli and American Zionists twenty years ago.

Before this recent détente, however, Western Jews had won their semantic argument. Indeed, in recent years *Diaspora* has been used as the generic term for all non-Israeli Jewish communities, and it is in that sense that it is used here.

The Diaspora, therefore, is not an institution or a community; it is a concept. It is not organized in any collective sense. It has no decision-making mechanism and no formal representatives. One can perhaps talk about a Diaspora identity that Jews outside Israel share. This is to say that one important dimension that Israel has contributed to the Jewish consciousness of Diaspora Jewry is the sensitivity of many to the fact that they do not live in Israel. This sensitivity, however, has not formed the basis for a mutual identity among Diaspora Jewry, in part because, while many Jews are conscious of the fact that they don't live in Israel, they tend to view this fact from different perspectives. Some feel sorry about it, some defensive, some guilty, some apologetic, some pleased, some expecting to change their status, some expecting their children to go to Israel, and so on. Certainly American Jews do not feel more closely identified with French Jews because neither of them live in Israel. Whatever other consequences a Diaspora consciousness may have, and I believe it has many, it does not lead to a Diaspora political interest.

The Diaspora, in fact, consists of subcommunities that are

themselves loosely organized in some cases and virtually un-
organized in others. Even within each subcommunity Jews do
not always share the same interests and do not necessarily relate
to Israel in the same way.

My use of the phrase *Israeli-Diaspora relationships* will refer,
therefore, to relationships between Israel and subcommunities
or organizations of Diaspora Jews. The organizations and subcommunities are defined as groups of Jews living outside Israel
who sense themselves united to each other through some Jewishly relevant concern.

Political Relationships.[1] Obviously the Diaspora (i.e., the
subcommunities and Jewish organizations within the Diaspora)
does not relate to Israel in the same manner as do two sovereign
states, two subcommunities, or two organizations. Nevertheless
political relationships exist. *Politics* has been variously defined.
One definition widely in vogue views politics as "the authoritative allocation of values."[2] The State is the instrument that can
allocate values authoritatively. Political relationships between
Israel and the Diaspora may exist, therefore, in two senses. First,
Israel, like any other state, has various political values or objectives that it seeks to realize through the instrumentalities of
other states. States seek favorable alliances, protection, grants,
military aid, or general goodwill from other states. In pursuit of
its objectives, Israel receives assistance from various Jewish subcommunities and organizations. Such assistance may involve a
very minimal political relationship, in which both sides cooperate
independently of each other and remain aware of each other's
activities only through the medium of the general press. But
relationships are more likely to be overt. While this is a delicate
matter involving charges of dual loyalty or dual political allegiance, the fact remains that Israel is by no means unique in
carrying on political relationships with citizens of a foreign
state.

There is a second sense in which political relationships may
exist between Israel and the Diaspora. Diaspora Jewry may seek
to realize its values through the instrumentality of Israel. It is

with this type of political relationship that this volume is concerned.

One may of course deny the existence of political relationships by citing certain formulae that have entered the vocabulary of Israeli-Diaspora relationships. This vocabulary, as I hope to demonstrate, is hopelessly inadequate.

In 1950 Israel's Prime Minister David Ben-Gurion, in an exchange of views with the president of the American Jewish Committee, Jacob Blaustein, said:

> The Jews of the United States, as a community and as individuals, have only one political attachment and that is to the United States of America. They owe no political allegiance to Israel. In the first statement which the representative of Israel made before the United Nations after her admission to that international organization, he clearly stated without any reservation, that the State of Israel represents and speaks only on behalf of its own citizens and in no way presumes to represent or speak in the name of the Jews who are citizens of any other country.[3]

Subsequent prime ministers of Israel have endorsed this statement as reflecting both their own views and those of the Government of Israel.

The problem is that statements denying that Diaspora Jewry has political attachments to Israel or owes it political allegiance or denying that Israel speaks for or represents Diaspora Jewry are either inaccurate or, more properly, far too simplistic to comprehend the real political relationships that have developed between Israel and the Diaspora. This is true for many reasons. I shall elaborate upon three.

First, the conditions place an unreasonable limitation on the State of Israel and the Jewish people of Israel. They suggest that Israel, unlike any other state, should not utilize on its own behalf the sentiments that exist among a portion of a foreign population. Friendship leagues between one country and another exist throughout the world. There are British-American or Franco-British or even Israeli-Soviet friendship leagues. They are based on mutual cultural, economic, ideological, racial, religious, and ethnic interests. Virtually every state maintains special relations with these leagues and organizations, which operate to promote their mutual interests. Indeed, a state will often initiate as well as encourage the formation of such friendship leagues and organizations. Why should it be legitimate for importers to promote economic policies that benefit the interests of a foreign country, or for ideologically committed groups to promote friendship between their country and another foreign state with which they identify ideologically, but not be legitimate for Israel to exploit the sense of Jewish peoplehood or the sympathy of Jews to Israel? Of course, one may argue that this is not "political allegiance." But what, then, does "political allegiance" mean? That Israel cannot draft Diaspora Jews into its army? That Israel cannot tax Diaspora Jewry? That there is a qualitative difference in the nature of an Israeli Jew's attachment to Israel compared to the attachment of a Diaspora Jew? Who ever thought otherwise?

Limiting Israel's right to interfere in Diaspora affairs is an unreasonable and impractical limitation on the Jewish people of Israel. If one can talk of a paramount Jewish "interest" or a Jewish "value," it is surely the survival of Jews. Jews desire Jewish survival. In pursuit of Jewish survival, they seek to encourage the sense of Jewish identity among Jews, to further Jewish education, to strengthen the ties among Jews throughout the world and, at a more basic level, to protect Jewish rights, to promote Jewish economic welfare, and to fight anti-Semitism. In the U.S., England, France, and Germany, national Jewish organizations were formed to assist Jews domiciled elsewhere. Since World War II in particular, American Jewish organizations have been active in efforts to help reconstitute Jewish life in many other countries. Samuel Castro, President of the European Council of Jewish Community Services, pointed out that the existence of a more or less structured European Jewish Community was the result of the American Joint Distribution Committee, which not only provided financial assistance but trained lay and professional leaders in community organization, modern financing, and fund-raising methods.[4]

Such activity necessarily involved the interference of Jewish organizations in one country in the internal affairs of Jewish communities in other countries. Furthermore, in defense against anti-Semitism, Jewish organizations have entered into direct relationships with foreign governments on behalf of Jews domiciled in foreign countries and have pressured their own Governments to act on behalf of Jewish interests in other countries. The outcry on behalf of Soviet Jewry and the efforts to use the United States Senate as an instrument in achieving greater freedom for Soviet Jews is only the most recent instance in a long history of such efforts. American Jewish organizations, for example, are proud of their record of both direct and indirect intervention on behalf of Jews outside the United States. Needless to say, on such occasions, American Jewish organizations necessarily claim to speak on behalf of Jews who live outside the United States. And yet, Israel is to be denied this right.

To put it another way, the Jewish people who live in Israel are to be denied the right to insist that *their* Government do what American Jews demand that *their* Government do. Israel is to proscribe itself from activities, such as assistance to Diaspora communities, that Jewish organizations outside Israel permit themselves. The argument is not only inadequate; it is also unrealistic.

The statement that Diaspora Jewry has no political attachment or owes no political allegiance to Israel or that Israel will not speak on behalf of Diaspora Jewry is inadequate for a second reason. The statement assumes that the initiative on behalf of establishing political relationships between Israel and the Diaspora would come from Israel, that it is Israel that would make political demands on Diaspora Jewry, and Israel that would insist on the right to speak on behalf of Diaspora Jewry. But in many instances the role of spokesman and representative has been thrust upon Israel, whether it sought such a role or not, and in some instances even where it sought to avoid it.

Israel's concern has been to establish friendly relations with all Diaspora communities and to strengthen their Jewish identity. But in many instances it is these communities themselves that have turned to the Israeli representative for guidance and instruction, actually soliciting his active interference in Diaspora life.[5] One former Ambassador related in a personal interview how he was forced to reject demands of the Jewish community that he designate its leader. In the late 1940s and early 1950s Israel was as embarrassed as it was heartened by the outpouring of emotion on the part of Soviet Jewry on behalf of Israel. Israel at that stage did virtually nothing to encourage this emotion. Indeed, some even charged that Israel sought to dampen this enthusiasm in its efforts to behave absolutely correctly toward the Soviets in order to retain the favor of the Soviet Government.[6]

On the other hand, in many other countries the government and society recognize Israel as the spokesman and leader of the local Jewish community, and Israel really has no choice in the matter. Natanel Lorch, in recounting his experiences as Israeli Ambassador to Peru, notes that when a Peruvian non-Jew talks to a Peruvian Jew, he will refer to the Israeli Ambassador as "your Ambassador." In an audience that Lorch had with the Catholic hierarchy, the senior Catholic Cardinal referred to Peruvian Jews as "your people."[7] When anti-Greek rioters plundered Jewish property in Istanbul, the Turkish Government thought it perfectly natural to express its regrets to the Government of Israel.[8] One would not expect this to happen in the U.S. or Great Britain.[9] The reason it does not happen more often may have more to do with American or British notions about the propriety of Israeli-Diaspora relations than as to how Americans or British really feel. In point of fact, it is widely believed that Israel sought to influence the American Jewish community to moderate its stance against the war in Vietnam in order to please the American Government. According to a knowledgeable person who prefers to remain anonymous, President Johnson raised the issue of Jewish opposition to the war in Vietnam in conversations with Israeli Prime Minister Levi Eshkol in January 1968. At a meeting of 300 to 400 Jewish leaders in New York, shortly before his return to Israel, Eshkol defended American intervention in Vietnam. The sequence of events suggests recognition by the U.S. of Israel as capable of influencing American Jewish policies on matters that one might have thought to be entirely internal to the American Jewish community. More recently it was reported, for example, that Washington requested Israeli leaders to influence American Senator Henry Jackson to withdraw his proposed amendment that would deny the Soviet Union "most favored nation" treatment unless it permitted its citizens the right to leave.[10] Another report cited a request transmitted through the Israeli Ambassador that Israel exercise its influence on American Jewry to defeat the Jackson amendment.[11]

The U.S. has also sought to use American Jews as a pressure on Israel, or has threatened American Jews, in however subtle a fashion, that America's policies toward Israel were likely to be affected by what American Jews did or did not do in relation to American policy in a different area of interest. One does not know how often these instances occurred, because they do violate the proprieties that govern Israeli-Diaspora relations and even international relations. They are necessarily couched in great secrecy and when overtures are made by one side or the other they tend to be highly informal and conducted through very irregular channels. Nevertheless, it was reliably reported that in February of 1957 American Secretary of State Dulles called in eight leaders of American Jewry. Most of the invitees were non-Zionists who were large contributors and fund-raisers for Israel. Dulles's purpose was to persuade these Jewish leaders to exercise a restraining influence on Israel during a period in which Israeli-Egyptian relations were quite tense.[12]

Ten years later an example of this type of pressure came to the public's attention. In a meeting with leaders of the Jewish War Veterans, President Johnson was reported to be puzzled at the opposition to his Vietnam policies by so many Jewish leaders in view of their eagerness for U.S. support for other small countries such as Israel. According to the press, his visitors came away determined to persuade American Jews "that they could not expect the United States to live up to its commitments to Israel if they opposed respect for much more explicit commitments in Southeast Asia." [13]

The point of all this is that even in the United States, where issues of "dual loyalty" or "unAmerican activity" are most likely to surface, and where Jewish organizations led the fight to deny political attachments between Israel and the Diaspora, the Government itself recognizes the reality and even the legitimacy of these attachments by seeking to utilize them for its own ends. America recognizes that ties between Israel and the Diaspora are far too subtle to be adequately defined or limited by simple formulae pronounced before the United Nations or in official exchanges of views. This is true regardless of how sincerely these statements are meant at the time they are made.

There is a third reason why denying political attachments between Diaspora Jewry and Israel, or denying that Israel has a right to speak on behalf of Diaspora Jewry or interfere in its affairs is inadequate in defining political relationships between Israel and the Diaspora. These statements say nothing about a most significant kind of political relationship—the pursuit by Diaspora Jews of their own political interests within Israel. There are, of course, additional formulae that proscribe this kind of activity as well. Indeed, in the public exchange of views between Ben Gurion and Blaustein referred to above, Blaustein stated:

> Jewish communities, particularly American Jewry in view of its influence and its strength, can offer advice, cooperation and help [to Israelis], but should not attempt to speak in the name of other communities or in any way interfere in their internal affairs.[14]

This has also been the position of the Israeli Government and its leaders—a position that, as we shall see in later chapters, Israel has sought to enforce vigorously. But this too is unrealistic, for technical and ideological reasons.

I shall return to the technical reasons in the chapter on the reconstituted Jewish Agency. Here I note only that the American Jewish gifts to Israel through the United Jewish Appeal represent a major source of income to Israel. These gifts are tax exempt under American law. The tax exemption is possible only so long as Americans exercise control over the expenditure of the funds they raise. The tax-exempt status of American contributions to Israel has come under increasing challenge in the last decade, and for this as well as other reasons American Jewish control over expenditure of American Jewish funds in Israel has been expanded and in all probability will continue to expand. Once a mechanism for influence and authority is created, it tends to generate its own momentum for expansion.

However, a far more important reason is ideological. Jews have so great an interest in Israel and so large a stake in its existence that they want some involvement in its policies. Furthermore, Israel's policies are far too important to Diaspora Jewry for the Diaspora not to want to influence Israel. This results not only from a perceived association of interest but may also arise from a conflict of interest. Precisely because Zionist and Israeli interests as perceived by some, and Diaspora interests as perceived by others may conflict with each other, the Diaspora is concerned with Israeli and Zionist policy. This concern and possible conflict should not be exaggerated. Indeed, the point of this study will be to demonstrate how little conflict actually exists. But there is some, and it necessarily engenders a kind of political relationship for which once again no simple formula can suffice. Since this volume is addressed to a discussion of this kind of relationship, it is well to place the conflict between Israel and the Diaspora in some historical perspective.

ISRAELI-DIASPORA CONFLICT

The creation of Israel added a revolutionary dimension to Jewish public affairs. Nevertheless, the leaders of Israel and the

Zionist movement had a long history of political relationships
with other organizations and subcommunities of Diaspora Jewry.
The difference is that, before the creation of Israel, pressures
were generally from the leaders of the World Zionist Organization
(the "State in the Making" as Herzl called it), seeking to influence
Diaspora Jewry, whereas since 1948, pressures have been more
balanced. But even in the pre-State period there were attempts
by Diaspora Jews both inside and outside the Zionist organization to influence the course of events in Palestine or to influence
leaders of the Yishuv (the Jewish community in Palestine) in
directions that the Yishuv leaders would not have chosen had
they been left to follow their own volition. Behind this conflict
rested, in many instances, the fear that the Yishuv and the Zionist leadership were willing to sacrifice the greater interests of
Diaspora Jewry in pursuit of their own interests.

Almost from its inception Zionism not only pressed its particular claims on the international community but claimed to
speak in the name of the Jewish people. Indeed, its initial success
was in achieving some degree of recognition as *the* authoritative
voice of world Jewry. There is reason to suspect that the Great
Powers even exaggerated Zionist influence within the Diaspora.
As a result, what Zionists did and said had consequences for
Jews everywhere. The bitterness with which Zionists were attacked by their Jewish opponents in the West stemmed not only
from the latter's opposition to the reconstitution of a Jewish
national homeland, but from their fears that Zionists' demands
would reflect on their national loyalty. Zionists became all the
more threatening as they took independent action within the
countries where their opponents lived.

History cannot but judge the anti-Zionists with narrow self-
interest and blindness. The "Jewish" credentials of most anti-
Zionists are badly tarnished. This is true of the Bundists committed to revolution and class warfare who pitted Jew against
Jew; wealthy notables who were far more concerned with their
standing in Gentile society than with the needs of the Jewish
people; or even the Orthodox anti-Zionists who passively ac-

cepted their social and political environment, who remained largely indifferent to the abysmal conditions of East European Jewry, and who only aroused themselves to concerted activity by threats to their spiritual hegemony from within the Jewish community. It is well to note, therefore, that much of the criticism of Zionist activities was motivated by base motives, hardly in the interest of the Jewish people. Nevertheless, there were those not only outside but even among the ranks of the Zionists who felt that the actions of Zionist and/or Yishuv leaders were in conflict with the larger interests of the Jewish people.

Any decision involves choices between alternative courses of action whose consequences are not without some ambiguity. There have been, and are likely to be, numerous instances where what is good for one portion of world Jewry is not good for another portion. In making decisions between alternatives one must also weigh relative costs. Zionists were accused in the past of having a distorted concept of relative costs—of placing too high a value on achieving their own goals and too low a value on the interest of local Jewish communities; of being too quick to conclude that, since the Jewish condition in the Diaspora was hopeless, it was a waste of resources to aid and assist the Diaspora communities.

An early example of a conflict of interest between Zionism and Diaspora occurred around the question of Jewish immigration to England at the turn of the century. English public opinion was concerned with the steady influx of East European Jews into England, and in 1902 the British Government appointed a Royal Commission to investigate the question.[15] Zionists sought and finally succeeded in having Herzl invited to testify before the Royal Commission "in the belief [that] that would have a tremendous effect." [16] It was Nathaniel Meyer Rothschild, only Jewish member of the Commission, who objected to Herzl's appearance before the Commission. He told Herzl that he was being invited "so that the opponents of the Jews might be able to say, 'Dr. Herzl is undoubtedly the best Jew, and it is his opinion that a Jew can never become an

Englishman.' " [17] Rothschild requested that Herzl not raise the
specter of Jewish discontent in Eastern Europe because, should
the Commission become aware of the hopeless condition of that
Jewry, "it will lead to restrictive laws." But Herzl refused. He
told Rothschild:

> I would be a wicked sort of person if I would say only that
> which might lead to the restriction of immigration. But I
> would be one of those wicked persons to whom the English
> Jews ought to raise a monument, because I would be protect-
> ing them from an influx of eastern Jews and therefore perhaps
> from anti-Semitism. But I have a plan of help, and I want to
> submit that to the Commission.[18]

Herzl's solution was to find some place for Jews other than
England. Herzl was willing to utilize the British desire for
restrictive immigration to press for a Zionist solution. He
balanced the risk of raising questions that might result in restrictive immigration against the hope that it would lead the British
Government to adopt Zionist proposals.[19] Even if one accepts
the judgment that it was a good risk that the Royal Commission
would not propose restrictive immigration without also proposing some alternative solution, one wonders why nobody thought
it worthwhile to consider the wishes of the vast majority of East
European Jews, who surely preferred England to any alternative
Herzl might persuade the British to consider. Fortunately or
unfortunately, the Zionists were organized, the British-Jewish
establishment was organized, but the masses of East European
Jewry were without a voice.

The willingness of Zionists to cooperate with everyone, including anti-Semites, in order to achieve their objectives, was
troubling to many non-Zionists. Non-Zionists suspected, and
with some justice, that Zionists and anti-Semites agreed about
the Jewish condition in the Diaspora. Herzl's warnings often
sounded very much like those of anti-Semites. He was not
above threatening countries of the West such as Austria that
unless they helped secure a Jewish homeland, they would be
inundated by Jews from the East. But the Zionist solution,

he said, would "eliminate a latent but constantly erupting trouble." [20] Both the Zionists and anti-Semites believed that Jews were and would always remain strangers in the lands where they were domiciled and therefore the only solution to the Jewish question was either total assimilation (many anti-Semites were willing to accept assimilated Jews on the assumption that they also converted) or emigration. As long as Zionists sought to achieve their ultimate objectives in the short run, it also allied them, at least theoretically, with those anti-Semites who objected to strengthening the Jewish position, materially and/or culturally, in the lands in which they were domiciled. This was expressed in Herzl's 1903 meeting with Plehve, Russian Minister of the Interior, whom Jews held responsible for the Kishineff pogroms.

There were two aspects of that meeting that might have led to the feeling that Herzl permitted Zionist interests to displace larger Jewish interests. First, there was the very fact that the meeting took place. Bein notes that "this journey of Herzl's to Russia was bitterly condemned later on: no Jewish leader, it was said, should have negotiated with Plehve. . . ." [21] In this respect, however, it is difficult to sympathize with Herzl's detractors. If some good could come of the meeting, why should it not take place? But in another respect, criticism of Herzl seems more legitimate. One of the issues that divided the Zionists themselves was cultural versus political work. It was Herzl who stressed that Zionist activity must be devotel to securing a charter to permit Jewish settlement of Palestine. This type of activity was preeminently political. Others, however, who looked to Ahad Ha'am as their mentor, stressed the necessity for cultural activity to arouse the Jewish people to a sense of mutual responsibility and to rekindle their national loyalties. Plehve informed Herzl that "we used to be sympathetic to your Zionist movement, as long as it worked toward emigration . . . but . . . there is less talk now of Palestinian Zionism than there is about culture, organization and Jewish nationalism." [22] Herzl responded by drawing an analogy to a revolt of sailors against their captain.

"Help me to reach land sooner," he told Plehve, "and the revolt will end. And so will the defection to the Socialists." [23]

As Bein notes, "Herzl skillfully exploited Plehve's concern over the foreign reaction to the Kishineff pogrom to obtain his tolerance, and even support, of the Zionist movement if it returned to its old program of action." [24]

One cannot help wondering whether Herzl might not have gained greater benefits for Russian Jewry had he exploited Plehve's concern over foreign reactions for more general Jewish objectives. In fact, however, Herzl wrote to Lord Rothschild that it would be preferable "if the pro-Jewish papers stopped using such an odious tone toward Russia. We ought to try to work toward that end in the near future." [25] Second, by using Plehve as a weapon against the cultural Zionists who were concerned with spiritual survival of Russian Jewry, was not Herzl again sacrificing greater Jewish interests for the benefit of the much smaller group of Russian Jews who wanted to leave the country? The argument reminds one of the 1971 controversy over Nahum Goldmann's statement that world Jewry must concern itself with the cultural rights of Soviet Jewry within the Soviet Union rather than focusing exclusively on the rights of Soviet Jews to emigrate to Israel. In the controversy that erupted over these remarks, Goldmann was denounced by the Zionist and Israeli establishment and an invitation to him to present the opening address to the World Zionist Congress then about to convene was withdrawn. Goldmann, a former president of the World Zionist Organization, might have been wrong for tactical reasons in saying what he did. One might have argued that neither the best interests of world Jewry nor of Russian Jewry would be served by anything but exclusive focus on emigration. But the manner in which the Zionist protagonists dealt with the opposition in 1903 and in 1971 suggests that not strategies but values were at issue. And, in both these instances, it is clear that Zionists were opposing their own values to those of the majority of local Jews.

One might argue that Herzl was justified in acting as he did because a non-Zionist position was really not articulated. In the British immigration instance, Herzl's opponent, Lord Rothschild, finally accepted his stand. In the Russian instance Herzl had only to contend with internal Zionist opposition. He might well have argued that as between himself and Ahad Ha'am, his position was the more popular one among Russian Jews. But there have been instances when Zionists have placed their own interests above those of the organized Jewish world and have not hesitated to press their own interests even when it should have been quite clear that they were acting against the wishes, if not the interest of the Jewish majority. Indeed, at the 1935 meeting of the World Zionist Congress itself, it became clear according to some "that it would not always be possible in the near future to reconcile the Zionist political course with that required for the defense of the Jewish position in the lands of the Diaspora." [26] Some governments adopted a favorable attitude toward Zionism while pursuing a domestic policy of Jewish discrimination, and the Zionist organization was not free to adopt a militant stand against these governments.[27]

Zionist attitudes toward Nazi Germany were especially troublesome to many. On August 23, 1933, an agreement between Germany and Syria-Palestine was announced, providing that Germany would import eight to ten million marks' worth of Jaffa oranges and that Palestine and Syria were to receive twenty million marks' worth of German industrial products, to be shipped on German vessels. Coinciding with these agreements was one between the Anglo-Palestine Bank and Germany in which Jews desiring to emigrate from Germany could take up to six million marks' worth of wares and merchandise. Jews would turn their money over to a special Reichsbank fund and then be compensated in goods. This agreement, known as the Transfer Agreement, had been reached between the Nazis and Chaim Arlosoroff, representing the Jewish Agency.[28] In September 1933 the second World Jewish Conference convened. (The Conference was really a preliminary meeting to the convening and establishing of a World Jewish Congress, which was eventually

formed in 1935.) The 1933 World Jewish Conference unanimously adopted a resolution calling for a global boycott on all German goods. Stephen Wise, American Zionist leader and the
moving force in the creation of the World Jewish Congress,
termed the Transfer Agreement a "new golden calf—the golden
orange." [29] Wise's allusion was to the benefits that the Yishuv
would derive by securing a market for their oranges and the
benefits their economy would derive by permitting German Jews
to leave Germany for Palestine along with goods and merchandise. Of course, nobody in 1933 believed that German Jews faced
serious physical danger. The German Jewish Community certainly did not believe so. The agreement, on the other hand, was of
great importance to Germany, as we shall see. But Wise, and
others like him, were incensed that the Zionist leadership was
defusing the only real weapon that Diaspora Jewry might hold
over Nazi Germany in order to mitigate Hitler's anti-Semitic
policies. Wise said:

> I think I speak the mind of Jews everywhere when I say we
> hold in abhorrence any Jew, whether in or out of Palestine,
> who undertakes to make commercial arrangement with the
> Nazi government for any reason whatsoever.[30]

All evidence points to the fact that Germany feared an
economic boycott in 1933. Indeed, the German Consul in Palestine supported the Transfer Agreement as a way of breaking the
boycott. The Gestapo representative in Palestine in 1935 wrote
that a Boycott Conference scheduled to take place in London
was torpedoed from Tel Aviv. Acknowledging the influence of
the Zionists in world Jewish politics, and perhaps taking more
credit than was his due, the Gestapo representative nevertheless
felt justified in defining his "main function" to his superiors as
preventing "from Palestine, the unification of world Jewry on a
basis hostile to Germany." [31] The German Consul in Palestine
also made it clear that those Zionist leaders responsible for the
Transfer Agreement prevented "the adoption of a resolution

calling for a boycott of Germany at the Zionist Congress held in Prague in September 1933." [32]

Yigal Ilam, in his recent monograph on Zionist history, concludes that it was the desire to strengthen the economic position of the Yishuv rather than the desire to save Jewish property in the Diaspora that lay behind the Transfer Agreement. He quotes Sharett (then Shertok) as saying:

> On this matter there is a conflict between the Diaspora and Palestine. . . . The fate of Zionism is, on occasion, to be cruel to the Diaspora, when the upbuilding of the land requires it. [33]

Berl Katznelson is quoted as saying:

> Herzl saw the whole war against anti-Semitism and anti-Semites as destined to sterility and therefore demanded the concentration of all our powers in the efforts toward upbuilding the land and in public policies directed toward saving of Jewish lives and upbuilding. [34]

According to Ilam, from its very outset Zionism

> cut itself off from considerations tied to the condition of the Jewish people in the Diaspora, except to the extent that they could contribute to the Zionist effort. [35]

Even the saving of Jewish lives might conflict with the interests of the Yishuv, and in such cases the decisions of Zionist leaders were not always as unambiguous as one might have hoped. *Aliya,* immigration of Jews to Palestine, not only fulfilled the vision that Zionism shared with the religious tradition—the gathering of the exiles in the Land of Israel—it also served the purposes of the Yishuv itself by increasing the number of Jews relative to the number of Arabs and providing manpower for settling new areas in Palestine, thereby bringing them under effective Jewish control. Settlers in Palestine, as Ben Halpern has noted, were inclined to regard immigration as a solution to *their* problem. [36] But, when it served their purposes, in the 1920s and 1930s Zionists adopted a policy of selective immigration. They were attacked for this by the Zionist opposition who favored mass evacuation of the Jewish populations of Poland and Rumania.[37] Ilam notes notes that no Zionist leader opposed mass immigration on principle, but many expressed their reservations about the nature of the *aliya* and the relative importance of saving Jewish lives as opposed to the needs of the Yishuv. Citing the 1935 meetings of the Zionist Actions Committee in Jerusalem, he notes that Yitzchak Tabenkin, a labor Zionist leader talked about the "private home" (the Land of Israel) as being more important than the "general home" (world Jewry). In his autobiography, Weizmann notes that his derogatory comments about the middle-class immigrants during the 1920s earned him the hatred of many Polish Jews, particularly the religious ones. He complains that these immigrants

> were little disposed to pull their weight in a new country. A few, in their struggle for existence, showed antisocial tendencies; they seemed never to have been Zionists, and saw no difference between Palestine as a country of immigration and, for instance, the United States. Many of them had no knowledge of Hebrew, and it was soon being said, rather ruefully, that at this rate Tel-Aviv would soon be a Yiddish-speaking town. Even to the casual observer, the new immigration carried with it the atmosphere of the ghetto. In the end, I felt that I had to give warning. . . . I feared that in the early stages of our growth a too-high proportion of them might unduly weight the balance.[38]

Utilizing a religious metaphor that contrasts "the world to come" with the life of "here and now," always to the favor of the former, Weizmann was quoted as saying ". . . Zionism is the eternal life, and compared to this, the saving of thousands of Jews, is only the here and now." [39]

Policy formation with respect to mass immigration continued to trouble the Zionist leadership after creation of the State of Israel. Even then, despite the desperate need for increasing the number of Jews, it was clear that not all immigrants were able to make a contribution to the welfare of Israel. In the 1950s a selective system of immigration was in force with respect to immigrants from Morocco. Each family was permitted to immigrate only if there was a father or son between the ages of 18 to 45 capable of earning a living for all and in good health. The entire family was rejected if any member was paralytic, mentally ill, or afflicted with a serious, incurable, or contagious disease.[40]

A system of quotas was also in effect for North African Jewry to control the rate of immigration. North African Zionist leaders demanded a policy of mass immigration instead of quotas because, in their opinion, the impending independence of North African countries might result in the prohibition of emigration. Significantly, it was Nahum Goldmann who said, "For me, the economic stability of Israel . . . tops the list of priorities even if it should mean that the transfer of Moroccan Jews should take a decade or even two." [41]

This policy did not go unopposed. North Africans in Israel demonstrated against what they felt was the complacency of Government and Zionist leaders. The Knesset itself approved a resolution stating that emigration of North African Jewry was the only solution to their problems and insisting that the Government present a program for increased immigration and absorption.[42] At the 1954 meetings of the Zionist General Council, Mapam (a party of the left) unsuccessfully submitted an amendment resolving "to discontinue the policy of selection of immigrants." [43] In defense it was argued that invalids were permitted to come in cases where immigration of an entire community occurred. But:

> it would be equally wrong to arrange for emigration to Israel of the invalids and the aged from countries from which the number of immigrants is not large and thereby to free the local wealthy Jews of their responsibilities for the maintenance of hospitals and old-age homes. Of course, when a whole family migrates to Israel a single member of that family cannot be left behind. But we cannot bring only the sick to this country and leave the healthy and the wealthy members of the community behind.[44]

It was easy and I should add even popular for the opposition to criticize this policy. In all fairness, one must bear in mind both the severe economic conditions prevailing in Israel in the 1950s and the leadership's evaluation of the condition of North African Jewry. They did not foresee an immediate crisis. According to Berl Locker, then chairman of the Zionist Executive, Israel would bring in immigrants even at the expense of endangering the structure of its economy if they judged the situation as reaching a crisis.[45] On the other hand, one's definition of a crisis depends on how one wants to evaluate. Zionist and Israeli leaders denied that one existed. A representative of the French Zionist Federation declared in impassioned tones:

> I turn to you with the call: Don't be so smart, so careful; if you had always been so careful the State of Israel would not have arisen; exert yourselves on behalf of immigration of Moroccan and Tunisian Jewry.[46]

At the 24th Zionist Congress in 1956 the opposition levelled more serious charges with regard to the leadership's evaluation of whether North African Jewry did or did not confront a crisis. According to them, a member of the Zionist Executive had stated, in Committee, that the 300,000 Jews in North Africa were threatened and that 100,000 must be brought out immediately. However, Goldmann and Josephthal (another Zionist leader) requested that no numbers be mentioned in the Committee resolution because there was no money to bring that many North Africans to Israel. According to Goldmann only 15,000 North African Jews could be brought out. The majority of the Committee agreed. When these charges were made on the floor of the Zionist Congress, they were denied by the Committee chairman.[47]

True or not, there is no question that Israeli and world Zionist leaders found themselves in conflict with spokesmen for the Diaspora community in question. North African Zionists demanded an increase in immigration quotas from about 3,500 to 5,000 a month and the easing of selective immigration policies.

They agreed that immigrants with incurable or contagious diseases should be denied entrance but they found especially objectionable the policy of denying immigration to a family with a healthy mother and children, only because the father was sick or over 45. [48]

The leadership replied that the problem was money. According to one member of the Zionist Executive, if the representatives of various Zionist organizations would rise and assume responsibility for immigration of so many thousand immigrants, the Zionist Executive would support them and help raise the money.[49] But since there were no resources to bring all the healthy Jews, a policy of no selection would mean only bringing sick in place of healthy immigrants and relieving the wealthy Jews in North Africa of their responsibility.[50]

There is no intention in all of the foregoing to cast aspersions on the moral commitment of Zionist or Israeli leaders. It would surely be unfair to judge them without a prior knowledge of all the facts. The point here is not to allocate blame but merely to indicate that there was a very real conflict of interest between Israel and North African Jews, as Israelis and North African Jews perceived their interests, and that, not surprisingly, Israel favored its own interest above those of a Diaspora community.

There are other instances of conflict, though none so well documented. Israel has been charged with excessive caution in pressing the problem of Soviet Jewry in the 1950s and early 1960s in order to attain Soviet support for Israeli foreign policy. According to an observer:

> It might be said that Israel's hope of altering the Soviet imbalance in favoring the Arab world created an Israeli neutralism with respect to the status of the Jews in the USSR. Israel had long maintained a discreet distance, and her relationship with the Soviet Union's Jewish community even became a political liability when the USSR from time to time would accuse the Israel diplomats of seeking to use the synagogue as an espionage base.[51]

According to foreign affairs observer Louis Shub, Israel changed her posture in 1965 because the Soviet Union's continued pro-Arab stance demonstrated that Israel had nothing to gain by her silence on Soviet Jewry, and Israel could not continue to maintain her silence in the face of world Jewry's "increasing solicitude, whatever Israel's reservations may have been with respect to the effect on her relations with the USSR." [52]

The interests of another Diaspora community were juxtaposed to those of Israel in the case of South Africa, which I shall discuss in greater detail below. Briefly, Israel had to choose between condemning South Africa for its policy of *apartheid,* thereby endangering the security of South Africa's Jews, and refusing to condemn South Africa, thereby endangering its cordial relations with other African states.

It is obvious from the foregoing that conflicts of interest can and do exist between Israel and the Diaspora and that these conflicts are political in the sense that each side seeks to impose its values as authoritatively as it can over the other. That which Israel would like Diaspora Jewry to do, or that which Diaspora Jewry would like Israel to do, is not necessarily what each would do were it not subject to influence by the other. The concern here is with conflict—with those instances in which differences arise between Israel or governmental agencies within Israel and Diaspora Jewry or subcommunities and organizations of Diaspora Jewry. The specific concern will be with the efforts of Diaspora Jewry to influence Israel, that is, to encourage it to adopt policies that it would not adopt were it not for the efforts of Diaspora Jewry.

There have been some proposals to regularize the political relationships and provide more explicit political instruments for their expression. The first proposals all took it for granted that the Zionists would represent Diaspora Jewry. The most radical suggestion to receive a hearing was raised by Dr. Manfred Reiffer on the pages of the Zionist weekly *Ha' Olam.* Reiffer proposed in 1948 that Israel adopt a two-house legislature with a Senate, half of whose membership would be appointed by the World Zionist Organization.[53] Reiffer's proposal received little echo. During the 1950s and 1960s Nahum Goldmann, who as leader of both the World Zionist Organization and the World Jewish Congress was the preeminent leader of the organized international Jewish community, pressed for a greater voice for Diaspora Jewry in Israeli policy decisions. In an address before the 1971 annual meeting of the American Jewish Committee, William Frankel, editor of the *Jewish Chronicle* of London (the best and probably most influential Jewish weekly in the world), noted the conflicts of interest between Israel and the Diaspora and the fact that what Israel does has repercussions on the Diaspora. He noted the need to bring to Israel's attention the opinion of world Jewish leaders and suggested a "consultative assembly of Jewish leaders on the best and most representative level to meet regularly with Israel's leaders and to communicate to them Jewry's opinion on those subjects which, as I say, are their legitimate concern." [54] He felt that the Zionist Organization could not serve this function since its leaders were too old, its representation too narrow, and even the reconstituted Jewish Agency was more Israeli than Diaspora-oriented.

What, in fact, Frankel was proposing was some kind of a world Jewish structure in which Israel would not be represented, in order that a Diaspora interest could somehow crystallize and then be presented before Israeli leadership. The problem with all of the present international Jewish organizations is that thy are either dominated by or so influenced by Israeli representatives that a true Diaspora point of view never emerges. It is not at all clear that such a point of view would emerge even without Israeli participation. It is not at all clear, as I suggested earlier, that there is such a thing as a single Diaspora interest as opposed to an Israeli interest. But there is certainly no instrument at present which would allow the crystallization of such an interest.

In the final chapter I shall return to a consideration of proposals to provide the Diaspora with such a voice. But even in the absence of institutionalized channels of political influence, Diaspora voices were not entirely silenced. The Diaspora does indeed speak. The nature and power of its voice will be the main consideration of the chapters that follow.

2
Mutual Dependence

Is Israel so important to Diaspora Jewry that we might anticipate a political interest on the part of Diaspora Jews in Israeli policies? Second, does Diaspora Jewry command sufficient political resources to effectuate its demands? In other words, is the Diaspora so important to Israel that the latter must take account of the demands of the former? Superficially, at least, the answer to both these questions, which are explored in this chapter, is Yes. Israeli-Diaspora relations are best expressed in the concept *interdependence,* which assumes a variety of forms.

ISRAEL'S IMPORTANCE TO THE DIASPORA

What is Israel's importance to the Diaspora? To answer that question properly one must distinguish between the part of world Jewry that lives under conditions of stress and the part that lives under conditions of freedom. To the former (Jews of Arab and most Communist-dominated countries), Israel represents the major direct and indirect support in their battle for physical and spiritual survival. Paradoxically, Israel's existence is also a major cause for the acute distress in which Jews of Arab coun-

44

tries find themselves. Jews have lived under conditions of stress in Arab countries, but if it were not for the existence of Israel and the enmity of the Arab States toward it, it is unlikely that the Jews of those countries would suffer to the extent they do today.[1] On the other hand, under Israel's leadership, world opinion has been mustered to protest outrages against Jewish persons and property. These campaigns on behalf of Arab and Soviet Jews have met, in some instances and in some periods, with success. A prime example was the campaign on behalf of the 2,500 Jews of Iraq. After June of 1967 Iraqi Jews lived under severe economic prohibitions and fear of arrest, torture, and death. These repressions reached their climax in public hangings in 1969. Israel was instrumental in galvanizing world public opinion and under this pressure the condition of Iraqi Jews improved and the majority were permitted to leave. In October 1972 new arrests and murders prompted Israel to undertake a new campaign on behalf of Iraqi Jews. Efforts to mitigate the repression of Syrian Jews have been less successful. On the other hand, efforts on behalf of Soviet Jews have met with some success. Israel has been a catalyst in worldwide efforts to obtain the release of imprisoned Soviet Jews and to gain permission for Soviet Jews to leave the Soviet Union. There have been other, less publicized, activities on behalf of Jews in Arab countries and the Soviet Union that have borne fruit, but about which, from their very nature, little is known other than the fact that they were directed from Israel.

Israel is important therefore in providing for the security of the portion of world Jewry that lives under conditions of stress. But it is even more critical in terms of their survival as Jews. For large portions of Soviet Jewry, particularly the estimated one-and-three-quarter million Jews of the Russian, Ukrainian, Byelorussian, and Moldavian Republics—that is, not the more traditional Jews of the Central Asian and Caucasian Republics (Georgia, Armenia, Kazakhstan, etc.) or the western Republics annexed during the 1940s (Latvia, Lithuania, and Estonia)— Israel's survival and success is the catalyst to their own desire for survival as Jews. Concern for and about Israel is the pivot of their own Jewish expression and identity.

Many Jews who live under conditions of freedom also feel that their survival as Jews is linked to Israel's existence. The fact that it is more difficult to explain this phenomenon in the West makes it no less true. No one has put the case more forcefully than the social commentator and critic Milton Himmelfarb, a "non-Zionist." Speaking of American Jewry, he said:

> The Jews' overriding foreign-policy interest is Israel. More accurately, our overriding interest of any kind is Israel. If—which God forbid—Israel should cease to exist, do we not know in our bones that the Jews would cease to exist? We have not in us the stuff of our *galut* ancestors, and what they were able to do in the absence of a Jewish state we and our descendants will be unable to do; for we are barely able to do it in the presence of a Jewish State.
>
> American Jews and Israelis must agree with Ben-Gurion: It is not that the Jews are for the sake of Israel but that Israel is for the sake of the Jews.[2]

Others go even further and attribute the security of American Jewry to Israel's existence. Putting less stress on "will" to survive and more on physical well-being, Richard Hirsch, executive director of the World Union for Progressive Judaism (the international organization of Reform Jewish Synagogues), said:

> For us, the Middle East represents a domestic issue, for there is a direct relationship between the security of the State of Israel and the sense of security of the Jews in the United States.[3]

Perhaps this statement is extravagant. But Himmelfarb and even Hirsch were expressing beliefs widely held within the American Jewish community and shared, as we shall see by Western European and Latin American Jewry as well. It is, therefore, no surprise that Israel is a matter of vital concern to the Diaspora. Israel is the necessary condition for their own existence.

Israel, however, is important to Diaspora Jewry in other

respects. The very effort made by Diaspora Jews on behalf of
Israel contributes to Jewish survival. One commentator observed:

> the American Jewish community is alive today in no small
> measure because of its great task of supporting and helping to
> create another society and another state. That task has been
> keeping the American Jewish Community going. Fund raising
> has made a life not only for Israel but for American Jews.[4]

Although American Jewish identity is preeminently "religious" rather than "national," it has been argued that Israel has
increasingly become the content or expression of Jewish religious identity.[5] As other foci of Jewish expression—such as the
fight against anti-Semitism, social justice, Jewish peoplehood,
theology and belief, and synagogue activity—receded in importance during the 1960s, Israel remained one of the few legitimate
outlets for Jewish expression. Its importance, in turn, increased
because of the real stakes in its existence; because of the rein-
forcement to its importance through attention from the mass
media; because it became for some a substitute for their ideal-
ized version of Jewish life in Eastern Europe before the holocaust; and because of the rewards that Israel is able to bestow
on its supporters.

Observers make many of the same observations about West
European Jewry that were made about American Jewry. In 1967
Arnold Mandel, literary editor of *L'Arche*, the leading Jewish
periodical in the French language, and a foremost commentator
on European Jewry, observed that a new major psychological
manifestation cuts across all Jewish communities of Western
Europe. It is, he noted,

> the substitution, as a bond uniting all Jews, of a sentiment for
> Israel and anything affecting the state, for religious feeling.
> . . . As a matter of fact, the sentiment for Israel can be
> regarded as religious, for its content and expression are of a
> truly religious character.[6]

According to the President of the European Council of Jewish
Community Services, "European Jewry's present and future are

. . . related to Israel's life, security and perspectives; no meaning for Israel in a world without Diaspora, no existence possible for a Diaspora without Israel." [7]

In a study of Jewish identification among British students, the author notes that Jewish students display their Jewish identification most strongly in relation to Israel. He concludes that there is nothing that unites, concerns, and identifies Jewish students in England as a group more than their relationship to Israel. This, he observes, is not a phenomenon unique to England, nor does he believe it to be a temporary one.[8] Similarly, an observer of South African Jewish students notes that the facts "seem to point quite clearly to the conclusion that students identify as Jews to a greater extent through attachment to Israel than through ethnocentric sentiments, or through alignment with the local community." [9]

Similar notions are expressed by Latin American Jews, whose community leaders deny that any differentiation is possible between Zionism and Judaism.[10]

I have indicated the critical importance and hence the dependence of Diaspora Jewry on Israel—at least in the eyes of many observers. But it is important to understand the nature of the dependence. It is really Israel's survival that is desperately important, primarily, I suggest, because Israel is the preeminent Jewish symbol. Israel, therefore, is recognized as important less for what it *does* than for what it *is*. Israel is important because it is Israel. Whether, therefore, Diaspora Jewry could really not survive without Israel is a moot question, the answer to which one hopes we shall never learn. But theoretically, Diaspora Jewry could survive without Israel as long as it could find a substitute symbol. The fact that the Diaspora does not realize that substitute symbols might be available only demonstrates the strength of Israel as a symbol. Indeed, no symbol of any consequence is ever consciously or existentially grasped as a symbol. If it were, it would lose its vitality. Nevertheless, not even the crassest skeptic can be certain that equally compelling symbols could be found to substitute for Israel. And whether they could be found or not, Israel as a symbol is *sensed* as crucial to Jewish survival. It therefore evokes particular forms of activity and behavior that themselves reinforce Jewish survival. I return to this question, with its implications for Diaspora political influence, in chapter 7.

Paradoxically, while Israel's importance is perceived by Diaspora Jews in symbolic form, and while they tend, therefore, to stress its importance in the sense of Jewish loyalty, allegiance, and unity that it evokes, Israel makes contributions of a far more material sort. Besides the physical protection and security it offers to portions of Diaspora Jewry, it makes concrete contributions to Jewish identity and education, both directly and indirectly. Indirectly, those who read about Israel, hear about Israel, and especially those who visit Israel learn not only about Israel but about Judaism. Directly, Israel supports Jewish education and culture in the Diaspora.

The needs of the Diaspora are expressed in the World Zionist Organization's own budget. Although income of the World Zionist Organization comes from the Diaspora, expenditures are, in fact, dictated by individuals whose first loyalty is to Israel. Israel does not entirely dictate how the World Zionist Organization should spend its money but it could probably insist successfully that a greater portion of funds be spent for the needs of the State. To those in positions of decision, Israel's needs and desires are paramount. It is therefore of some consequence that a large portion of World Zionist Organization (WZO) income is spent on behalf of Diaspora Jewry. Precisely how much is difficult to determine. For example, in addition to educational, cultural, and youth activities in the Diaspora, the WZO has undertaken a program called "Tur Vaaleh." This program subsidizes trips to Israel of potential immigrants from Western countries who can explore job opportunities in the country before they actually make a decision to immigrate. Its purpose is to encourage immigration. In fact, however, many if not most of those who take advantage of this and similar programs decide against immigration. In the interim, however, they have deepened their understanding of Israel and their own Jewish horizons, have met other committed Jews and have undergone, however vicariously, a profound Jewish experience. The program "Sherut La'am," an Israeli version of the Peace Corps, encourages young people to spend a year in Israel in voluntary labor. "The impact of this program is almost entirely in the realm of broadening the Jewish education and experience of the youth involved.

While the absolute sums involved are not great, they reflect concern and activity on behalf of Diaspora Jewry, which has no substitute. Whereas the Diaspora itself supplies the money which is simply channeled through the WZO, the Diaspora has neither the manpower nor the organized knowhow to substitute for the activities that the WZO or Israeli agencies and institutions perform, especially in the educational sphere. This is true not only of WZO activity, but of other Israeli institutions as well. For example, there are summer seminars in Israel for American Jewish communal workers. These seminars are paid for by American Jewry. The costs to Israel are incidental. But American Jewry can not provide the manpower to staff these seminars so effectively as Israel. The same is true for other types of support that Israel offers the Diaspora, even where such support involves relatively minor financial burdens. The teachers, communal workers, camp counselors, and youth leaders whom Israel sends abroad are a basic factor in Jewish survival in many countries of the world.

In addition, Israeli cultural exports (books, records, art objects, etc.), provide an important component of Jewish culture in the Diaspora. To some they provide virtually the sole content of Jewish culture. To others they provide only a part, albeit in many cases a significant part of the Jewish content of their lives.

Israel, therefore, is enormously important to Diaspora Jewry. However, my suggestions about the nature of its importance already raise questions as to whether the Diaspora's stake in

Israel is likely to be translated into concern over its public policies and hence into political pressure. This point will be discussed in subsequent chapters.

THE DIASPORA'S IMPORTANCE TO ISRAEL

It is difficult to categorize, much less measure Israel's dependence on Diaspora Jewry, but I shall try. Israelis are very conscious of this dependence. Indeed, there would be no Israel without Diaspora Jewry. This statement, at one level, is a tautology, since virtually all Israelis are descendants of someone who came from the Diaspora. But even the 650,000 Jews who lived in Israel in 1948 could not have withstood the pressure from their Arab neighbors if it were not for the additional one-and-one-half million Jews who have entered the country since then.

But it is not only as a source of *aliya* that made Israel so dependent on the Diaspora. Nor is Israel's dependence on *aliya* simply a result of its need for more manpower for military and economic growth. Let us begin with the latter point.

Aliya is important to Israel for psychological reasons, which are perhaps no less compelling than economic and military factors. Many Israelis, especially the elite, justify their own sacrifices and legitimate the very existence of the state as the creation of an instrument to bring Diaspora Jewry back to its ancestral homeland. The Knesset defined the "central task of the State of Israel" as "the mission of the Ingathering of the Exiles." [12]

If Diaspora Jewry, of its own choice, should lose all concern with *aliya*, Israel, for most of its present leadership, would have lost its *raison d'être*. Unquestionably this would bring in its wake a profound value crisis, sufficient to weaken and perhaps even destroy the state from within. A sense of that crisis and the consequent erosion of Israeli values and loyalties did occur in the 1950s and again in the 1960s when *aliya* fell. But important to Israelis as *aliya* is, they also depend on the Diaspora qua Diaspora. This dependence is economic, political, and psychological.

Economic Dependence

It is impossible to arrive at a precise figure that measures the contribution of Diaspora Jewry to Israel, but some notion of its importance can be ascertained from data gathered in various studies. Michael Brecher, relying on data presented by Halevi and Klinov-Malul, noted that world Jewry accounted for 59.2% of Israel's six-billion-dollar cumulative import surplus from 1948 to 1965.[12] Furthermore, most of the remaining 40.8% came from U.S. aid and German reparations funds, which might not have been so large except for the support that world Jewry, especially that of the U.S., gave to Israel. David Krivine noted that world Jewry accounted for 68.7% of the long-term capital transfers to Israel from 1949 to 1965, almost 70% of which came from State of Israel Bond sales.[13]

I will limit myself to one fiscal year, 1970-71, in an effort to estimate the assistance that Diaspora Jewry provides to Israel. Direct financial assistance from the Diaspora is of four types. Best known is "institutional transfers." This is the total sum transferred from abroad to institutions in Israel. The primary recipient of such funds is the Jewish Agency for Israel through the United Jewish Appeal and similar campaigns. Other major recipients of funds from abroad include Hadassah hospital, the Hebrew University, the Weizmann Institute, the Haifa Technion, and other religious, welfare, health, and educational institutions. In 1970 the total sum transferred from abroad to these institutions was $132,000,000.[14]

The second type of financial assistance was State of Israel Bonds. In 1970 the total sales of Israeli Bonds amounted to $210,000,000, although one should deduct from this figure the money Israel spent for redeeming Bonds sold in previous years.[15]

The third type of direct financial assistance is net "private transfers." This includes all private gifts to Israelis and assets that new immigrants bring with them in money and goods. In 1970 the figure was 383 million dollars. However, there is reason to believe that part of this figure includes money that Israelis earn within Israel, smuggle abroad in order to avoid taxes, then convert into dollars on the black market and return to Israel disguised as gifts from friends or relatives.[16] In addition, not all the institutional and private gifts and contributions or Bond income comes from Jews. The assumption is, however, that virtually everything that doesn't come from Jews comes as a result of their efforts.

To these figures must be added the fourth type of assistance: private assistance from abroad. Not all private investors are Jewish and not all Jews invest in Israel only because it is a Jewish State. But Government officials concerned with private investment estimate that from seventy to eighty percent of the total foreign investment in Israel comes from Jews.[17] The proportion suggests that Israel's Jewishness is an important factor in investment decisions.[18] Total foreign investment in 1970 was 53 million dollars and in 1971 the figure jumped to 121 million dollars.[19]

An additional source of income for Israel, not included under the rubric of direct financial assistance, is income derived from tourists. Not all tourists are Jews, but a high percentage is. During the 1960s the Ministry of Tourism commissioned surveys that estimated the proportion of Jews and non-Jews among the tourists and the amount of money spent by each group in Israel. In 1970 an estimated 246,000 Jewish tourists visited Israel and spent an estimated average of $370 each or a total of about 91 million dollars.[20] The addition of approximately $800,000,000 in foreign currency in one year to an an economy the size of Israel's is extremely significant. Most of this, as noted, is through the activity of Diaspora Jewry.

This figure still underplays the economic importance of Diaspora Jewry. Grants and loans from the United States must, at least in part, be attributed to the influence of American Jewry. In addition, Diaspora Jewry plays a crucial role in the sale of

Israeli products abroad. In the latter half of 1972 the Israeli press carried news of a debate in government and business circles over the question whether Israel should appeal to Diaspora Jews to purchase Israeli exports as a matter of Jewish loyalty. The implication was that up till that time Israel had made no concerted effort to sell its exports to Jews. In the light of that, a report prepared for the Ministry of Commerce and industry in early 1972 is of special significance. According to that study as reported in the press, Israel exported 185 million dollars worth of goods to the United States in 1971. The United States represents Israel's major market; it purchases 21% of Israel's total exports. Within that market, the report shows, "the final consumer for Israel products is primarily the Jewish public. . . ." [21] Indeed, the report itself recommends efforts to break out of the limitations of the Jewish market and to reach a wider public.

Political Dependence

I have already alluded to Israel's dependence on Diaspora Jewry, especially American Jewry, in the political realm. Some notion of American Jewry's importance to Israel is evident in a feature article on Prime Minister Yitzchak Rabin, who served as Israeli Ambassador to Washington from 1968 to 1973. The author of the article quoted a senior member of the Israel Embassy in Washington as follows:

Until Rabin . . . whenever a critical problem arose, it was customary to activate important Jews to go to the U.S. Government on behalf of Israel. Rabin stopped this custom. There is an Embassy and there is a Government. No Jews as intermediaries. [22]

But, the Israeli spokesman to the contrary notwithstanding, Israel continues to rely on Jewish political support and even on its mediation. The Israeli press regularly reports on visits by leading American Jews with White House and State Department officials on behalf of Israel, particularly in times of crisis. This was certainly true in the period between 1968 and 1970 when Israel was most anxious about the sale of U.S. planes and President Nixon seemed in no hurry to grant Israel's requests.

Psychological Dependence

It is difficult to pinpoint the sense an observer has that Israel fears "being alone" and feels that it is not alone only because it can rely on Diaspora Jewry. Israeli leaders have certainly repeated this time and time again. Typical is Ben-Gurion's statement that "Israel's only absolutely reliable ally is world Jewry." [23] Israel may be the only country in the world without any natural cultural, historical, racial, religious, or ethnic ties to at least one other state.

Isolation has serious cultural consequences and Israel, like many other nations, fears these consequences quite apart from their political and economic implications. Diaspora Jewry's support provides a bulwark against the sense of isolation. It is difficult to document this phenomenon. It is not always apparent or readily expressed in daily life. It is somewhat more evident in a time of crisis. This is perhaps the best explanation for the reportage in the Israeli press in the period of the Six Day War. Between June 1 and June 12, the period immediately surrounding the war, *Ha'Aretz* devoted 45 stories and 206 columnal inches to world reaction to the Israeli crises. Obviously, some of these stories also included anti-Israel reactions. Of the total, 22 items covering 90 columnal inches concerned the reaction of world Jewry.

Israel Kolatt has pointed out that Israel's revaluation of the importance of the Diaspora was strengthened precisely in that period after 1956 when it felt most isolated—when the Soviet Union on the one hand and Eisenhower and Dulles on the other were unsympathetic to her needs.[24]

In summary, therefore, the Diaspora contribution to Israel is of enormous importance. The Diaspora, therefore, possesses great potential political resources.

POLITICAL INFLUENCE

The concern here is with Diaspora Jewry's influence on Israeli public policy. Such influence can take two forms—direct influence expressed in efforts by Diaspora Jewry to influence Israeli policy, and indirect influence expressed in the consideration that Israeli policymakers pay to Diaspora Jewry or their perception of Diaspora Jewry and its needs. I shall consider the first type of influence devoting some attention to the second.

I have indicated the potential that exists for mutual influence between Israel and Diaspora Jewry. It is unlikely that Israel could survive without the material and political support of the Diaspora.[25] This suggests the enormous influence that Diaspora Jewry ought to be able to exercise over Israel. But influence is not only a function of the resources that one side holds, but it is also a function of the degree to which one side seeks to exercise its power and of the degree to which the other side is receptive to the exercise of power. Finally, the influence that one side can yield by virtue of its resources may be offset by the resources of the other side, so that instead of a condition of mutual influence there is a condition of mutual noninfluence. This last condition does not hold in the case of Israel-Diaspora relations. In fact, whereas Israel exercises enormous influence over world Jewry, the opposite is not the case, despite the fact that the resources of the Diaspora, certainly of a community like that in the U.S., are much more critical for Israel than are Israel's resources for the American Jewish community. If, therefore, there is an imbalance between potential influence and the actual exercise of influence by Diaspora Jewry, it is to the first two conditions that one must look: the degree to which the Diaspora actually seeks to exercise its potential power, and the degree to which Israel is receptive to the exercise of such power. I shall examine these questions in chapter 7 and eight after we have looked more carefully at case studies of Diaspora pressure on Israeli public policy.

THE CENTRALITY OF U.S. JEWRY

As was noted, Diaspora Jewry is not cut of one cloth. One cannot talk in general terms of the influence of Diaspora Jewry. One must specify what group or groups are the subjects. Of those Diaspora groups or communities that might exercise power, we may first consider international Jewish organizations, such as the World Zionist Organization and the World Jewish Congress. Israelis participate in both organizations and hold a dominant position in the former and veto power in the latter. Both organizations are decentralized, and to the extent that they command effective sources and potential influence, these rest (outside Israel) in their American constituencies. Thus, to the extent that these organizations are influential, it is to the American Diaspora to which one must look as a source of power.

In addition to the international Jewish organizations, individual Diaspora communities may be influential. Among the various countries of the Diaspora it is again only in the United States where a truly great reservoir of resources and potential influence exists. There are an estimated 11,700,000 Jews living in countries with more than 1,000 Jews.[26] (Obviously no community with less than 1,000 Jews could possibly exert influence.) Of the 11,700,000 Jews, an estimated 3,500,000 live in the Soviet Union, Soviet-dominated countries, or Moslem countries. All of them lack the resources or capacity to influence Israel directly. Of the remainder of Diaspora Jewry, seventy-five percent live in the United States. If for no other reason alone, U.S. Jewry assumes vital significance. The numerical preponderance of U.S. Jewry is more than reflected in its financial contributions to Israel. Roughly eighty to eighty-five percent of all monies raised by Bonds for Israel, and sixty-five percent of money raised by the United Jewish Appeal and similar campaigns throughout the world, come from the United States.

Second, Israel looks to the United States for basic support of its international position. Its relations with the U.S. are of paramount concern to Israel and therefore it is the American Jewish community more than any other to which Israel looks for political support. Even if U.S. Jewry were far fewer, or their financial contributions far more niggling, their location would provide them with the potential for enormous influence on Israeli policy.

Finally, it is to American Jewry that one must first look to find examples of Diaspora influence on Israeli policy, because American Jewry is second only to Israel as a leader of international Jewry. Canadian, British, South African, and to a lesser extent French Jewry look to the U.S. for leadership. American Jewry has provided aid to Jewries of these countries. It is American Jews (along with Israelis) who take the lead in the international organizations to which the Jewish leaders of these countries belong.

Thus, the focus in the case studies that follow will be primarily on Amercan Jewry's efforts to influence Israel. This focus, however, in no way distorts the reality of influence. For with very few exceptions, it is only from American Jewry that Israel has sensed any political pressure.

PART 2

Case Studies

In this section we shall turn our attention to the exploration of instances where Diaspora Jewry sought to influence policy formation. Attempts at influence, as noted above, are defined as the exertion of direct pressure on Israel rather than the consideration by Israel of the needs of Diaspora Jews. In the following chapters I discuss religious policy, other domestic policy, foreign policy, and finally, the specific role of the reconstituted Jewish Agency. Most of the material is organized around case studies. One of two criteria was utilized in selecting the case studies. In some instances, there were fairly well publicized efforts by Diaspora Jewry to influence Israel. In such cases, such as the "Who Is a Jew?" controversy or Israel's policy toward the World Zionist Organization, I am concerned with tracing Diaspora Jewry's strategy, tactics, and relative success in influencing public policy. In other instances, I chose cases or policy areas where, in view of the interests of Diaspora Jews or in light of the very structure of the relationships, one would have anticipated efforts to influence Israeli policy. Examples of such cases are Israel's economic policies, or the status of Conservative and Reform rabbis and institutions in Israel. The discussion of the reconstituted Jewish Agency also falls into this category, since the reorganization presumably took place in order to increase the involvement of world Jewry in Israeli affairs, thereby opening ostensible channels for greater influence.

3
Religious Policy

The policy area in which Diaspora Jewry has been most concerned and most anxious to influence Israel is that of religion. With exceptions to be noted below, virtually all of the pressure on Israel came from Orthodox Jews in the United States. The one man most closely involved in these continuing efforts by Orthodox Jewry to influence Israel was the late Yaacov Herzog. Herzog, son of the late Chief Rabbi Herzog, was an Orthodox Jew and Director of the Prime Minister's office at the time he died in 1972. Herzog was probably the only Orthodox Jew who was privy to the highest policymaking councils of the State of Israel and who did not achieve his status as the candidate, nominee, or representative of a religious party. By virtue of his personal and familial connections in the Orthodox world and his associations in the government world, Herzog was in one way or another approached and consulted by one or both sides in most of the religious-political struggles that took place since the creation of the state. Even when not personally involved, he was certainly informed. Considerable importance was, therefore, attached to Herzog's statement that there were five instances concerning religious policy when the government was most conscious of Diaspora pressure.[1] These instances were:

61

1. The controversy over education of children in immigrant camps in 1949-50.
2. The National Service Law controversy in 1953-54.
3. The "Shalom" Kashrut controversy in 1963-64.
4. The "Autopsy" controversy that flared up on many occasions and upon which I will focus in the 1965-1970 period.
5. The "Who Is a Jew?" controversy in 1959 and again since 1970.

I will limit my attention primarily to these controversies since, if the Diaspora was able to influence Israeli religious policy at all, it should be in those instances where the Government was conscious of its pressure. Other efforts at influence will be noted briefly and in passing. Following this, I will attempt some summary statement about the nature of Orthodox Jewry's influence since Orthodox Jews were the source of pressure. Then, in the final section of the chapter, I will turn my attention to the case of Conservative and Reform in Israel— asking, as it were, a negative question. Why, given the ostensibly far more important role that American Conservative and Reform Jews play in activity on behalf of Israel, have they exercised so little influence or even exerted so little pressure on behalf of their own interests? However, before I begin with case studies of Orthodox pressure, it is important to understand the constellation of Orthodox forces in the United States who concern themselves with Israeli affairs.

THE CONSTELLATION OF ORTHODOX FORCES IN UNITED STATES

American Orthodoxy is divided into two camps.[2] In one camp are those committed to the State of Israel whose dedication to achieving religiopolitical goals in Israel is balanced by their desire to protect the good name and interests of Israel. The second camp is made up of those whose primary concern is

with political-religious issues rather than Israel's general interests. Some, of course, rationalize this by the notion that Israel's
interests are ultimately a function of their acting as Orthodoxy
would have them act. Others are avowedly hostile to the State.
For purposes of nomenclature, I shall label the first camp
religious Zionists and the second *religious non-Zionists*. In the
United States, the first camp includes the Religious Zionists of
America (RZA), formerly separated into the Mizrachi and Hapoel
Hamizrachi organizations (their women's organizations are still
distinct), and the Rabbinical organization, composed primarily
of rabbis of a "modern Orthodox" orientation. The Israeli counterpart to this camp would be the National Religious Party
(NRP) at the political level and, to a lesser extent, as we shall
see, the Chief Rabbinate of Israel at the authoritative religious
level. Organizations and institutions in the United States that
fall quite clearly into the second camp include Agudath Israel
of America, and most of the Yeshivot (institutions for advanced
Talmudic training based on traditional European modes of study
and life styles), whose leaders constituted the spiritual leadership
of Agudath Israel, and most Hasidic *Rebbes* and followers, some
of whom are very hostile to Israel, the most important being
the *Rebbe* of Satmar. The Israeli counterparts of this camp are
Agudath Israel and the Yeshiva and Hasidic leaders who closely
resemble their American partners. The Union of Orthodox Rabbis of the United States also falls very clearly into this second
camp today, although many of its leaders were associated with
Mizrachi in the 1940s and 50s and many had personal ties
with the Israeli Chief Rabbinate. The Young Israel and the
Union of Orthodox Jewish Congregations of America (UOJCA),
the two largest Orthodox congregational bodies, fall between
the two camps, with the Young Israel tending toward the first
camp and the Union toward the second. Both, however, played
a very minor role in all the cases I shall describe.

Tension between the two camps is mitigated by a number
of factors. Divisions between the constituents are not so clear-
cut as divisions among the leaders. Leaders of the religious

Zionists cannot afford to be indifferent to charges of anti-religious coercion in Israel or to fears that Israel may lose its Jewish character. Not only are they not indifferent, but they must also legitimate themselves religiously against charges by the religious non-Zionists that they are too passive, moderate, and accommodating to the Israeli-Zionists establishment. Furthermore, both the religious Zionists in America and the NRP in Israel owe ostensible allegiance to the Chief Rabbinate, whose policies, in fact, are often closer to the policies of the religious non-Zionists than to those of the religious Zionists. Many of the religious non-Zionist leaders, on the other hand, are not indifferent to the long-run consequences of their action on the State of Israel, nor can they afford to be too extreme and thereby stand indicted of the charge that the Zionists level against them: hostility to Israel.

THE IMMIGRANT CAMP EDUCATION
CONTROVERSY—1949–1950

The controversy that follows can only be understood against the background of the mass immigration to Israel in the early years of statehood and the highly politicized nature of Israeli society. Deep suspicions and ambitions divided the parties of the Left and the Right, and the religious parties. The religious parties saw in the influx of new immigrants, many from traditional religious cultures, the opportunity to gain new adherents and perhaps even become a majority within Israel. The dominant party of Israel, Mapai, sought to capitalize on the innocence, simplicity, and sense of gratitude of these immigrants toward the State of Israel to turn them into adherents of their own ideology. Each side acted through a combination of honest conviction that what it was doing was in the best interest of Israel and in the best interests of the immigrants themselves, and of partisan political motivation.

Israel was unable to provide housing for the masses who

arrived immediately after the founding of the state. They were initially absorbed, therefore, in immigrant camps. Schools within the camps were placed under the control of the Cultural Department rather than the Education Department of the Ministry of Education and Culture. Israeli parents, at that time and until passage of the education law of 1953, could send their children to one of four types of school systems—the Labor school system, the General school system, one of two religious school systems under control of the Mizrachi, and Agudath Israel respectively. However, in the immigrant camps, there was only one "unified" school system which, under the Cultural Department, was controlled, in fact, by Mapai. By late 1949 stories began to spread of anti-religious coercion, of children having their earlocks shaved, of being denied the use of religious articles or opportunity for prayer and—of greatest long-run significance—of being denied religious education despite their own and their parents' requests. In late 1949, representatives of the Religious Front[3] raised these issues in the Knesset. They demanded that education in the immigrant camps be placed under control of the Department of Education, where the religious parties had far greater representation and where the principle of education, according to the parents' ideological orientation, was recognized. They also demanded the appointment of a committee to investigate the charges of religious coercion. What the religious parties were most anxious to secure was control over the education of the religious immigrants. This demand was far more difficult to explicate. Consequently, at the public level, the religious parties tended to phrase their demands in terms of more generalized charges of "religious coercion."

The religious parties engaged in an extensive public campaign to alert the Israeli public to these charges.[4] The campaign was also carried on among Orthodox Jews in the Diaspora, especially in the United States. But the evidence suggests that Diaspora Jewry was not simply a tool that the Israeli parties manipulated. There is some evidence that Orthodox Jews abroad sought not only to assist the Religious Front in influencing the

Government of Israel, but to invigorate the campaign within Israel itself. For example, the Union of Orthodox Rabbis cabled Israel's Chief Rabbi Herzog as well as other religious leaders asking what steps they had taken concerning the problem of coercion in the immigrant camps.[5]

Of course, one cannot dismiss the possibility that some Israeli organization or personage requested the cable from the Union of Orthodox Rabbis to increase the pressure on the Chief Rabbi, but there is no direct evidence in this regard. In general, the interplay of pressure is of interest. The membership of the Union of Orthodox Rabbis is made up of older, European-trained rabbis, many of whom are personal friends of the senior Israeli rabbinate. Their leaders are held in high regard by Israeli rabbis. Organizationally, the Union of Orthodox Rabbis is inept, strife-ridden, and virtually without influence on the American scene. Nevertheless, its own ties to the Israeli rabbinate were such that it commanded respect and deference from them. Since they, in turn, were unquestionably influential in religious-political circles within Israel and these circles, in turn, carried influence within the Government, we have the phenomenon of influence operating in quite the reverse direction from what might normally be expected.

Most of the Diaspora effort, however, was directed toward influencing Israeli policymakers directly. This was the first such effort since the creation of the State, and everyone was concerned about its legitimacy. For example, the Mizrachi Organization of England, at its national convention, demanded religious education in the immigrant camps. The President, Rabbi Kopul Rosen, stated that Jews must support Israel and this obligation entitled them to involvement in what takes place in Israel. Jews, he observed, must not interfere in purely internal matters, but anything that occurs in Israel and affects Jewish life in general is a legitimate matter for their concern.[6] By implication, the religious education of children in Israel was a legitimate matter for Diaspora interference. Not only did Mapai leaders dissent from this interpretation of legitimacy, but at least

one prominent, religious, political leader did as well. Rabbi
Judah Leib Maimon, the Minister of Religion and leader of
Mizrachi, declared his opposition to the interference by Diaspora
rabbis in the internal affairs of Israel in the immigrant education
controversy.[7] He also objected to the public demonstrations
organized by Orthodox organizations in New York, to which I
shall refer .

The Government itself was intensely sensitive to the efforts
by Diaspora Jewry to bring pressure upon it. In response to the
demands of the Religious Front, the Government did appoint
a committee to investigate accusations respecting religious coercion in immigrant camps, but added that the committee was
also to inspect the manner in which parties outside Israel were
mobilized to level these accusations.[8] The five-member committee was chaired by a former Supreme Court Justice, Gad
Frumkin, and included four Knesset members, two of whom
were from the Religious Front and one of whom was the subsequent President of Israel, Yitzchak Ben Zvi.

The Committee was appointed by the Government (i.e., by
a decision of the Cabinet) on January 17, 1950, a day after
various cabinet members, including Prime Minister David Ben-
Gurion, had received a cable signed by the United Religious
Front, a roof organization representing virtually all the Orthodox
organizations in the United States. The cable requested that the
Government ". . . examine anew the problem of integration of
children in order to avoid the perversion of justice to the children and their parents and to the foundation of religious Jewry
and in order to avoid a world-wide scandal." [9] The Cabinet was
also informed of the fact that on January 13 the executive director of the Zionist Federation of England had cabled Zalman
Shazar, another future president of Israel but at that time minister of education, informing him that news of the Orthodox
charges of religious coercion, which had been aired in the
Jewish Chronicle of London, were endangering the UJA campaign, which was about to open.[10]

The Committee, whose appointment was probably a partial

response to pressure from the Diaspora was, as noted, charged
with exploring the problem of who initiated the pressure. It
found no evidence, after examining cables sent from Israel in
December and January, that the initiative had come from Israel.
It found, rather, that Diaspora Jewry had turned to religious
leaders in Israel, demanding to know what steps Orthodox
groups in Israel were taking to combat "the anti-religious in-
quisition in the immigrant camps." [11] On the other hand, the
chairman of the Mercaz Olami (International Center) of Mizrachi had cabled the New York office on January 8, asking for
moral and financial help in the battle.[12] On January 10, he
again cabled to Mizrachi in New York, noting that:

> dramatic action is necessary for the final settlement of this
> tragic episode. Please pass this information along to the Union
> of Orthodox Rabbis, the Rabbinical Council of America,
> Hapoel Hamizrachi, and the press.[13]

Orthodox organizations in the U.S. planned a mass meeting
for January 23 at the Manhattan Center in New York to air
their grievances and their demands. Rabbi Maimon cabled
American Mizrachi urging them not to participate and "not to
interfere in the internal problems of the State of Israel," but
Leon Gellman, chairman of the Mercaz Olami, urged participation, as did other leaders of the Mizrachi and Hapoel Hamizrachi of Israel.[14] However, they also cautioned against "dramatic
activity" until the Government's Committe had completed its
investigation.

The Government, as was noted, was both sensitive to and
resentful of these activities and pressures. The question is, how
responsive were they? Publicly, they expressed indignation. Ben-
Gurion, in reply to the cable, referred to earlier, from the United
Religious Front in America, charged them with reaching conclusions without knowing the facts. But most of his reply was
directed to their "threats." The cable to Ben-Gurion had maintained that the Government must act "to avoid a world wide
scandal bearing tragic long-run implications." To this Ben-
Gurion said:

I am especially astonished at the peculiar threat with which you turn to the Government of Israel. The State of Israel is a democratic republic based on liberty, freedom of conscience and the freedom of religion and all her affairs are determined by the decision of a majority of her citizens in accordance with their best understanding. You can rest assured that we will do nothing under the pressure of threats if the matter is not of itself just and necessary. If you want to exercise direct influence on the direction of the State of Israel and strengthen certain tendencies among us, the most efficient method for you and for those on whose behalf you speak is to come to us and settle in our midst.[15]

Shazar, referring to the Manhattan Center meeting of the Orthodox groups said:

Since the creation of the State of Israel, this is the first act, the first organized protest among the Jews of the world against the State of Israel.[16]

He went on to say that anyone who knows American Jewry knows the meaning of "meetings" (he used the word in English although his statement was in Hebrew); as he put it, "we were accustomed to have 'meetings' like this against Hitler." According to Shazar, even if all the charges of coercion were correct, they were an internal matter and the responsibility of the Government and the Knesset "and the matter should not be passed outside the country or come to us from outside the country." [17]

The representatives of the Israeli religious parties denied, in turn, that they had made any effort to organize Diaspora Jewry.[18]

In its conclusions, the Committee addressed itself to the general question of world Jewry and Israeli public policy. They noted that Diaspora Jewry had the right to take an interest in Israeli affairs, especially in the areas of culture and religion, and especially at a time that the State was so dependent on their help. They also had the right to criticize, but they did not have the right to interfere in matters that should be left to the State to decide, and they must even refrain from activity that could be interpreted as such interference.[19]

The statement is, of course, self-contradictory. But it expressed the self-contradiction that was inherent in the prevailing attitude of Israel toward Diaspora Jewry. No one wanted to deny world Jewry's right to criticize. But the line between criticism and pressure is not only a thin line, but it is also a line that no one can realistically draw in circumstances where Israel was so dependent on Diaspora Jewry for assistance and therefore necessarily sensitive to their opinion.

The same day in which the Government had appointed the Committee, it also appointed a five-man Ministerial Committee (two of whose members represented the religious parties), to make recommendations respecting the problem of education in the immigrant camps. Since the Investigating Committee only issued its report in May, and the Ministerial Committee had completed its work in a matter of weeks, we may assume that it was not influenced by the Committee's conclusions that religious coercion had indeed taken place. The Committee's appointment does suggest the Government's recognition that some new steps were necessary; this despite the fact that it did not accept the Committee's recommendations, which tended to be favorable to the religious position. After further negotiations, the Government, however, did approve, and the Knesset did adopt on March 14, 1950, a proposal to transfer educational responsibility in the immigrant camps from the Department of Culture to the Department of Education and to insure that there would be provision for religious education under the supervision of religious educators and administrators.[20]

The conflict over religious education in general, and the education of new immigrants in particular, continued, but the Knesset's March decision represents the concluding phase of one round in that conflict and the one in which Diaspora Jewry's role was most pronounced. Policies more or less in line with the demands of the religious parties were adopted. Three questions offer themselves. First, would the government have acted any differently had there been no pressure upon it by the religious parties? Second, assuming that the government responded to pressure of religious groups, were they responding to domestic or Diaspora pressure? Third, assuming the Government was responding to Diaspora pressure, was Diaspora Jewry acting only as an instrument for Israeli religious groups or was Orthodox Jewry in the United States acting independently and on behalf of its own interests as it perceived them? I shall discuss each question in turn.

1. Was the Government influenced by the pressure of religious groups?

It is fairly obvious that the Orthodox did influence the Government. Although placing control over education in the immigrant camps in the hands of the Department of Culture was contrary to the law, the question was how soon this would be rectified. As we shall see, the Orthodox perceived their real fight to be getting the Government to move as rapidly as possible. The fact that a Ministerial Committee was appointed on January 17 indicated that the Government was willing to take action, but it also served to delay immediate action. The Orthodox, therefore, saw their fight as one against time, and the fact that they forced a Government decision and a Knesset law within the period of about three months is an indication of success.

The Orthodox influence is all the more noteworthy because of a powerful constraint, which one assumes led Ben-Gurion in particular to resist them—surrendering to pressure from Diaspora Jewry on the religious issue might lead to Diaspora intervention in other social and economic policies. Ben-Gurion and other leaders of the State were sensitive to the threat of pressures from American Zionists allied to the right-wing General Zionist Party in Israel. This is even hinted at in the final conclusions of the Investigating Committee's report, which acknowledged the special privileges, as it were, of Diaspora Jewry to concern itself with cultural and religious matters and, by implication, not with social and economic matters, which were of greater concern to the General Zionists. But surely, the very fact that Diaspora Jewry did intervene must have led Ben-

Gurion to consider the possibility that precisely because of their intervention he could not set a precedent by giving in to their demands.

2. Did the Government respond to domestic or Diaspora pressure?

This is a more difficult question to answer unequivocally. In the very nature of political influence, the major pressures, no doubt, came from the Religious Front in Israel. Their threats of resignation made as early as November of 1949 and their refusal to participate in Cabinet meetings in early 1950—that is, their direct political pressure on the Government was, perhaps, the strongest influence. On the other hand, Ben-Gurion was apparently willing to risk a Government crisis on the issue. Therefore, domestic pressure alone might not have sufficed. Furthermore, the political leaders of religious Jewry in Israel themselves felt that they needed broad public support of religious Jews.[21] This point of view was expressed in the communications with Orthodox Jewry abroad.

The Religious Front, as before noted, supported the mass meeting in New York. Throughout the period of negotiations between the Religious Front and the Government, Leon Gellman, Chairman of the Mercaz Olami, cabled information to the United States and on two occasions asked the American Mizrachi to send cables "and to get other influential religious bodies to send cables of protest to the Government on this situation."[22] He wrote that the Religious Front could be strengthened to a considerable extent by the backing of strong organizations throughout the world. In a letter to the Union of Orthodox Rabbis on March 4 he stated that "religious Jewry here requires in the highest measure possible help and assistance from the Diaspora."[23]

Hapoel Hamizrachi leader Moshe Shapiro, the man who would eventually become undisputed leader of the National Religious Party (formed from a merger of Mizrachi and Hapoel Hamizrachi), stressed that left wing parties in Israel were happy to delay any changes since the chlidren were under their influence. The real hope, he argued, was pressure from the Diaspora.[24]

Diaspora Jewry, by and large, is unable to make specific demands with respect to Israeli policy. In this and, as we shall see, in other cases as well, Diaspora Jewry can raise general demands—it can charge religious coercion, it can protest religious discrimination—but it cannot involve itself in the details of policy or administrative execution. Diaspora Jewry tends to respond, and indeed is only really aroused over what it views as religious and moral imperatives. It was pointless to try to educate the masses or even the leaders of Orthodox Jewish organizations about the Religious Front's demands to move educational authority from one ministerial department to another, much less to educate it on on the details of who should serve on a ministerial or administrative committee to oversee the changes, or what *type* of referendum should be held in the immigrant camps. This necessarily was left to the politicians of the religious parties. But this constitutes a serious limitation of their effectiveness. For, in fact, what the religious parties really wanted was control over immigrant education—at least over the education of those children whose parents desired religious education for them. This necessarily became an administrative political battle in which the Religious Front could no longer count on Diaspora support once the general moral issue of "religious coercion" was resolved. It seems quite proper to attribute an important role to Diaspora Jewry in contributing to the sum total of pressure on the Israeli government; but this pressure led to victory in a battle that was only part of a much broader conflict.

3. Did the initiative come from Israel or Diaspora Jewry?

This question is the most difficult of all to answer. Apparently, influence worked both ways. Information, of course, flowed from Israel and without this information, Diaspora Jewry would have done nothing. Specific requests for help also came from Israel. On the other hand, once alerted, some Orthodox elements were quite willing to work independently. We have noted the cables from the Union of Orthodox Rabbis to Israeli religious authorities, including the Chief Rabbi, which insisted on knowing what steps were being taken—almost implying that they were not sufficiently militant. Indeed, some political leaders of religious Jewry in Israel found themselves constrained to moderate the militancy of Diaspora Jewry. For example, Mizrachi and Hapoel Hamizrachi leaders Gold, Gellman, Shragai, and Raphael cabled the American Mizrachi, urging that drastic action not be taken and that they were "on alert to protect demands religious Jewry" and that they would "keep you informed further development and advise you on necessary steps." [25] There is an implication in this cable, as well, that Israeli leaders were fearful that Diaspora protests might get out of hand and they were anxious to maintain control of the situation. Religious forces hostile to Israel within the Diaspora required very little encouragement to demonstrate against the State. As we shall see in the next section, once these forces were aroused, even Agudah was unable to control them.

In summary then, it is clear that Diaspora Jewry by itself could have accomplished little or nothing, since they would have been hard pressed to know what to ask for other than a generalized demand to stop religious coercion. On the other hand, it also seems clear that religious politicians in Israel were assisted by Diaspora Jewry, whose help might even have been critical in the influence they were able to exert over Israeli policy. Finally, Diaspora Jewry was aroused, and its leaders were capable of arousing it, because they viewed religious education of immigrant children as their own self-interest, a matter to which I shall return in chapter 7.

THE CONTROVERSY OVER THE NATIONAL SERVICE
LAW FOR WOMEN: 1953–54

In August 1953 the Knesset adopted the National Service Law for Women. That law has never been enforced. The decision, first to moderate the law and finally not to enforce it at all, came within a year from the time it was passed. My concern in this section is to determine to what extent Diaspora pressure was influential in that decision.

The background for the adoption of the law was, very briefly, as follows. Under the provisions of a 1949 act, any girl who declared her objection to military service on religious grounds was exempted from any obligation to serve. Many Israelis were unhappy with this law, which they felt was inherently unjust and which furthermore led to false declarations of religiosity. The religious parties that had objected to military service for all girls were most anxious to retain the 1949 law. In early 1951, after the religious parties had resigned from the Government on a different issue, a caretaker government proposed a law that provided for the creation of Boards before which girls claiming a religious exemption had to appear in order to substantiate their claims. Second, the bill provided for a Civilian National Service for girls exempted from military service. All the religious parties expressed their opposition and mass protests and demonstrations took place within Israel. There is no evidence of any pressure from the Diaspora. The bill passed a first reading in the Knesset but was never pushed to further stages.

In July 1951, elections to the second Knesset took place. Each of the four religious parties entered its own slate. The religious Zionist parties, Hapoel Hamizrachi and Mizrachi, won eight and two seats respectively and the non-Zionist and more militantly religious parties of Agudath Israel and Poalei Agudath Israel won three and two seats respectively. All four religious parties entered the new coalition with the understanding that no legislation respecting the draft of girls would be proposed for a year but that after a year the Government would propose some kind of a National Service Law. The issue was not raised again, therefore, until late 1952, whereupon the two non-Zionist religious parties resigned from the Government. The two religious Zionist parties, in turn, entered into lengthy negotiations on the detailed provisions of the bill. (Since these two parties,

Mizrachi and Hapoel Hamizrachi, later merged into the NRP [National Religious Party], and since there were no discernible differences between them in the negotiations that took place and in the subsequent controversy, I shall, for the sake of convenience, refer to them as the NRP, although it should be clear to the reader that the NRP did not exist at this time.) Within Israel, Agudath Israel was far more vociferous than Poalei Agudath Israel in opposition to the bill. Indeed, the latter's position was quite ambivalent. Since Poalei Agudath Israel is a very small party in Israel and virtually nonexistent in the United States, I shall, for the sake of convenience, refer to the religious political party in opposition to the bill as Agudah, the name by which it is generally referred to in English. Agudah, as noted, exists both as a political party in Israel and as an organization within the United States.

Agudah attacked the Government for proposing any changes and the NRP for agreeing to a change and not resigning from the Government. The law was presented to the Knesset in July and passed its final reading in August of 1953. It provided that girls who were released from military service on religious grounds would be required to serve for two years in a National Labor Service under control of the Ministry of Labor, rather than the Ministry of Defence as had originally been suggested. They would work in new immigrant camps, religious kibbutzim, or hospitals. Girls for whom such service would be in sharp contradiction to their life style, i.e., leaving home before marriage, were to be exempted from any form of national service.

In the Knesset vote, the NRP abstained on the first reading of the bill but voted in favor on the final reading. The NRP's position was a difficult one. The Chief Rabbinate had originally expressed strong opposition to the law although, in light of concessions which the NRP obtained, it specifically refrained from insisting that the NRP resign from the Government. Agudah capitalized on NRP acquiescence in order to charge it with insufficient concern for religious law. On the other hand, the NRP was under a threat from Mapai that should they oppose the law, the Government would oppose passage of a bill establishing rabbinical courts. The NRP considered this law extremely important.

During July, while the bill was before the Knesset, protests were heard from Agudah circles in Israel, England, and the United States. At a New York demonstration, protestors carried placards reading, "Don't Turn Us Into Enemies of the State," and threats against the UJA and Bonds for Israel drive were aired.[26]

The attack against the law in the United States was led by the Union of Orthodox Rabbis and an Agudah-oriented organization, The National Committee for the Repeal of the Women's Draft, which operated out of the Union of Orthodox Rabbis' offices. Agudah and, as we shall see, more extremist religious elements also participated.

Despite the demonstrations or resolutions of the Union of Orthodox Rabbis,[27] Diaspora pressure prior to passage of the law was negligible.[28] The religious Zionists were certainly passive. In fact, in 1951 at least one Mizrachi leader in America apparently felt that even the NRP was too militant in its opposition to a draft of girls.[29]

Four days after final passage of the law, Mordecai Kirshblum, at the time President of the American Mizrachi Organization, wrote to Israel that members of his organization opposed National Service.[30] The tone of his letter was one of surprise. Kirshblum had just returned to the United States from a visit in Israel and he wrote as follows. (The passage is quoted at greater length than necessary because it contains other aspects of interest.)

I found here quite a different climate for our movement and our thinking. Not only staunch Agudists but also good Mizrachim who are naturally ignorant of the basic and fundamental facts have become influenced by Agudath Israel propaganda in regard to Sherut Leumi [National Service]. The Agudah could never have captured these people if not for the so-called signal of the chief rabbinate to oppose the government on this score to the fullest extent. In view of such development (*sic*), we naturally have a big job to do and must start unwinding ourselves from this very complicated and twisted situation. We will require a great deal of enlightenment, information and even a suggested line of approach. I am sure that you people will guide us steadily and promptly so that we can fulfill our mission to the full extent of our responsibility.[31]

Thus, the indications are fairly clear that neither Kirshblum nor presumably his correspondent, Bezalel Bazak, an intimate associate of NRP leader Moshe Shapiro, knew of this opposition before passage of the law. This is not to suggest that had they known of it they would have voted against it. Indeed, Mizrachi was never a very formidable organization on the American scene and the NRP was aware that there was no reason to take it seriously when it opposed NRP policies. Furthermore, as is evident from Kirshblum's letter, relationships between the Israeli and American organizations were hardly those of equality. The point is that Mizrachi people do not behave very differently from any of the other Orthodox Jews in the religious Zionist camp. And if the NRP did not know about currents within Mizrachi, they would not suspect that anyone besides Agudah people opposed them. One could hardly anticipate, therefore, that they would be influenced by demonstrations in the United States in their negotiations over the law. Furthermore, while we may infer from Kirshblum's letter that opposition forces were at least quietly at work, there is no evidence in the press of a great deal of activity in opposition to the law in the United States prior to its passage.

The question to which we turn now is: was Diaspora Jewry influential in the Government's decision not to enforce the law? There are three alternative possibilities. The Government might have been influenced by the demonstrations within Israel and by its conviction that it could never enforce the law but would be confronted instead with religious girls and their parents who would prefer jail to national service. It is also conceivable that the decision was made under continued NRP pressure, even after the law was passed. Finally, since the decision not to enforce the law was made under the government of Prime Minister Moshe Sharett, whereas the law was passed during Ben-Gurion's first tenure as prime minister, we cannot dismiss the possibility that the change in personnel accounted for the new policy.

None of these possibilities are mutually exclusive. Indeed, they were probably all factors in the final decision. My concern is only to demonstrate that the Diaspora factor was also present. In doing so, I will also note that the explanatory powers of the other factors, by themselves, have certain weaknesses.

It is clear from Kirshblum's letter that a large portion of Orthodox Jewry opposed the law. Those who did not oppose it remained silent. By the end of August, Kirshblum reported that "the tumult is greater here than it is in the homeland." [32] NRP circles in Israel sought to quiet the protests against the law,[33] but the mood not only became increasingly militant but was accompanied by sharp attacks on Israel.[34]

The most widely publicized demonstration took place outside the Israeli Consulate in New York in February 1954 to protest "religious persecution" in Israel.[35] Israel was sharply attacked, people leaving the consulate were assaulted, and an effort was made to overturn a consulate car. One leaflet distributed at the demonstration asked that thousands of telegrams be sent to President Eisenhower and to the Congress calling on them to stop U.S. aid to Israel because Israel denied its citizens freedom of religion.[36] According to the *Jewish Chronicle*, the demonstration was organized by the National Committee for the Repeal of the Women's Draft, whose leaders lost control of the demonstration.[37] The Israeli press, including the Poalei Agudah press, held Agudath Israel responsible, although Agudah denied responsibility. In the wake of the bitterness that the demonstrations aroused, Agudah also announced that it would not bring a complaint about the national service for women before the U.N. Commission on the Status of Women. The complaint had been filed in December 1953 by Harry Goodman, the political secretary of the world organization, although even at the time, the move had been opposed by other figures within the organization.

But the demonstrations and protests apparently had their effect on the Government, especially, perhaps, on the new prime minister. Ben-Gurion announced his temporary retirement from public office in December 1953, and Moshe Sharett assumed the office of prime minister in January 1954. Sharett was more moderate than Ben-Gurion in most matters and the issue of the National Service Law did not carry the same emotional ideological overtones for him that it did for his predecessor. Consequently, he may have been more yielding to Diaspora pressure, to NRP pressure, and to the fear of widescale resistance within Israel. In a speech to the Knesset on February 14, Sharett referred to the demonstrations in New York and had this to say:

> I know that the National Service Law caused sincere excitement among various sectors of Orthodox Jewry. This resulted from the completely false information and vicious propaganda which circulated concerning the National Service Law, its true contents and on the procedures which the Ministry of Labor —with the approval of the Government—intends to utilize in executing the law.[38]

The procedures to which Sharett referred were publicized, at least in part, in a letter he wrote on that same day to Chief Rabbi Herzog.[39] They weakened the force of the law beyond anything the NRP had hoped for a few months earlier. They specifically provided that the Minister of Labor should act "most generously" in exempting from national service any girl who requested an exemption on grounds of conscience or family background, and that the majority of the members of each exemption board were themselves to be religious people. If any doubts were to arise in the minds of the exemption board members as to whether the girl in question really had a legitimate basis for arguing that her life style was such as to entitle her to a complete exemption from any form of national service, then the board was to grant her an exemption. That the demonstrations and protests provided at least a partial explanation for this letter is evident in both the text itself and in Herzog's response to it. Sharett noted that

> the Government which I have the honor to lead, and I myself, are most sensitive to the delicate character of the problems involved in executing the law. We are definitely anxious to do everything to quiet the storm that has been aroused in certain circles in this country and the Diaspora concerning this law." [40]

Herzog, in turn, cabled rabbinical organizations in the U.S., asking them to use their influence to halt the campaign of slander against Israel.[41] It is reasonable to assume that Herzog's cable was a response to Sharett's letter, although he must also have been taken aback by the vehemence of the last New York demonstration. His cable may have had some impact in averting further demonstrations against Eban and in front of the U.N.[42]

Agudah, while still demanding that the law be rescinded, maintained that "their protests and demonstrations secured the more lenient provisions" contained in Sharett's letter to the Chief Rabbi.[43] Shortly thereafter, word was passed on to religious circles in America that the law would not be enforced. Unfortunately, we do not know the precise date when the decision was reached or word was sent to New York. However, external evidence suggests it was some time between March 18 and April 4. A bulletin of the Mercaz Olami dated March 18 and intended for circulation to Mizrachi leaders notes that "there is no hope of a full freezing of the law much less rescinding it." [44] On the other hand, the National Committee for the Repeal of the Women's Draft protested statements made at a Mizrachi convention held in the U.S. on April 4. They cabled their protests to the Chief Rabbi, noting that ". . . after the quieting notice about postponing enforcement of the National Service Law arrived it was agreed to refrain from any activity." [45]

The evidence suggests not only the importance of Diaspora

activity but also the weakness of alternative explanations to account for the change in Government policy. It is difficult to attribute this to NRP pressure alone, since the NRP had resigned itself to the National Service Law after obtaining what it thought were the maximum concessions. Even the Chief Rabbinate had resigned itself to the law when it withdrew its strongest card—the demand that the NRP resign from the Government. While the Chief Rabbinate no doubt rejoiced when it learned that the law was not to be enforced, and NRP circles may also have been satisfied, it can hardly have been primarily through their efforts that the decision was made. Alternatively, the Government may have feared widespread resistance to the law within Israel. But one must recall the lenient provisions of the law which, in fact, provided that those most likely to resist the law would be unaffected by it. Perhaps many girls might not only claim exemption from national service, but refuse even to appear before the exemption boards to claim this exemption. But the fear that the jails might be filled with girls unwilling to do their national service was eliminated by the provisions of the law. It is not unreasonable, therefore, to conclude that what the Government most feared were continued demonstrations and protests in the Diaspora, with their negative impact on Israel's image.

THE *SHALOM* CONTROVERSY

The *Shalom* controversy refers to the issue of whether the Israeli ship *Shalom* should be equipped with a nonkosher as well as a kosher kitchen. The Zim Israel Navigation Company Ltd., (ZIM) which operated the *Shalom,* is a government-controlled corporation. The Jewish Agency and the Histadrut (the national federation of workers) held minority shares. While still under construction in a French shipyard, the management of Zim ordered that it be equipped with two kitchens. Their rationale was that a considerable number of potential passengers would sail aboard the ship only if nonkosher cuisine was available. The Board of Directors approved the management decision on condition that within a month none of the three owner groups raised objections.[46] The ministers representing the religious parties (Poalei Agudath Israel as well as the NRP were then members of the Government) raised the issue and the Government appointed a three-man Ministerial Committee to investigate the matter.[47]

At this point, Israeli political leaders turned to Diaspora Jewry for help. There is no question as to where the initiative came from. No word was heard from the Diaspora on the *Shalom* matter until mid-1963. Then appeals were made for help. For example, the Mercaz Olami wrote to Mizrachi in the U.S. stating that

> the Cabinet Committee is to meet in the next few days [;] we are turning to you, therefore, with a special request because it is desirable, important and urgent to organize protest cables against a treife [non-kosher] kitchen from all religious circles and especially American rabbis—not only the Union of Orthodox Rabbis but also the Rabbinical Council of America. Since Government circles here argue that the Conservative rabbis agree to a treife kitchen on the boat, it is especially important, if possible, that they should also express their opposition to this tendency. The cables of protest should be sent to the Prime Minister and the Minister of Religion.[48]

Kirshblum's response, as we shall see, indicates that the Mercaz Olami was not the only group to request his intervention. He refers to a cable from NRP cabinet member Joseph Burg. Furthermore, he refers to a meeting with an Israeli representative, which we know from other evidence took place on June 18. Given the fact that it would probably require two or three days to organize the meeting, it could not have been done in response to a letter from Israel, which was dated June 12. Kirshblum's response is here quoted at some length to provide a sense of the organization of pressure by the Orthodox camp.

As for the matter of the S.S. Shalom, I have done whatever I possibly could under the circumstances. Delegations of the Rabbinical Council of America and Union of Orthodox Rabbis and our own Vaad Lichizuk Hatorah conveyed their feelings to Ambassador Katriel Katz, who listened attentively and respectfully, even as he promised to register with the Government of Israel the feelings and statements which were conveyed to him.

In response to a cable by Dr. Burg, I categorically denied the wild rumor mentioned by Zvi Herman [a director of Zim, the individual most prominently identified with the demand for a non-kosher kitchen, and the man who eventually concluded an agreement with Sanheder Harabbanim to be discussed below] that the great and famous Rabbi Moshe Feinstein had indicated his willingness to give a hechsher [certification of kashrut] to the S.S. Shalom on the basis of two kitchens. Similarly, I have cabled to Dr. Warhaftig c/o Mercaz Olami that Professor Shaul Lieberman assured me that there is no chance whatsoever that the Conservative Rabbis will possibly condone the action about to be taken by the Zim Lines.

I don't believe that we can do more than we have done. I assure you that the minute a decision is made that the Shalom will include also a non-kosher kitchen, there will be violent action against the Zim Line, the kind that will convince them that they are absolutely insane in irritating religious Jewry, which has been their best and most reliable customer.[49]

The Ministerial Committee, in fact, decided in favor of only one kitchen. According to one report, the deciding vote, cast by a Mapai minister, came after he heard the opinion of a representative of the RCA in Israel that two kitchens would lead to the debasement of Israel's name among American Jewry.[50] The Government, however, ignored the recommendations of its own committee and decided to leave the decision in Zim's hands, insisting only that it weigh the matter again.[51] A week later, Zim decided on two kitchens.[52]

The RCA issued a press release expressing "shock" and "dismay" at the decision of the Zim Line.[53] In September their leaders wrote to all members asking them to send letters or telegrams to Zim's New York office "urging, requesting and demanding that they change their avowed plans." The rabbis were told "to announce this from the pulpits and perhaps in your bulletins and newsletters asking the members of your congregation to do likewise. The heavy flow of letters and telegrams might be just what they are waiting for in order to help them change their plans." [54] The same circular contained a sample letter from a rabbi to Zim, which included the following paragraph:

> We, who have been urging our people these many years to buy Israeli products and to travel Israeli lines, will feel compelled to re-evaluate our feelings and our opinion regarding your line should you persist in this move.

On September 25 two separate delegations of rabbis (one representing Conservative and Reform as well as Orthodox rabbis) met with an Israeli representative on the *Shalom* issue. Kirshblum, after reporting on the meeting, observed that "tension within religious Jewry is constantly growing as a result of the S.S. Shalom" and that U.J.A. and Bonds will definitely be hurt when the demonstrations and advertisements will begin to manifest themselves." [55] Kirshblum was not issuing a threat but stating what he considered to be a fact. He assumed that the religious non-Zionists would seize upon the issue and use it as a stick to beat Israel. Perhaps he had the demonstrations surrounding the National Service Law in mind when he made this statement. It is probable that, bearing in mind the Government's surrender in that affair, he had no doubt that it would give in on this matter as well. But his confidence and his fears for Israel were misplaced. The religious non-Zionists never became as involved in the Shalom controversy as they did in the other cases to be discussed in this chapter. The reason for that rests, no doubt, on the fact that they were neither so personally affected nor so committed to the "good name" of Israel as to be disturbed by nonkosher facilities aboard an Israeli ship. It was rather the religious Zionists, whose sense of identification with Israel was affected, who became demonstrative over the issue. On the other hand, as we shall see, Israel was less susceptible in 1963 to the kind of pressure it had been susceptible to ten years earlier.

Israelis continued to inform their American allies of developments and continued to suggest certain steps.[56] But, as I have indicated in other cases, once aroused, the protests of American Jews, even those of the religious Zionists, developed a momentum of their own. The Israeli rabbinate had consistently maintained that it would not certify the *Shalom* kitchen as kosher so long as there was a nonkosher kitchen aboard. When no respectable American rabbinical figure or organization was willing to do so, Zim entered into an agreement with Sanheder Harabbanim, a rabbinical group of questionable status and of very bad repute, to provide rabbinical certification. A month later, they canceled the agreement,[57] after it aroused the protests of Conservative and Reform as well as Orthodox groups in the United States, and of secular as well as religious Jews in Israel.[58] But, Zim's act served to heat the passions of the Orthodox. Israel's Sephardic Chief Rabbi Nissim threatened to withdraw the Kashrut certification of all Zim ships. Rabbi Joseph Soloveitchik announced his readiness to sign a statement prohibiting all travel on any Zim Line. Whereas rabbis of the non-Zionist camp had been prepared to do so for some time, the fact that Soloveitchik was willing to join with them (the RCA also expressed its willingness to do so), indicated how deeply the heretofore moderate forces in the religious Zionist camp felt about the *Shalom* issue in general and the agreement with a "rump" rabbinical organization in particular. Soloveitchik urged the NRP not to compromise. "The future of our movement depends on the results of the confrontation on the matter of the ship. Any compromise is likely to destroy the movement and alienate its finest people." [59]

The political leaders of religious Zionism on both sides of the ocean now undertook to "cool" the tempers and prevent the issuing of "prohibitions," which they feared would not only harm the State of Israel but backfire against the religious Zionists by arousing the sensitivity of the nonreligious.[60] The conflict was therefore returned to the political arena. As the politicians returned to the fray, the rabbis and Zim directors withdrew. But one cannot dismiss the possibility, and I shall return to this point, that it was the militancy of the religious forces, in both Israel and the Diaspora, that forced the politicians on both sides to reopen the issue. Indeed, the NRP reportedly told Prime Minister Levi Eshkol that one reason they could not compromise on the *Shalom* issue was the unhappiness that this matter caused among American Jewry,[61] although earlier the Minister of Religion had purportedly been amenable to some arrangement that would permit two kitchens on the *Shalom*.[62]

The religious parties threatened to resign from the government a number of times during the next month. Finally, under pressure from both the Government and the Jewish Agency and lacking even the support of the Histadrut, Zim gave in. *Ha'Aretz* reported that those favoring two kitchens "were disappointed by the lukewarm attitude of public political forces and especially from the Histadrut." [63] According to the press, the major pressure on Zim came from Eshkol and other Mapai Ministers. *Ha'Aretz* reminded its readers that the chairman of the Zim Board of Directors was also the general director of the Ministry of Finance, which Eshkol had headed before his designation as prime minister. Referring to the Zim chairman, *Ha'Aretz* said "no one will doubt that he has again carried out, in the Shalom case, the wishes of the man who is now Prime Minister." [64]

Zim's agreement with the Israeli chief rabbinate specified that for at least a reasonable period the *Shalom* would sail with only one kosher kitchen. I might add that the following year, the rabbinate agreed that on those cruises where the *Shalom* did not touch an Israeli port, there would still be only one kitchen, but this time nonkosher. Shortly, thereafter, Zim sold the *Shalom* and the matter ceased being a subject for dispute. The concern here, however, is with the earlier decision.

The *Shalom* controversy ended in an acknowledged victory for the religious parties. There is no question that despite the activity of Diaspora Jewry, the victory was a political concession by Eshkol to the religious parties. Indeed, from January to February 1964, two months after Diaspora Jewry had issued its most serious threats, Eshkol switched positions three times. At the beginning of the year, he was reportedly insistent that there would be two kitchens.[65] But a day after he met with NRP leaders, an unnamed Mapai leader suggested that Mapai was prepared to compromise.[66] On February 7, Eshkol was reported to have switched from a readiness to compromise to a new intransigence, because the left-wing party, Mapam was prepared to join the coalition and the threats of the religious ministers to resign no longer frightened him.[67] But Mapam did not join the coalition and Eshkol did give in.

Three respondents, one an NRP political figure, the other the Israeli ambassador to the U.S. during this period, and the third a member of Zim's Board of Directors, felt that it was the NRP alone that achieved the victory and that Orthodox Jewry abroad, if it played any role at all, served only as an instrument of the religious parties.[68]

Other observers credited a more significant, though indirect role to Diaspora Jewry. *Ha'Aretz* felt that Eshkol's decision was not simply a matter of coalitional politics. A correspondent argued that the necessity to consider the demands of the religious parties stems "from the fear of the unpleasant echo that open conflict between the State and the religious would arouse in the Diaspora and especially in the U.S." [69] But even if we accept this interpretations, Diaspora pressure operated indirectly and was utilized by the NRP rather than operating directly on the Israeli Government. There is no question, therefore, that the fight was led by the NRP, Diaspora support providing an element in its strength. The question is, did Diaspora Jewry's attitude also strengthen the NRP conviction not to compromise, as it was purported to have been willing to do at one stage? How influential was Rabbi Soloveitchik's warning against compromise or the militancy of the generally moderate RCA? If these factors were of no influence, then one must conclude that

Diaspora Jewry was not influential in the formation of public policy but was merely a valuable asset for one side or another in a basically domestic affair.

The questions do not admit of any clear-cut answer. But, the *Shalom* case does evoke another interesting conclusion. The threats of economic sanctions—that Diaspora Jewry would boycott the Zim Lines or the rabbinate would withdraw kashrut certification from all Zim ships—were not persuasive. They may have had some impact on Zim's decision to withdraw from its agreement with Sanheder Harabbanim, but its final decision to maintain only a kosher kitchen was an expression of Eshkol's wishes. His decision, in turn, was a function of NRP pressure. If Diaspora influence was effective, therefore, it was because it was able to influence the NRP. The contrast between the *Shalom* case and the previous case is highly instructive. Over a ten-year period, the structure of pressures had changed dramatically. Whereas in the National Service Law instance, the extremist element of American Orthodoxy was able to operate directly on the government, in the present instance, the combined voice of American Orthodoxy, with the cooperation of Conservative and Reform Rabbis, was unable to influence the most compromising, least ideological, least militant, most Diaspora-oriented prime minister that Israel has ever had. The *Shalom* case suggests the possibility that a decade-and-a-half after its foundation, the Diaspora was no longer able to operate directly on the Israeli Government but could be effective only to the extent that it was able to influence established domestic political forces. In the remaining cases, I shall seek to explore this hypothesis.

THE AUTOPSY CONTROVERSY: 1966–1969

The lengthiest and bitterest religious controversy in Israel concerned the rights of a deceased or his family to prevent a postmortem examination. The Anatomy and Pathology Law of

1953 permitted autopsies without the approval of the deceased
or his family if three doctors, authorized to do so, signed a
certificate stating that an autopsy was necessary in order to
determine the cause of death or to use parts of the deceased's
body to heal another person. The law therefore gave wide
latitude to medical judgment, and less consideration to the
wishes of the deceased's family than is true, for example, in the
United States. The medical profession felt that it needed this
authority in a society where a large proportion of the population
was religious (and there are severe religious restrictions on
autopsies) and/or came from societies and cultures in which
attitudes about what constituted proper respect toward the
dead constrained families from granting permission for autopsies. But this very sensitivity of a large segment of the country's
population to postmortem operations made a head-on clash almost inevitable.

Protests from religious circles began shortly after the law
was passed and they continued throughout the 1950s. There
were many complaints; the most relevant for my purposes were
protests that the law made insufficient provision for the wishes
of the deceased's family and that doctors permitted postmortem
operations in an unnecessarily large number of cases. It was
also charged that two doctors commonly signed blank certificates,
thereby permitting one doctor alone to authorize an autopsy.

In negotiations surrounding formation of a coalition government, following the fifth Knesset election in 1961, the dominant
party, Mapai, agreed to appoint a committee to investigate the
1953 law with a view to recommending amendments to the
1953 Anatomy and Pathology Law that would make greater
provision for the wishes of the deceased's family.[70] The committee's recommendations were satisfactory to the religious
parties. However, in order to secure the approval of the Government, they agreed to a proposed bill that was less favorable from
their point of view. It provided that no postmortem could be
performed within five hours of the announcement of a death,
in order to give the deceased's family time to register its objec-

tion. Autopsies against the objection of the deceased or his family could be performed only in cases of death by violence, if three authorized doctors stated that not determining the cause of death constituted a threat to the public health, or if there was reason to suspect that the death was caused by a medical error. The medical profession expressed its objections to the proposed amendment,[71] but the chief rabbinate also opposed it because they felt that doctors maintained too much authority to authorize autopsies against the wishes of the deceased or his family. Due to the rabbinate's objection, the NRP withdrew its support and the amendment was not brought to a final vote.

In 1967 the NRP undertook new negotiations with Mapai concerning the amendments. Orthodox organizations in the U.S. also mounted a campaign to amend the law. The initiative for these efforts did not, however, come from the NRP. Requests for assistance came from the chief rabbinate, but primarily from the Public Committee to Safeguard Human Dignity, headed in Israel by Rafael Soloveitchik, a religious leader of pronounced right-wing, non-Zionist tendencies. The Public Committee operated through an American counterpart organization, The American Committee for Safeguarding Human Dignity, and through a number of prominent non-Zionist religious leaders, who identified with the committee and its activities in the United States.[72] They, in turn, influenced the religious Zionist organizations. The religious Zionists were forced to adopt a more aggressive stance than they might otherwise have been prepared to do by virtue of their interrelationships with other Orthodox organisations [73] and out of fear that they might be accused of indifference to legitimate religious demands.[74] As we shall see, they did, however, seek to moderate the tactics of the extremists.

In January, the Association of Orthodox Jewish Scientists, a small but prestigious organization, two of whose leaders were medical doctors, issued a statement supporting the demands of religious Jews while suggesting, however subtly, that rabbinical leaders in Israel had not done all that was possible to find solutions to the need for postmortem operations within the framework of religious law.[75] The thrust of the statement was to support the demand for giving greater authority to the wishes of the deceased or his family. In February a delegation met with Israeli Ambassador Avraham Harman and later with the President of Hadassah, Charlotte Jacobson. In their discussion with Harman they noted that

> while many of the accusations made against the physicians with respect to their motivations deserve to be rejected, it is clear that physicians have too often ignored the specifics of their agreements with regard to the indications for autopsies and to the manner of performance of autopsies, with resultant offense to the sensitivities of families of the deceased. . . . The religious leaders, who had previously shown good faith almost to the point of naiveté, have now responded much more militantly, and in the resulting conflict, the flames of emotion have been fanned to a dangerous level, bordering on hysteria.

The statement was issued on February 28 and mailed to all members of the Orthodox scientists group on March 14.[76] Members were urged to write to Israeli Government officials and to the Director of the Hadassah Hospital in Israel. Special pressure was exerted on Hadassah Hospital in Israel, but especially on the parent women's organization in the United States in an effort to force it to change the Israeli hospital's procedures. The Union of Orthodox Jewish Congregations also met with Hadassah leaders, and carried on a sometimes acrimonious, sometimes threatening correspondence with them.[77] In more militant tones, the Committee for Safeguarding Human Dignity attacked Hadassah in a *New York Times* advertisement[78] and the Agudath Israel Youth picketed its offices.[79] The pressure on Hadassah did result in the hospital's exhibiting greater sensitivity to the deceased's family's wishes and a consequent drop in the number of autopsies it performed,[80] but that is beyond the purview of this case study.

NRP leaders urged their American allies to exercise restraint. They pointed out that the Government was committed to amending the law and that only the opposition of the chief rabbinate had persuaded the NRP not to press for the amendment.[81] Although the NRP never encouraged any action other than restraint, the Religious Zionists of America continued to assist in the campaign within the U.S. for the amendment of the law. Indeed, the RZA president even took credit for convincing the leaders of a number of non-Orthodox organizations that they should cable Prime Minister Levi Eshkol on the matter.[82] On April 5 the presidents of the American Jewish Committee, the Union of American Hebrew Congregations (Reform), the United Synagogue of America (Conservative), the Rabbinical Assembly of America (Conservative), and the American Jewish Congress (which later retracted its endorsement of the message) wrote that

> motivated solely by humanitarian considerations, we urge adoption in Israel of compassionate procedures prohibiting autopsy without family consent, except in cases under coroner's jurisdiction or where there is a threat to public health.[83]

The more militant Orthodox organizations, led by the American Committee for the Safeguarding of Human Dignity, carried on a far more aggressive campaign of meetings, petitions, and demonstrations against Israeli policy and in favor of amending the law. They planned a mass demonstration in front of the United Nations for April 10. The demonstration was postponed at the last minute. According to RZA president Hershel Schachter, he was instrumental in persuading the leaders to postpone the demonstration, in return for which he, Schachter, obligated himself to secure the signatures of at least forty well-known and wealthy Jews to a cable identical to the one sent by the presidents of the non-Orthodox organizations. He reported that he had secured promises from Rabbis Joseph Lookstein, Norman Lamm, and Emmanuel Rackman (three of the most prominent rabbis of Orthodox synagogues in the United States), and of Wolfe Kelman, executive vice-president of the Conservative rabbinical body, to assist him in gathering the signatures.[84] The Yiddish press reported that the demonstration was postponed because "influential personalities" assured the organizers that the law would be amended.[85] Left unclear, however, was whether the amended law would be the one that the Government had already agreed to or what the chief rabbinate and the Committee for the Safeguarding of Human Dignity wanted. The differences between the NRP and the chief rabbinate were never mentioned in the N.S.. In fact, even the religious Zionists phrased their demands in terms of support for the chief rabbinate, virtually ignoring the fact that the NRP and the Government had arrived at a compromise amendment a year earlier. In one resolution, for example, the religious Zionists expressed their "sharpest protests against ignoring of the just demands of the united Israeli rabbinate." [86] In other words, the thrust of the attack was against the Government of Israel, a more convenient target than the NRP.

Perhaps the religious Zionists felt that they had no alternative. Even if one assumes that they were fully informed about the Government-NRP agreement, they could hardly put themselves in the position of publicly disputing the stand of the chief rabbinate, a position that the NRP itself was reluctant to assume. But there is no evidence that religious Zionist leaders who did know of the differences of opinion between the NRP and the rabbinate gave even private support to the NRP. In both the National Service Law and Shalom controversies, there had been differences of opinion between the rabbinates of Israel and the NRP. In both cases, the religious Zionists in America identified themselves with the NRP in their private if not their public statements. This was not the case in the present instance. It is unlikely that any individual or organization in the religious Zionist camp, short of Rabbi Joseph Soloveitchik himself,[87] could have persuaded the Israeli rabbinate to compromise its position. But the fact that the American religious Zionists offered so little support to the NRP certainly was of no help to it in its efforts to persuade the rabbinate to adopt a more flexible stance.

On April 10, Eshkol announced that the autopsy law would be amended at the next Knesset session.[88] While the announcement may have been made as part of an effort to calm the protests in the U.S. (significantly, the announcement was made by Agudath Israel leaders in Israel after their meeting with Eshkol), the evidence suggests that Eshkol was really only promising what he had already promised the NRP. A few weeks later, NRP leader Moshe Shapiro expressed his optimism in a letter to Rabbi Joseph Soloveitchik, stating that the matter, presently under negotiation within the Government, would be settled.[89] American Orthodox pressures on Israel continued, however, through letters and delegations.[90]

The Knesset took up the proposed amendment in the second week of May, but the rabbinate again expressed its opposition and the NRP again requested that the bill be withdrawn.[91]

In the wake of the Six Day War and the general feelings of conciliation that followed, American Orthodoxy ceased its activity on behalf of changes in the law. In mid-1968, however, Yeshiva circles in Israel once again requested assistance on behalf of the Committee for the Safeguarding of Human Dignity.[92] Pressure was again mounted, only this time with less intensity, due, no doubt, to the renewed sense of American Jewish identity with the State of Israel. Legislation was again introduced in the Knesset, but the rabbinate once again informed the NRP that the proposed amendment, which the NRP supported, was in conflict with Jewish law.[93] NRP Minister Burg blamed extremist religious circles in general, and Agudath Israel in particular, for the failure of effective legislation to provide greater deference to the wishes of the deceased's family,[94] but the effective opposition apparently came from the chief rabbinate, against whose wishes the NRP refused to act. The rabbinate, however, was itself subject to pressures from the extreme right. Two respondents, both American rabbis closely involved with Israeli activity, blamed the religious right wing for failure to achieve a solution. According to Rabbi Simon Dolgin, it was the unwillingness of the Committee for Safeguarding Human Dignity to compromise that prevented a satisfactory solution.[95] According to the executive vice-president of the Rabbinical Council of America, the delegation that his organization had sent to Israel in 1967 could have worked out an acceptable compromise on the autopsy issue, but there was no individual of sufficient stature and courage in the camp of the religious non-Zionists who was willing to risk his reputation or who could prevail on his peers to accept a compromise.[96]

The Anatomy and Pathology Law was never amended. Religious groups, however, did gain some satisfaction in 1969. The state comptroller's report of that year pointed out that postmortem operations had been illegally conducted in a number of government hospitals. In the ensuing outcry, the Minister of Health reminded all hospital directors of their obligations under the law and appointed a committee to check procedures and recommend further revisions to insure full implementation of the law. In addition, all hospitals were instructed to submit monthly reports to the Ministry of Health on postmortem operations "and implementation of the ordinance concerning the requirements for the signature of three doctors for all such operations performed." [97] The controversy within Israel, however, did not abate. In fact, it assumed violent proportions in 1971. In 1973 new regulations of the Ministry of Health provided increased protection for the family's wishes by greatly simplifying the manner in which it could prevent a postmortem operation. Since then, the controversy has abated.

In the autopsy controversy, Diaspora pressure appears to have achieved nothing, although in retrospect it is not clear what it could have achieved. The Government was willing to accept an amendment which, at least in theory, would have provided a great deal more consideration to family objections to autopsies. The fact that the medical profession opposed the amendment in 1965 and continued to do so at later stages[98] suggests that the amendment may have been of real consequence. The Government agreed to the compromise before Diaspora pressures were felt. It is unlikely that it would, under any circumstances, have agreed to all the rabbinate's demands, which included a rabbi's consent before a certificate signed by three authorized doctors could override family objections. In any event, the NRP did not pressure the government to agree to this. The amendment, therefore, failed to pass because the Israeli rabbinate refused to support it.

Diaspora pressure, in fact, supported rabbinical demands, which had no effective political expression in Israel. Efforts to influence Prime Minister Eshkol were simply misdirected. The only hope for the forces favoring the rabbinate's position would have been to apply pressure directly on the NRP. This might or might not have succeeded. Had it succeeded, the NRP, in turn, might or might not have successfully influenced the Government. But this was not the tactic employed. The entire battle in the U.S. was, therefore, doomed to failure regardless of how impressive a list of non-Orthodox supporters the religious Zionists were able to muster and regardless of how extreme the demonstrations by the non-Zionists became. It must have become increasingly obvious as time went on that the most effective influence on the religious policy of the Government was that exercised by the NRP. In the final case study we find American Orthodox circles finally adapting their tactics in the reality of Israeli politics.

THE "WHO IS A JEW?" CONTROVERSY: 1970–1973

Among the bits of personal information that the Ministry of the Interior records for each resident of Israel are his religion and his *leom*. The term *leom* is officially translated as "nationality" but in fact the terms *people* or *folk* are more accurate precisely because, like *leom,* they lack precision. The question "Who is a Jew?" has been fought out at the political level around the criteria by which one is registered as Jewish according to *leom* and/or religion.[99]

By the end of 1973 the question "Who is a Jew?" had led

to four governmental crises: one in 1958, two in 1970, and on
in 1972. Following the 1958 governmental crises, after length
delay, indecision, threats, counter threats, and new elections, i
was decided to let the Minister of the Interior decide who wa
or was not to be registered as a Jew. Since the Minister of th
Interior was from the NRP, and since that party has continue
to hold this post since that time, the Government's decision wa
a *de facto* victory for the religious position.

In that instance the Government of Israel actually invite
the involvement of Diaspora Jewry. In the throes of the crise
Ben-Gurion requested a number of rabbis and Jewish scholar
from the Diaspora to express their opinion on appropriate criteri
for establishing who is a Jew. The fact that even a majority c
the non-Orthodox respondents felt that traditional religiou
criteria should be determinative eased the Government's retrea
from its original position, which had been to register anyone a
Jewish who declared he was Jewish.

In 1970 the question "Who Is a Jew?" was first raised wit
respect to *leom*. Could someone who was incontrovertably nc
Jewish by religious standards, and who did not wish to b
registered as Jewish by religious standards, nevertheless b
registered as Jewish according to *Leom?* Can one be part of th
Jewish folk or people without being Jewish by religious star
dards? The question ultimately rests on whether there is such
thing as a Jewish *leom* independent of the Jewish religion. Th
question formed part of the early constitutional debates in Israe
The unwillingness and/or inability of the Government to resolv
this question, their fear of bitterly dividing the country shoul
they reach a decision one way or the other, was a factor in th
decision not to formulate a constitution.

But the Government was forced to decide the issue in 197
because of a decision of the Israeli Supreme Court in the Shal
case. Benjamin Shalit's wife, a naturalized Israeli citizen of nor
Jewish parents had no desire to convert to Judaism and regi
tered her religion as *none*. The Shalits also registered their chi
dren as having no religion, but they did wish to register them a

Jewish under the category of *leom*. The court upheld Shalit in a five-to-four decision on the technical grounds that, in the absence of legislation to the contrary, registration clerks of the Ministry of the Interior had no authority to inquire into the veracity of a resident's statement, the clerk's role being merely to record what the registrant claimed in good faith.

The court's decision forced the Government's hand. By indecision it would confirm the court's opinion, thereby permitting separation of religion and *leom* as a matter of public policy. The NRP insisted that the law be changed to provide that one who was not Jewish by religion could not be registered as Jewish by leom. Leaders of Orthodox Jewry in the Diaspora, on their own initiative, also demanded a change in the law.[100]

A substantial portion of the Labor party (including Prime Minister Golda Meir) also favored a change in the law. But, whereas a majority of the Labor party, all the religious parties, Herut, and some individual members of other parties agreed that one who was not Jewish according to religion ought not to be registered as Jewish according to *leom*, the question became: how was one to define the "religious" criteria? Proponents of the change agreed to accept traditional religious criteria which defines a Jew as someone born of a Jewish mother or converted to Judaism, and they all agreed that even if one met with these criteria he could only be registered as Jewish if he had "not become an adherent of another religion." The controversy centered on the meaning of the term *converted to Judaism*. The NRP (the only religious party then represented in the Government) wanted to add the provision that only someone converted in accordance with Jewish law or by an Orthodox rabbi would be recognized as being Jewish by conversion. In other words, they wanted the law to read that someone is defined as Jewish if he was born of a Jewish mother or was converted to Judaism *in accordance with Jewish law,* and was not an adherent of another religion. The Government majority, however, rejected the NRP request and submitted its bill (in fact, the bill was an amendment to the Law of Return) without the addition that the

NRP requested. In the Knesset vote the NRP nevertheless supported the law, whereas Augdath Israel and Poalei Agudath Israel abstained. Following the vote, the Minister of Justice announced that the Government interpreted the bill to mean that conversions by non-Orthodox rabbis abroad were acceptable; that is, for purposes of registration a convert would be considered Jewish whether he underwent conversion by an Orthodox, Conservative, or Reform rabbi. The law, however, did not bind the Israeli rabbinate in determining who is a Jew in cases that would arise before them—principally questions of marriage and divorce.

Representatives of both Conservative and Reform Judaism had lobbied on behalf of this interpretation. Prior to the cabinet's decision they met with the Prime Minister and the Minister of Justice. The Reform representative also met with a number of other Knesset leaders and cabinet members [101] including Minister of Tourism Moshe Kol, at the latter's request.[102]

The Conservative and Reform representatives elicited a promise from the Prime Minister that the changes in the law that the Government would submit to the Knesset would not be so worded as to preclude non-Orthodox conversions in the Diaspora.[103] But participants were not of the opinion that their meetings with the Prime Minister influenced her. According to Rabbi Ralph Simon, who represented Conservative Judaism, Golda Meir told them that in her trips through the U.S. many American Jews expressed their unhappiness to her about the lack of recognition for non-Orthodox rabbis in Israel. In return for the NRP'S insistence on the amendment precluding a secular or national definition of a Jew, she insisted, therefore, that the amendment recognize the validity of conversions by non-Orthodox rabbis, at least when performed in the Diaspora. She felt that this was a first step in breaking the Orthodox monopoly in Israel, but that, at this stage, it was all that could be expected.

Many of the NRP representatives in the Knesset were unhappy with the final wording of the amendment. They agreed to support the bill only because of their leader Moshe Shapiro's firm conviction that under no circumstances would a Govern ment majority agree to any provision that denied recognition to non-Orthodox conversions; the proposed bill, therefore, was the best they could hope for.[104]

After the bill's adoption, pressure immediately developed to amend the law by adding the words "according to Jewish law" to the term "conversion." The effort in the U.S. was supported by all Orthodox groups, but the initiative, impetus, and greatest effort came from the non-Zionist religious groups and especially from the Lubavitcher *Rebbe*. Ad hoc organizations were created in both Israel and America to lead the campaign. The leader of the American group, The Committee for Jewish Survival, denied that it was organized by Lubavitcher people.[105] Other respondents, even in the non-Zionist religious camp, referred to the organization as a Lubavitcher front, although it certainly had the support of non-Lubavitcher people as well.

Whereas the campaign to amend the law engaged the intense energy of only a small part of the Orthodox world, it was an effort that no Orthodox leader could afford to oppose. All Orthodoxy, both in Israel and the Diaspora, was united in its desire to amend the law in such a manner that only Orthodox conversions would be recognized. Thus, proponents of the amendment were able to secure the signatures of the presidents of every national Orthodox organization in the U.S. to an ad placed in three large Israeli dailies on June 2, 1971, maintaining that Israeli recognition of non-Orthodox conversions encourages assimilation.[106]

In the "Who Is A Jew?" controversy, special efforts were made to appeal directly to Israeli public opinion, as for example, in the ad just mentioned or in letters to the press to be cited below. As in other cases, Diaspora Jewry also sought to exercise pressure through mass meetings [107] and through a campaign of letter writing, cables, and petitions to Israeli public officials and, as noted, to the Israeli press.[108] There were also meetings with Israeli leaders in the U.S.[109] and in Israel itself.[110] Although representatives of the Israeli Committee to amend the law visited the U.S. in November 1971 to organize and coordinate activity to amend the law,[111] the Americans would have proceeded with out this encouragement.

The campaign to amend the law, however, differed from al others. First, it encountered active opposition from Conservative and Reform groups. Second, the Orthodox adopted a new tactic They not only sought to influence the Government by direct pressure, but also indirectly by pressuring the NRP to threaten to resign from the Government unless the law was amended. As suggested in the last case study, if proponents of change had any hope of success, it was in the pursuit of this strategy.

Pressures were exerted from both Israel and the Diaspora or the NRP. In Israel it came primarily from rabbinical circles Followers of the Lubavitcher *Rebbe* in Israel were also extremely active, but they, in turn, acted under basic guidelines that came from the Diaspora. I will confine my discussion to the Diaspora campaign.

In general, the pressure from all sources failed. It succeeded only in influencing one NRP Knesset member, Avner Shaki, and that came at the cost of Shaki's political future (at least in the short run). Furthermore, it is highly unlikely that Shaki, a leader among Sephardi Jews, was sensitive to Diaspora pressure. Indeed, he announced that he voted as he did in response to the rulings of the Israeli rabbinate and, he claimed, in accordance with the NRP's own platform.

Diaspora pressure on the NRP included resolutions by Orthodox groups,[112] messages from distinguished rabbinical leaders in America,[113] and meetings and demonstrations, including protests against an NRP Minister's visiting the U.S.,[114] but principally in direct attacks by the Lubavitcher *Rebbe,* whose prestige, even within the NRP, was enormous.[115] These attacks by the *Rebbe* and the Committee for Jewish Survival[116] sought to embarass the NRP by citing statements of the Israeli chief rabbinate that insisted that the NRP resign from the Government if the law was not amended. The NRP, in turn, was active in mobilizing counterpressure on the chief rabbinate to rescind their decision They were partially successful and the rabbinate's position or whether the NRP was or was not obligated to resign became ambiguous.

Pressure on the NRP reached its peak in the spring and summer of 1972 when Agudath Israel introduced an amendment providing that conversions must be in accordance with Jewish law. Even the Young Israel cabled the NRP urging them "to vote in accordance with our principles."[117] The NRP, in fact, asked its coalition partners to permit it to vote for the bill, which in all events had no chance of passage—but the Cabinet rejected the NRP request. It did permit NRP Knesset members to abstain. (This was part of a package deal that involved other parties and other issues, a discussion of which would take us too far afield from the main topic).

Although the Agudath Israel amendment never had any hopes of passage, Liberal party Knesset member Zalman Abramov, a friend of and legal adviser to the Reform movement in Israel, suggested that Conservative and Reform groups in the Diaspora mobilize a counterattack.[118] The presidents of the world organizations, American congregational organizations, and American rabbinical organizations of the Conservative and Reform movements signed a statement that urged the Government

> to reject the misguided advocacy of those who would insert the words "according to Halacha" in the Law of Return. . . . When the Law of Return was revised in 1970, the Knesset in its wisdom understood that yielding to the pressures of some Orthodox Jewish leaders would have deleterious consequences for aliyah and for the sense of participation of non-Orthodox Jewish communities in the drama of Israel. The very same considerations of the government of Israel at this time.[119]

The NRP, however, did not surrender to Orthodox pressures. On the contrary, they chose to respond to the pressures from Orthodox groups in the Diaspora by conducting their own campaign to explain their position abroad and by denying the fact that the Israeli rabbinate had demanded that they resign from the Government.[120] To this end, the NRP sent a representative abroad to explain his party's position to Orthodox groups.[121]

In summary, the influences on the NRP from the Diaspora had only a marginal effect. The only significant outside influence on the NRP comes from the Israeli rabbinate [122] and in this case, even that pressure did not prevail. The Committee for Jewish Survival continued to bring pressure on the NRP [123] with even fewer noticeable consequences.

In the negotiations over formation of a Government following the Knesset elections of December 1973 the NRP sought a commitment to amend the Law of Return. But it would certainly have done so without Diaspora pressure. The events of 1974 carry us beyond the limitations of this study. They were complicated by internal conflict within the NRP over personal and foreign policy issues in which the "Who is a Jew?" issue became an instrument for one side to obtain concessions on other issues from the other side. But, in the final analysis, the law remained unchanged.

Another question that might be raised is, would the Government have been more amenable to NRP requests to amend the law if it had not been for the counterpressure of Conservative and Reform groups in the Diaspora? This is a difficult question to answer and the reader may more readily arrive at his own conclusion after reviewing the final section of this chapter. But in all likelihood the Government in general, and the Labor party in particular, did not respond to direct pressure of non-Orthodox Jewry. They did consider the desires of Conservative and Reform Jewry and the implications of denying the legitimacy of conversions performed by non-Orthodox rabbis. But the direct pressures of non-Orthodox Jewry were at most of only marginal influence.

ORTHODOXY'S INFLUENCE ON ISRAEL

I have discussed the five instances in the area of religious policy where the government was most aware of pressure from Diaspora Jewry. There were other instances where one or more sections of Orthodox Jewry sought to influence Israel's public policy. The most important such efforts were:

1. Opposition to the drafting of Yeshiva (advanced talmudic academy) students. This issue first arose shortly after the creation of the State and has recurred periodically.
2. The 1961 effort to transfer children of religious background within the *Aliyat Ha'Noar* program from nonreligious to religious auspices and to prevent the future placement of religious children in nonreligious environments.
3. The 1964 efforts to persuade Israel to restrict Christian missionary activity in Israel.
4. The 1965 efforts, limited to the non-Zionist religious elements, to close certain areas of Jerusalem to all forms of transportation on the Sabbath.
5. An effort to persuade Israel to soften its stand in negotiating with Arab terrorists who hijacked a TWA plane bound for Israel in 1970. As far as could be ascertained, this effort was confined to the UOJCA.
6. Opposition in 1972 to a proposed bill permitting civil marriage in Israel.
7. 1972 efforts to persuade the major fund-raising agency on behalf of Israel to allocate large sums of money for the religious needs of new immigrants coming from the Soviet Union to Israel. Strictly speaking, this was an effort to influence fund-raising agencies and the Jewish Agency, not the Government of Israel.

In my general conclusions about the effectiveness of Orthodox influence from the Diaspora, I will also refer to these issues. First, however, let us turn to a set of more prosaic questions concerning initiative, tactics, and channels of influence.

Initiative

Respondents were asked from where the initiative to pressure Israel arose? A number noted that in the 1970 "Who is a Jew?" issue, Orthodox concern was an almost spontaneous reaction to developments in Israel as reported in the American press. Otherwise, respondents from the religious Zionist camp noted that initiative came from NRP leaders, from the chief rabbis, or from the non-Zionist religious "yeshiva world."[124] This third camp often charges Israel with religious coercion or gross violation of religious rights. The RCA, for example, will first check the facts with the Israeli consulate before it adopts a stand.[125]

In general, American Orthodox leaders who were interviewed see themselves as "manipulated"[126] by Orthodox forces within Israel.[127] In addition, the religious Zionists tend to be "manipulated" by the non-Zionists. The pressure that some American Orthodox organizations exert upon Israel tends to be a response to "pressure" upon them. In fact, one Orthodox leader viewed his organization's primary role as a compromiser and protector of Israel against the demands and tactics of religious extremists.

Tactics

Orthodox organizations employ a wide variety of tactics. Probably least effective are letters and cables to Israeli officials[128] and threats against fund-raising campaigns on behalf of Israel. Only such non-Zionist religious organizations as the Union of Orthodox Rabbis or the Rabbinical Alliance threatened to encourage a boycott of fund raising on behalf of Israel. The effectiveness of such threats is reduced to a minimum since everyone knows that these organizations exercise practically no influence on any major contributors. In fact, such obvious attempts at blackmail probably have a backlash effect. Israel could never afford to give in to such threats. Religious Zionists, however, believe that Israel is conscious of the fact, and they often remind Israelis of the fact that if Orthodox Jews are unhappy with Israeli policy, fund-raising efforts will necessarily be hurt no matter how strongly the leadership itself may support the campaign.[129] But there is no evidence that even this tactic has had any noticeable success. Perhaps, however, threats to establish a competing campaign, as was done in the effort or behalf of religious needs of Soviet Jews in 1972 has an impact on the allocation of funds.

A frequently employed tactic is the sending of delegations to Israel to meet with Israeli leaders. Delegations of Orthodox leaders find it relatively easy to meet with top Israeli officials in the U.S. or in Israel. Sending a delegation assures the organization of publicity, and serves other obvious organizational needs. There is little evidence that it is particularly successful in persuading Israeli officials to alter their point of view, although logically many such delegations from many organizations should have some cumulative impact.

Demonstrations in the Diaspora against Israeli policy is probably the single most effective instrument of pressure. It is certainly the one to which Israeli officials are most sensitive. Israel fears mass demonstrations and protests. Its prestige depends, in part, upon its reputation as the leader and central figure of concern for world Jewry. Attacks upon it by other Jews harm its public image.

Related to this is the "nuisance" factor. As a former foreign office official noted, Israel does not like trouble. American Orthodoxy is capable of making trouble, and, other things being equal, it is better to come to terms with them.

With the exception of the immigrant camp controversy, only the non-Zionist religious groups have utilized this tactic. Even organizations such as Agudath Israel shy away from demonstrations, because they involve public attacks on Israel and, as we saw in the National Service Law controversy, can easily get out of hand. Outside of some religious extremists, most Orthodox groups are reluctant to attack Israel directly, in part because their leaders do not want to hurt Israel, and in part because of the tremendous sympathy for Israel even among their own supporters.

Orthodox respondents believed that to the extent they exercised any real influence it rested less on the pressure they exerted and more on their prestige. Yaacov Herzog shared this opinion. According to Herzog, the Government knows that the future of the Diaspora rests with the Orthodox youth: "They are the survivalists." The reason the Orthodox, unlike the Conservative and Reform, will demonstrate against Israel is that they feel themselves to be a part of Israel, whereas the Conservative and Reform are not sufficiently identified with what takes place in Israel to demonstrate, he said.[130]

Channels

American Orthodox organizations have relatively easy access to top Israeli leaders. At the first stage they will turn to the local Israeli consul or ambassador, who will always pass their requests on to the Israeli Foreign Office.[131] The next stage is a meeting between a delegation of Orthodox leaders and prominent Israeli officials, either in the U.S. or in Israel. The leader of one Orthodox organization, however, is convinced that this kind of direct pressure on Israel—letters, cables and finally direct meetings and confrontations—is futile. His organization, he says now seeks to influence Israel through the offices of the UJA (the major fund-raising agency for Israel in the United States) and the Jewish Agency.

The most effective channels of influence are through Israeli political parties, especially partners in the Government coalition. The one religious party that has almost always been a member of the Government is the NRP. But there are only a few instances where Diaspora Orthodoxy has a "religious" interest independent of the NRP's interests. Instead, in most instances, it was the NRP who used Diaspora Orthodoxy as a channel for their interests. However, in the "Who is a Jew" controversy, one segment of Israeli society (the non-Zionist religious camp) sought to utilize American Orthodoxy to influence another segment of Israeli society (the religious Zionists) to pressure the Government on behalf of interests that the latter, on their own, would not promote. Even this tactic has certain weaknesses.

First, many respondents do not believe that Israeli religious leaders (spiritual or political) have much respect for American

Orthodoxy. This lack of respect is a limiting factor in the exercise of influence.

A second limitation stems from the reticence of Orthodox Jews in pressuring the NRP. The NRP does not activate American Orthodox Jewry through "political" personalities but through Orthodoxy's "religious" leadership, who believe that they are being asked to act in the interests of Judaism and of religious Jews (few Orthodox leaders distinguish between them). The NRP could not activate American Orthodoxy for its overtly "political" as distinct from "religious" demands, nor has it tried to do so. By the same token, seeking to pressure Israel through the instrumentality of the NRP against the wishes of the NRP is not only a sophisticated operation that is beyond the capacity and interest of most Orthodox Jews but is also "inappropriate" behavior to many others because it too smacks of "political" as distinct from "religious" behavior.

Finally, the NRP is not easily pressured. It has many friends in the U.S. The Religious Zionists of America will never take public issue with the NRP.[132] In fact, they do not even expect to be consulted. In the cases we have studied as well as others, the RZA requested information and "a line of action" from the NRP. The RZA, in turn, does exercise some influence on the American scene where it defends the NRP from counterpressure. Many RCA rabbis and leaders are RZA members or are committed to its ideology. Other organizations such as Young Israel, which are quite independent of Israeli politics and under the influence of non-Zionist religious leaders, are extremely reluctant to clash with the NRP for fear of splitting their own organization. Obviously, the greater the ideological distance between an American organization and the NRP, the more willing they may be to take issue with it, but the less likely they are to be able to influence its stand.

The General Effectiveness of Orthodox Pressure

A survey of five cases suggests no simple answer to the question: has Diaspora Jewry (in this case American Orthodoxy) influenced Israel's religious policy? In two cases, immigrant camps and drafting of girls, there was evidence of influence; in one case, the *Shalom,* the influence was probably indirect; and in two cases, autopsies and "Who is a Jew?", there seems to have been no effective influence at all. The most striking fact in a comparison of these cases the time distribution. Diaspora pressure was successful in 1951 and 1954, of limited success in 1964, and unsuccessful in 1967 and 1972. This confirms the observation of a former adviser to Prime Minister Levi Eshkol on Diaspora affairs, Avraham Avi-Hai, according to whom the religious groups were more influential in the early years of the state because of a mistaken notion in Israel that all Diaspora Jewry were religious. This began to change in the 1960s. According to Avi-Hai, the *Shalom* controversy was the turning point.[133]

Paradoxically, though Orthodox influence apparently waned beginning in the mid 1960s, the Orthodox have become increasingly active in seeking to influence Israel on a wide variety of issues. Indeed, of the seven additional issues listed at the beginning of this section, six arose after 1960 and three since 1969. This is, in part, due to the increased strength of the religious right wing, the non-Zionist religious forces, within Orthodox circles in the U.S. It is they who increasingly set the agenda of public issues for American Orthodoxy and they are far more militant and aggressive in bringing pressure on Israel. Another factor was a greater feeling of confidence in Israel's physical security until 1973. As one Orthodox leader phrased it, "they can't sell the military danger to us so there is more pressure now."[134] The absence of pressure in 1974 and 1975 suggests that Israel's security affects religious non-Zionists as well as religious Zionists.

Perhaps I have underestimated the significance of Diaspora pressure. Certainly, my assertion that in some cases the NRP achieved its goals without Diaspora assistance can be challenged. In the first place, part of the NRP's influence within the Government rests on the assumption that it has a great hinterland in the Diaspora. Second, Orthodox pressure is most effective when American and Israeli religious forces work together. A former Israeli Ambassador to the U.S. commented that whereas it is pressure from within Israel and not the Diaspora that influences the Government, the fact that demands within Israel find an echo in the Diaspora also has an impact.[135] Nonetheless, there is no escaping the fact that Diaspora interests are not really autonomous; their pressure is invited from Israel and they exercise an influence only because they are allied with active forces within Israeli society.

This serves to explain, in part, why Orthodox pressures in the Diaspora have generated so little counterpressure. One might have anticipated the mobilization of non-Orthodox groups against the Orthodox. I have noted one such occasion: the "Who is a Jew?" controversy. Even then, however, when their direct interests were involved, the non-Orthodox acted only on a suggestion from a member of the Israeli Knesset. The best known counterreaction to Orthodox pressure was in a 1964 telegram to Levi Eshkol signed by the American Jewish Congress, the American Jewish Committee, B'nai Brith, and the Conservative and Reform American rabbinical and American synagogue groups. The telegram called upon Eshkol to resist the pressures of Orthodox groups for legislation restricting Christian missionary activity in Israel.[136] Obviously, any legislation in Israel that might be interpreted as restricting religious freedom would be extremely damaging and dangerous to Diaspora Jewry. A delegation of French Jews also expressed its hope that Israel would exercise great caution in the matter of legislation affecting missionary activity.[137] But despite the importance of the matter to the Diaspora, the intervention of American non-Orthodox organizations only came after a suggestion from an Israeli official in New York.[138]

Thus, in the two cases where American non-Orthodox groups opposed American Orthodox pressure on Israel, their intervention came at the request of Israelis. In other cases the non-Orthodox were either entirely passive, or were silent partners to Orthodox pressures.

In part, this is a result of the non-Orthodox Jew's lack of commitment to his non-Orthodoxy. In part, it results from a true communality of interest among "religious" Jews of America as opposed to the "secularists" of Israel. But, by and large, it stems from non-Orthodoxy's lack of alignment with any specific forces within Israeli society that would "manipulate" them into activity. And as long as no one in Israel takes the initiative, political pressure on Israel, as suggested in chapter 2, is quite inappropriate to Diaspora Jewry's image of Israel and Israel-Diaspora relations. To put the matter more simply, there is no significant force within Israel to legitimate the pressure from non-Orthodox forces in the Diaspora. In the absence of such legitimacy, Diaspora Jewry itself refuses to act.

ISRAELI POLICY TOWARD CONSERVATIVE AND REFORM JEWRY

Most Conservative and Reform Jews feel that Israel discriminates against them. Their rabbis are not authorized to perform marriage, divorce, or conversion ceremonies in Israel. The Israeli rabbinate does not even recognize the authority of much of what they do abroad. Their synagogues, as a general rule, receive no Government subsidy and on many occasions local political pressure impedes the establishment of new congregations.

Despite these disabilities, despite the fact that the bulk of financial support that Israel receives from the U.S. comes from Jews affiliated with Conservative and Reform synagogues, and despite the fact that most of the lay readers in the U.S. who mobilize political support on behalf of Israel are members and leaders of Conservative and Reform synagogues—these two movements have done virtually nothing until recently to acquire recognition and status in Israel nor have they, until recently, acted together in their mutual self-interest.

The Conservative movement was divided on the proper strategy to pursue in Israel. Until recently, some of its top leadership was essentially Orthodox in outlook [139] and saw no special need to achieve status and recognition in Israel and abjured cooperation with Reform. Their attitude was that if they kept quiet and maintained a traditional front, they could achieve recognition for at least a selected number of Conservative rabbis. They could point to the fact that until 1963 the Israeli rabbinate recognized divorces performed by those Conservative rabbis in the Diaspora whose rabbinical-scholarly-pietistic credentials were known to them. In 1963, however, a special delegation from the Union of Orthodox Rabbis, on a visit to Israel, apparently received a pledge from the Israeli rabbinate to no longer recognize divorces granted by Conservative rabbis. Less than a year earlier an Israeli rabbinical court had refused to recognize divorces granted by two Conservative rabbis but, according to the president of the American organization of Conservative rabbis, "we were given assurances that there would be no repetition of such arbitrary action which represented a reversal of a policy that had obtained for 30 years." [140] Now, apparently, the policy was to be reversed in principle.

This new policy was offensive to even the most traditional wing of Conservative Judaism since it denied recognition to acts of Conservative rabbis not on the basis of some criterion of knowledge or piety that the traditionalist wing itself was willing to accept, but simply on the basis of organizational affiliation.

In protest against the policy of the Israeli rabbinate, the Conservative movement canceled its international conference scheduled to take place in Israel. Further, Rabbi Louis Finkelstein, president of Jewish Theological Seminary, leader of the Conservative movement, and an arch traditionalist, wrote to Israeli officials requesting them to act to obtain rabbinical recognition for divorces granted by Conservative rabbis.[141]

The issue came to a head in September 1963, when the Tel

Aviv rabbinical court refused to recognize a divorce issued by
an American Conservative rabbi whose credentials, according
to the Conservative movement, were beyond dispute.[142] The
matter was raised at a cabinet meeting by then Foreign Minister
Golda Meir, who said she had received repeated complaints
from various religious leaders to the U.S.[143] The cabinet empowered Minister of Religion Warhaftig to try and work out an
acceptable solution.

The American organization of Conservative rabbis hired
former Israeli Attorney-General Gideon Hausner to explore ways
of compelling the Israeli rabbinical courts to recognize the
divorce in question.[144] However, the matter was not pressed.
According to a Rabbinical Assembly leader,

> there were all kinds of pressures, internal and external, to have
> us drop the lawsuit which we had asked Gideon Hausner to
> initiate. . . . While these tensions were being debated and
> resolved, the young lady got tired of waiting. She returned to
> the United States and her marriage was performed in the
> chapel of the Seminary Synagogue.[145]

The case illustrates the weakness of the non-Orthodox pressure. The Conservatives were finally moved to activity. But,
what triggered it was, in fact, an assault upon their acts in
America rather than a denial of their privileges within Israel.
In other words, as long as Israel refused to accord to Conservative Judaism in Israel the same rights and privileges that Orthodoxy had, Conservative movement maintained its silence. It
broke this silence only after the Israeli rabbinate challenged the
legitimacy of what Conservative rabbis in America had done.
Whereas the challenge from Orthodoxy is nothing new, the fact
that the authority of Israeli law stood behind the Israeli rabbinate's challenge made the matter a very serious one. Conservative
rabbis would now have to tell those coming to them for a
divorce that this divorce would not be recognized in Israel.

Ostensibly, the Conservative movement had powerful allies
in the Israeli Government. The issue was raised on their behalf

by the Foreign Minister herself. Other personages added their cries of indignation against the Israeli rabbinate. But the support really bordered on lip service. None of the nonreligious ministers or parties had enough of a stake in the matter to turn it into a Government crisis. Instead, the Government handed the matter over to the Minister of Religion, an NRP representative. The Conservatives, in turn, were neither sufficiently united nor sufficiently committed, nor had they sufficient patience to press the issue any further.

Recently, the Conservative movement has cooperated politically with the Reform[146] in the "Who is a Jew?" controversy, and in all likelihood there will be more and more joint activity on the part of both these movements to secure recognition in Israel.

Reform has been far more outspoken in publicizing its demands and in protesting discrimination against it. A meeting of the World Union of Progressive Judaism in July 1968 presented three demands to Prime Minister Levi Eshkol. They included the recognition of the right of Reform rabbis to perform marriages in Israel, recognition by Israel of conversions performed by Reform rabbis, and "full support and aid from the Ministry for Religious Affairs and local Religious Councils, in full equality with Orthodox congregations" for Reform synagogues in Israel.[147] Reform demands have not been met (except on the matter of conversions in the Diaspora), nor will they be short of a major upheaval in the Israeli political system. As of 1973 the Conservative and Reform movements had a total of 22 synagogues with perhaps 1,000 family members. They are too weak to fight their own political battles and depend upon Diaspora support. Why has such support not been forthcoming?

There are many reasons for this. One reason is that the non-Orthodox, however strong or weak their commitment to Israel, are more committed to Israel than to Conservative or Reform Judaism or to the principle of complete religious freedom in Israel. This is true even of many Reform Jewish leaders, not to mention rank-and-file Reform rabbis and laymen.

In 1968, for example, the World Union of Progressive Judaism held their conference in Israel.[148] Local Reform rabbis were especially anxious to demonstrate a Reform presence in Israel by holding a prayer service at the Western Wall without any separation of sexes. Separation of sexes during prayer is not only an issue of importance to the Orthodox as a matter of Jewish law but it is also the major symbolic distinction between Orthodox and non-Orthodox religious movements in Jewish life. Separation of the sexes is adhered to at the Western Wall. The Reform movement conveyed its request to the Ministry of Religion, which is responsible for arrangements at the Wall. The Minister of Religion stated that the Conference could hold a service either at the Wall, with men and women separated, or on the slope overlooking the Wall, with men and women together. The local Reform rabbis insisted on pressing for the right to pray at the Wall with men and women together. Reform leaders consulted with the Prime Minister. Eshkol said he would support their right to pray at the Wall as they wished, but added that since this would inflame the Orthodox he would also have to provide police protection. The Reform leadership, over the objection of their local rabbis, decided that this would be too embarrassing to the Israeli Government and satisfied themselves with issuing a "strong statement."

Within the U.S., those influential laymen who are not very involved in support for Israel would like Reform to adopt a more aggressive stand in Israel. But those who are primarily responsible for Reform Judaism's Israel policy "have a tremendous loyalty to Israel" [149] and are less militant. They fear that arousing American Reform to a more militant posture could also arouse anti-Israel sentiment. Only a general loss of confidence in Israeli leadership on the part of American Jewry might arouse the Conservative and Reform movements to increase their pressure on Israel.

Aside from the fear of harming Israel, there is the general apathy of non-Orthodox Jews to their own movements. Furthermore, neither Reform nor Conservative Jews relate to Israel as Reform or Conservative Jews. In this respect they are at a tremendous disadvantage alongside the Orthodox, many of whom have a particular religious perspective of Israel. But there is no unique Reform or Conservative vision of Israel. Hence, they do not relate to Israel as an arena in which it is proper, necessary, or legitimate for one to pursue self-interested objectives. One difference betwen th Orthodox and the non-Orthodox is precisely that in pursuing their objectives within Israel the Orthodox firmly believe that they are not pursuing self-interested objectives but rather advancing Judaism and Israel. The non-Orthodox self-conception is neither so grand nor so daring.

If the Reform or Conservative movements in Israel were of any substance, the Diaspora might be activated to greater activity. But even this would be no guarantee of success. Given the present political structure, the non-Orthodox would have to find an Israeli party willing to fight, that is, to compromise other issues for the sake of advancing Conservative or Reform interests. Furthermore, as far as Conservative and Reform groups are concerned, their own religiopolitical commitments, or lack of such commitments, creates built-in problems that the Orthodox do not have. In the long run, Conservative and Reform political demands can only be met by the depoliticization of religion in Israel. Their problem is that to depoliticize religion requires a political decision. Only a group willing to become a virtually "one-issue" party could wage this fight successfully.

4

Other Domestic Issues

While religious policies aroused the greatest interests and efforts on the part of Diaspora Jewry to influence Israel, other aspects of domestic policy also attracted Diaspora intervention. In this chapter let us turn our attention to four such policies. Three focus on specific events and one on a general policy area.

THE BEN-GURION-BLAUSTEIN "EXCHANGE OF VIEWS" AND ITS AFTERMATH

There is no question that prior to the establishment of the State and for more than a decade thereafter, the American Jewish Committee was the Jewish organization to whose views Israeli leaders were most sensitive. Israeli and Zionist leaders perceived the American Jewish Committee (AJC) as the Jewish organization with the best access to American policymakers and as most representative of wealthy American Jews. Thus, the AJC was an important link in securing political and economic support from the American government and financial assistance from the American Jewish community.[1]

Zionist leaders sought the cooperation of non-Zionists, in-

118

cluding AJC leaders, in the 1920s and invited them to participate in a Jewish Agency. Indeed, the agreement between Zionists and non-Zionists whereby the latter joined the Jewish Agency was largely the result of an agreement reached between Chaim Weizmann and Louis Marshall, leader of the AJC.[2] AJC leaders filled most of the important non-Zionist posts, although the AJC as such never entered the Agency structure. Both sides abandoned the idea of non-Zionist representation by the early 1940s, but a few years later the AJC appealed to Weizmann to reconstitute the Jewish Agency again with non-Zionist representation.[3] In fact, however, the AJC motive was to gain representation for their views in opposition to Jewish statehood.[4]

The AJC membership included some who opposed any cooperation with the Zionists. The leadership's position was to support the Jewish settlement in Palestine for humanitarian purposes but to vehemently oppose the legitimacy of Jewish nationalism. Opposition was both ideological and practical. The AJC feared that a Jewish state would lead to charges of dual loyalty against Jews and heighten anti-Semitism. In 1946, despite its reservations, the AJC supported the partition proposal.[5] Nevertheless, it was with mixed emotions that it confronted the reality of a Jewish state. As the chairman of its Executive Committee stated in 1950, "sympathetic though we were and are with the upbuilding of Israel, we have nonetheless realized that the new state could create serious problems for us." [6]

In 1948 Israel invited leaders of the AJC to comment on a proposed draft of the Israeli constitution. AJC sensitivity to the problems Israel might create for Diaspora Jews and the AJC mentality is reflected in its suggestion that references in the constitution to "the Jewish State" rather than to "the State of Israel" be deleted. An AJC leader also urged "that the oath of office pledge the incumbent to order service to the welfare of the people of Israel instead of, as proposed, to the welfare of 'the Jewish people.'" [7] The AJC noted with satisfaction that a number of their views were incorporated into the proposed constitution.[8]

As early as 1948 the Executive Committee urged upon Israel the importance "of avoiding any pronouncements from which it might be inferred that the State of Israel regards itself as the spokesman for the Jews of the world or for any Jewish community outside of its own border." [9] In May 1949, three AJC leaders were invited by Israel's Prime Minister David Ben-Gurion to visit Israel. On that visit the AJC received assurances that Israel would not represent itself as the spokesman of world Jewry or seek to promote large-scale immigration from the U.S.[10]

AJC concern focused increasingly on the question of Israel's demand for *aliya* from the U.S. The fear was that the very demand for *aliya* would raise questions about American Jewish loyalty. According to former President Judge Joseph Proskauer, who led the organization from 1943 to 1948, the AJC should "forcefully discourage Israeli propaganda for immigration from America." [11] Whatever assurances it may have received from Ben-Gurion in 1949 were shaken by a report that in an address to an American Jewish delegation Ben-Gurion had stressed the importance of large-scale immigration of American youth, threatening to appeal to the youth over their parents' head.[12] AJC President Jacob Blaustein wrote to Ben-Gurion on September 19 calling the statement "most unfortunate and most unexpected; and as contravening assurances given by Ben-Gurion to AJC officers last spring." [13] According to AJC Administrative Committee minutes, the letter intimated that if Israel contemplated a campaign for immigration from the U.S., AJC would have to reconsider its support for Israel. The minutes further report that Blaustein told Israel's American Ambassador Eliyahu Elath and its U.N. representative Abba Eban that the AJC must stand against interference by Israel in the internal affairs of American Jewry and the "propagation of Jewish nationalism in the U.S."

The day following the Administrative Committee meetings, Judge Proskauer wrote as follows to Ben-Gurion.

> I am reasoning with you and your answer to me, to my mind, is going to determine whether my attitude of reasonableness is to be thrown into the ashcan and the philosophy of the

American Council for Judaism is to prevail, for obviously people like myself cannot be expected to ask American contributions to funds intended in part to achieve such an un-American aim as the emigration of all American Jews to Israel. Nor can we be expected to sit silent under the attacks that will follow shortly unless this situation is corrected. . . . I implore you to issue a statement modifying your position and categorically disclaiming any intention on the part of the State of Israel to interfere with the life of American Jewry.[14]

A response came quickly. Blaustein reported to the AJC Executive Committee on October 22 that Ambassador Elath, after speaking to Foreign Minister Sharett, reported that Ben-Gurion's speech to the American Jewish delegation had been misquoted. Ben-Gurion's secretary cabled that the report of Ben-Gurion's speech was "unauthorized" and a letter from the Prime Minister was on the way. A cable of Ben-Gurion's speech to a U.J.A. delegation in Israel affirmed his policy of desiring only "selected immigration" from America. Finally, Elath wrote on October 21 noting that Ben-Gurion had clearly been misquoted and that Israel "has no desire to intervene in the internal affairs of the American Jewish community." [15]

The American Jewish Congress, AJC's traditional organizational rival, charged the AJC with "blackmail against the State of Israel." According to a Congress official,

what the Committee is doing in polite terms is to say to the government of Israel that if it does anything that causes us public relations problems in America and if it doesn't apologize and clean up the difficulty as the Committee believes it should be done, the Committee will withdraw support and will resume its old status as an organization sometimes non-Zionist and sometimes anti-Zionist.[16]

AJC leaders continued, however, to press their point of view upon Israel. In April, Blaustein reported that he had impressed on Elath the harmfulness to Israel itself "of any attempts by his government to agitate among American Jews in the interests of a world Jewish nationalist philosophy." [17] At stake in all this,

Blaustein declared in his "private conferences with Israeli states-
men," was

> not only the continuance of American philanthropic and
> economic assistance, but also the general good will of Ameri-
> can Jewry. And above all, the unassailable fact remains that
> for Israel's own security there must be a strong and indepen-
> dent American Jewry.[18]

Apparently Blaustein wanted a public statement by Ben-
Gurion himself. One can only guess why Blaustein was anxious
for such a statement after so many responsible Israeli and
Zionist officials had reassured him that Israel did not wish to
intervene in American Jewish life, and did not insist on mass
immigration of American Jews. We may conjecture, first of all,
that Ben-Gurion himself was the only real authoritative source
for a statement on immigration policy, particularly when it was
he who, as we shall see in chapter 8, saw Israel's *raison d'être*
in "ingathering the exiles." Second, what Blaustein had received
until then were private assurances, whereas what he really
wanted was a public statement that would not only be a more
authoritative expression of *intent*, but would in and of itself
constitute the very policy expression that the AJC desired. Third,
a statement from Ben-Gurion to Blaustein would constitute a
major public relations triumph for the AJC in general and
Blaustein in particular. Finally, assurances by Sharett, Elath,
and Eban to the contrary notwithstanding, Israeli emissaries in
the United States continued to demand mass *aliya* and continued
to point a finger accusingly at those American Jews who were
not prepared to resettle in Israel. Indeed, there is evidence that
Israel's assurances to the AJC on immigration questions were
not taken seriously by Israeli officials themselves. In July 1950,
the Foreign Office held a conference of Israeli representatives
abroad. Among the topics for discussion was *aliya*. Eban noted
that the AJC insisted that Israel should surrender its ideological
demand for *aliya* and instead stress Israel's need for assistance
and for *aliya* from democratic countries. In that manner, it

would make identification with Israel an extension of one's democratic values but the particularist Zionist argument should go unmentioned. According to Eban, "We have absolutely no right to accept this demand and to forgo the ideological principle." [19]

In August 1950, Blaustein visited Israel at the invitation of the Prime Minister. According to the AJC official biographer, "after many hours of negotiating with top officials, alternately cajoling and threatening, he secured his basic objectives." [20] On August 23, at an official luncheon tendered by the Prime Minister to Blaustein, an "exchange of views" between the two was announced. As noted above in chapter 1, Ben-Gurion declared that

> the Jews of the United States, as a community and as individuals, have only one political attachment and that is to the United States of America. They owe no political allegiance to Israel. . . . The State of Israel represents and speaks only on behalf of its own citizens and in no way presumes to represent or speak in the name of Jews who are citizens of any other country. We, the people of Israel, have no desire and no intention to interfere in any way with the internal affairs of Jewish communities abroad.

And finally:

> let me say a word about immigration. We should like to see American Jews come and take part in our effort. We need their technical knowledge, their unrivalled experience, their spirit of enterprise, their bold vision, their "know-how." We need engineers, chemists, builders, work managers and technicians. The tasks which face us in this country are eminently such as would appeal to the American genius for technical development and social progress. But the decision as to whether they wish to come—permanently or temporarily—rests with the free discretion of each American Jew himself. It is entirely a matter of his own volition. We need halutzim, pioneers too. Halutzim have come to us—and we believe more will come, not only from those countries where the Jews are oppressed and in "exile" but also from countries where the

Jews live a life of freedom and are equal in status to all other
citizens in their country. But the essence of halutziuth is free
choice. They will come from among those who believe that
their aspirations as human beings and as Jews can best be
fulfilled by life and work in Israel.[21]

In his response, Blaustein showered praise on Israel's achievements and progress and then reiterated the classic American
non-Zionist position that Israel's existence was for the benefit of
"other Jews."

While Israel has naturally placed some burdens on Jews elsewhere, particularly in America, it has, in turn, meant much to
Jews throughout the world. For hundreds of thousands in
Europe, Africa and the Middle East it has provided a home in
which they can attain their full stature of human dignity for
the first time. In all Jews it has inspired pride and admiration,
even though in some instances, it has created pressing head-
aches.

He conceded, however, that

coming after the tragedy of European Jewry in the 1930's and
in World War II [Israel] has done much to raise Jewish
morale. Jews in America and everywhere can be more proud
than ever of their Jewishness.

Blaustein then pointed out that to American Jews, America is
their home and their destiny. He went on as follows:

We have been greatly distressed that at the very hour when
so much has been achieved, harmful and futile discussion and
misunderstandings have arisen as to the relations between the
people of the State of Israel and the Jews in other countries,
particularly in the United States. Harm has been done to the
morale and to some extent to the sense of security of the
American Jewish community through unwise and unwarranted
statements and appeals which ignore the feelings and aspirations of American Jewry.
    Even greater harm has been done to the State of Israel
itself by weakening the readiness of American Jews to do

their full share in the rebuilding of Israel which faces such enormous political, social and economic problems.

Your statement today, Mr. Prime Minister, will, I trust, be followed by unmistakable evidence that the responsible leaders of Israel, and the organizations connected with it, fully understand that future relations between the American Jewish community and the State of Israel must be based on mutual respect for one another's feelings and needs, and on the preservation of the integrity of the two communities and their institutions.[22]

In retrospect, the "exchange of views" is remarkable. In the first place, the entire setting of the exchange, the very title *exchange of views* suggests a meeting or negotiation between two equal parties. Second, whereas Ben-Gurion's statement is modest and inoffensive, deliberately couched to say nothing to which the other party would not agree, Blaustein's statement is a denial of basic Zionist premises and openly critical of Zionist and Israeli spokesmen. If the setting for the exchange suggested a meeting of equals, the tone of the exchange suggested that Blaustein represented the dominant party.

The most difficult part of Ben-Gurion's statement was not his disavowal of political allegiance but his final comments on *aliya*. (Significantly, he uses the neutral term *immigration* rather than the value-laden term of *aliya* with its far more positive connotation.) There is nothing in the statement that directly contradicts Ben-Gurion's past pronouncements. (Who ever said that a decision to immigrate does not rest "with the free discretion of each American Jew"? Did anyone ever suggest that Israel would *force* American Jews to come?) Nevertheless, Ben-Gurion's silence on Israel's mission to "ingather the exiles" or the obligation of the Jew *qua* Jew to live in Israel, his tacit agreement that American *aliya* was desirable to provide Israel with needed technical skills rather than for meeting its need for more Jews—all this was contrary to everything he had ever said on the subject. The tacit admission that American Jews do not live in "exile" must have been difficult enough for the Prime Minister to swallow, but defining immigration to Israel as an act of *noblesse oblige* by citizens of an advanced country toward those of a more backward state was degrading to a man who so many times had spoken of *aliya* as Jewish self-fulfillment and who referred to the day of his own arrival in the country as a day of rebirth.

The "exchange of views" can only be understood as a response to the pressure from a part of Diaspora Jewry. Nor were the concessions extracted from the Prime Minister easily obtained. A sense of this can be gathered in a letter to his own director by an AJC staff member who accompanied Blaustein. The letter is dated August 23, 1950, the date on which the "exchange of views" took place:

> it was all the time touch and go; we had ups and downs and until last night we still did not know whether or not we will get a satisfactory letter.
> We met with Ben-Gurion twice . . . eight hours.
> The statement . . . is not all we have suggested. It is a compromise between our original suggestions and their proposals and they consider that they went as far as they possibly could to meet our point of view. You may note that Mr. Ben-Gurion is definitely stating that Jews of America are not exiles and by implication, that all their campaigns of "ingathering the exiles" do not apply to American Jews. This was a point very hard for him to accept but he finally did agree.
> We consider it important that the statement of Ben-Gurion be publicized even before the big U.J.A. Conference starts here on September 6th. It should in no way appear that this statement is a quid pro quo for the plans that this conference is going to devise.[23]

While this is an instance of successful pressures on Israel from Diaspora Jewry, one wonders about the consequences or the continuing impact of the "exchange of views" on Israeli policy. Israeli spokesmen continued to call for *aliya* from the U.S., a call that failed to meet with any positive response. Ben-Gurion, on the other hand, while continuing to insist on the necessity for *aliya* from the West, chose his language rather carefully in the period following the "exchange." Whether in response to his commitment to Blaustein or in response to the reality of *aliya,* the Prime Minister spoke in terms of Israel's need for an *aliya* of technical experts. For example, in his speech to the World Zionist Congress in 1951 he said:

> The shortage of doctors, nurses, teachers, kindergarden teachers, engineers, chemists, trained managers, men of science and research is becoming more acute—and threatens with all its severity the cultural level of the State and the capacity to provide public services: education, health, security (for the army cannot establish itself and cannot develop without a continuing and satisfactory increase of expert professional pioneers, educated and of broad spirit).
>
> These two things—wealth and professional expert pioneers —can only be provided by Jews of the free world.[24]

In other words, Ben-Gurion stressed Israeli needs rather than Jewish obligations. The following year, in his message to the Zionist General Council, he noted that one could be a Zionist even if one didn't "fulfill the most exalted Zionist obligation—*aliya*." [25] He noted that Israeli Zionists who tended to adopt a maximalist position on *aliya* were obliged to understand their opponents from the West; they were obligated to political background to the differences of opinion." [26] Ben-Gurion's associate, Zalman Aranne, put the matter more bluntly. He noted that this was not the time to open an ideological war for a radical Zionist position because Israel dared not antagonize potential friends on its path to economic independence.[27] But if in the following year or two Ben-Gurion did adhere to the "exchange of views" in his public statements, it is nonetheless true that these statements were of purely symbolic import. They had no impact, nor could they in the nature of things have had any impact on *aliya* from the West. Whether Ben-Gurion himself knew that is a moot question.

In later years the AJC felt that it had cause for complaint. Publicly, Israel's policy continued to be adherence to the 1950 agreement but, increasingly, the substance of the "exchange" appeared to lack content. One can demonstrate this by what Israel did and did not do. It is always dangerous to argue from negative evidence, but there is no sign that Israel refrained from doing anything or changed any policy it might otherwise have adopted, as a result of Ben-Gurion's "exchange of views" with Blaustein. On the other hand, a number of things that Israel did do gave the AJC cause for complaint. In February 1960 its senior staff member John Slawson wrote to AJC President Herbert Ehrman complaining that Israel was acting as a spokesman for Jewish citizens of other countries in violation of the 1950 "arrangement." He recommended "that you bring this matter to the attention of appropriate Israeli representatives in the U.S. requesting that Israel henceforth desist from such actions. . . ." [28]

In December of that year Blaustein wrote a letter to Ben-Gurion as follows:

> During past months . . . there have been a number of definitive violations of your August 1950 Statement. These departures are causing serious embarrassments and consequences. They are again opening up the furor that was existing at the time in 1950 when we got together and resolved the Statement we then issued.
>
> American, Canadian and English Jewries are up in arms about these violations—and I think I should tell you that some are charging me with having been naive in even having accepted the August 1950 Statement as bona fide . . .
>
> . . . Some of the violations to which I refer are as follows:
> 1) Israel's notes addressed to the United States, British and other governments regarding the swastika daubings in those countries last winter. . . . Israel should have confined itself to discussing [the issue] with the Jewish communities in those countries. . . .
> 2) General Moshe Dayan's incomprehensible March 9, 1960 statement in Canada that "his government should not only represent the people of Israel, but the interests of all Jews."
> 3) And Foreign Minister Golda Meir's reply to the delegation of the Anglo-Jewish Association which resulted in the startling headlines in the Jewish National Post (April 15, 1960): Israel will continue to speak for Jewry." . . . I assure you that if you wish your country to retain its friendships—at a time when

you sorely need them—it is essential that you promptly correct the wrong impression to which I have referred. . . .

Out of my closeness to you, I feel I can venture to say that you cannot expect diplomatic and financial cooperation from even friends, including me, when understandings with them, and principles dear to them, are violated or ignored.[29]

A memorandum to the AJC Executive Board in mid-December noted that after conversations with "Golda Meir and other Israel officials [we] found them firm in the conviction that Israel is the sole authority to speak and act for Jews everywhere." [30] The AJC also noted that Ben-Gurion, in his address before the 25th Zionist Congress, announced that

Jews living outside Israel were violating the precepts of Judaism and that in the free and prosperous lands Judaism faced the kiss of death, a slow and imperceptible decline into the abyss of assimilation.[31]

AJC President Herbert Ehrman notified Ben-Gurion of his "grave concern" concerning that statement as well as his dissatisfaction with Israel's Law of Return, which automatically granted citizenship to all Jews who came with immigrant visas.[32]

As before, the Israeli government remained sensitive to AJC criticism. In response to Blaustein's critical and threatening letter, Avraham Harman, Israeli Ambassador to the U.S., conveyed a message from Ben-Gurion to Blaustein affirming the 1950 agreement and stating that the government of Israel "speaks and acts only on behalf of its citizens." [33] But Blaustein and the AJC wanted another public statement and after further exchanges of letters the two met and on April 23, 1961, issued a joint statement. The statement, much briefer than the orginal "exchange of views," noted that both sides

agreed that everything should be done on both sides in order to obviate . . . misunderstandings in the future, so that it would be entirely clear to everybody concerned that the 1950 Agreement had lost none of its force and validity so far as either side is concerned. In particular Mr. Ben-Gurion undertook to do everything within his power to see to it that the agreement is in future kept in spirit and in letter.[34]

We might note, however, that the joint statement was not nearly so degrading as the "exchange" of a decade earlier. It acknowledged that "it is perfectly natural for differences of view to exist on the essence and the meaning of Judaism and Jewishness, both inside American Jewry and between various Jewish communities," [35] noting that regardless of the differences the parties must act in accordance with the 1950 agreement. It also permitted the Prime Minister greater ideological flexibility by noting that "some misunderstandings might have arisen owing to the fact that Mr. Ben-Gurion now and then takes the liberty of expressing views on a variety of topics that are his own rather than those of the Government of Israel." [36]

The 1950 "exchange of views" was reaffirmed by Levi Eshkol when he became Prime Minister in 1963,[37] and by the succeeding Prime Minister, Golda Meir, in a 1970 letter to Jacob Blaustein, where she wrote:

> As you know I was privy to the talks which you conducted on the occasion of your visit to Israel in 1950, and to the understanding which flowed from those talks. This has been a continuing understanding. On my part, there has been no deviation from it, and it is my intention that there will not be.[38]

It seems fair to say that the last decade has reduced the "exchange of views" to a document of purely symbolic importance, and only to the AJC at that. Perhaps nothing better expresses the meaninglessness of the document than the fact that Golda Meir could affirm its contents, could note that, on her part, "there has been no deviation" when in fact many of the complaints made by the AJC in the earlier decade concerned statements by Golda Meir herself. There is evidence that even the AJC no longer takes the contents seriously. It sent no protests, much less threatening letters of the Blaustein variety when

Israel called for mass *aliya* from the West after 1967, nor did AJC object to the very intensive activity on the part of the World Zionist Organization in promoting *aliya* from the United States. The AJC also kept silent in 1972 when the U.N. General Assembly President declined to rule on an Arab delegate's objection to Israel's claim to speak for the Jewish people, thereby granting de facto recognition to this claim.[39] But what could the AJC have done—defended the Arab point of view; denied that Israel has a special right to protest treatment of Jews in Arab countries or in the Soviet Union? Events and life have, at least for the time being, left the 1950 "exchange" without substance. It remains, however, an instance of successful pressure by Diaspora Jewry on Israel.

THE "STATUS" OF THE WORLD ZIONIST ORGANIZATION

The story of the World Zionist Organization (WZO)-Jewish Agency's (JA) "status" is an interesting one—so interesting that the temptation is to report *all* the events surrounding it rather than focusing on the particular concern of Diaspora Jewry's influence in shaping Israel's public policy. In the pages that follow the temptation is resisted as far as possible, although the pattern of the story is so complicated that not all the seemingly extraneous threads can be unwound without destroying the pattern itself.

We must deal here with three groups of actors. First of all, here is the WZO, which in the period under discussion was identical to the JA.[40] The WZO represents neither a peculiarly Israeli nor peculiarly Diaspora interest. The tendency was to Israeli domination; indeed, the dominant party in the Israeli Government also dominated the WZO. But Israeli parties in opposition to the Government were also represented in the decision-making councils of the organization, as were Diaspora Zionists. Having preceded the formation of Israel by some fifty years, the WZO had developed its own set of organizational self-interests. Its role, function, and prestige had been pre-empted, to a great extent, by the State of Israel. The Government, especially Ben-Gurion in his attacks on the WZO, in the recognition he had accorded to non-Zionists (especially in his "exchange of views" with Jacob Blaustein, referred to earlier), had created an impression that the state no longer accorded any special role to the WZO. In an effort to recoup part of its prestige the WZO sought recognition by the State of Israel as the representative of the Jewish people in the Diaspora in all matters affecting Israel. The WZO sought to achieve this recognition through passage of a law by the Knesset that would define the "status" of the WZO in Israel.[41] Of course, the very fact that the WZO felt that it required an act of the Knesset to buttress its prestige indicated more than anything else how rapidly the shift in status had taken place from the Zionist Movement to the State. But these were the facts.

The second group of actors is the Government of Israel led by Ben-Gurion. Ben-Gurion's position in opposition to the WZO represented an extreme view but, after some concessions, he prevailed upon the Government to accept his position. Theoretically, therefore, one can talk about a Government position or a conflict between the Government and the WZO, but this is only a partial truth. It was really Ben-Gurion's position as opposed to that of the WZO. Had anyone other than Ben-Gurion been Prime Minister, the outcome would have been more favorable to the WZO and hence less favorable to the WZO's major antagonist, the American Jewish Committee (AJC). The paradox, however, is that Ben-Gurion's position, which at the time was attributed to his peculiar and iconoclastic views respecting the WZO, was in effect a "statist" view that subsequent Israeli governments would have had to accept. To put it another way I am suggesting that Ben-Gurion was ahead of his time in his view of the relative role of the WZO and the Government. But precisely because he was the man he was, he was able to press this view on a reluctant government. Nobody else could have done it. Within a few years it was obvious that he was right. Since I have permitted myself the expression of a personal view, I will go a step further and permit myself the expression of a personal value. The fact that in retrospect Ben-Gurion was right does not heighten my sympathy for his position nor soften the tragedy of the blow that he dealt to the WZO.

The third major group of actors was the non-Zionists from the Diaspora.[42] The voice of Diaspora non-Zionists was expressed primarily through the representations of the AJC and its leader and major spokesman at that time in Israeli-Diaspora relations, Jacob Blaustein, to whom Ben-Gurion had made certain commitments in their 1950 "exchange of views."

The issue around which these three major groups clashed was what sort of status or legal authority Israel was to bestow on the WZO. Essentially, the objective of the WZO was to obtain the broadest authority and the maximum status; the AJC objected to conferring any special status on the WZO except in a very specific area of activity within Israel. As an opponent of the WZO, the AJC did not want Israel to lend its prestige to the WZO. The Government's objective is harder to infer. It seems most nearly correct to say that its efforts were directed toward conciliating between the contrary objectives of the WZO and the AJC so that neither side should be very unhappy, but doing so in a manner that retained the maximum degree of latitude for the Government and was least compromising to its own sovereignty. This is a perfectly natural position that one might expect any government to adopt. Since it was the WZO that was asking the Government to surrender a degree of sovereignty to it, one might have anticipated from the outset that the Government would adopt a position closer to that of the AJC, making the outcome of the controversy a foregone conclusion. It was not. The reason for this involves us in the additional complication of mixed motives and crosscutting allegiances. Members of the Government were, after all, past leaders of the WZO. Ties of party, ideology, and past institutional loyalty should have led them to a position much closer to if not identical with that of the WZO. That the Government did oppose the WZO was owing to Ben-Gurion. As the leading exponent of Israeli sovereignty, he formulated a new ideology and a new view of relations between the WZO and Israel that he succeeded in pressing upon the Government and, later, the Knesset. In many respects the "status" fight became the paradigm for a whole new set of relationships that were to emerge in the years that followed—relationships that are so clear today that it is difficult in retrospect to grasp what the argument was all about. But in those days things were not quite so clear.

The effective Jewish leadership of the Yishuv, the Jewish settlement in Eretz Israel prior to creation of the State was the Vaad Leumi. In preparation for eventual statehood, the Vaad Leumi decided on March 1, 1948, that the provisional Government of Israel would be a council composed of members of the Vaad Leumi and the JA executive, that is, the WZO executive. In other words, whereas the Vaad Leumi itself had been selected by a body representing the Yishuv and could certainly claim to voice the will of the Yishuv, it itself chose to co-opt the JA executive as the supreme representative body of the provisional government.

Two other examples illustrate the authority and prestige of the WZO even after the State was created.

In May 1950 the prime minister announced the formation of a Government-JA Coordinating Board with four governmental representatives, four JA representatives, and one representative from the Jewish National Fund. The Board's first responsibility was to be the coordination of activity in the sphere of *aliya*.[43]

As *Ha'Aretz* noted, "recognition of a majority rule [on the Coordinating Board] places the sovereign state under a higher authority. . . ."[44] In practice, this limitation had no practical import. But in theory, not only had Israel conceded part of its sovereignty to the WZO, it had done so without anybody finding it very startling or a subject of criticism. A more striking example of how lines between the Government-State of Israel and the JA-WZO were blurred in those early years of statehood came in the 1952 Knesset debate on the Status Law, which is the subject of this case study. Opposition speakers stressed the point that the Status Law that the Government proposed was contrary to the resolution that the World Zionist Congress had passed the previous year. Ben-Gurion found it necessary to remind the Knesset that despite the fact that they were all Zionists, the Congress resolutions were *not* the law of Israel and were *not* binding on members of the Knesset.[45]

Despite the administrative delineation of WZO and governmental activity as early as 1948 and later in 1950, the ideological distinction and theoretical responsibility of each was not at all clear. It is this lack of clarity in the minds of many of the principal actors that explains the subsequent events. As they unfolded, the role and status of each was clarified and Ben-Gurion's position emerged triumphant. This position was never set out on a point-by-point basis, but it emerged rather clearly in a series of speeches to the Knesset and the Zionist General Council and may be summarized as follows:

1. The State of Israel is a sovereign body representing its citizens, responsible to its citizens, and not accountable to any other body.
2. The State of Israel and not the WZO is the major institution around which the Jewish people are united and which evokes their sense of commitment and Jewish loyalty. The WZO cannot stand between Israel and the Jewish people.
3. Israel will not grant the title "representative of the Jewish people" to any organization. It is the State more than any institution that represents the Jewish people. (Ben-Gurion himself never actually said this. It was said, explicitly, as we shall see, by Bebah Idelson. It is implied, however, in many of Ben-Gurion's statements and was stated explicitly a few years later). In any event, for Israel to call any organization a representative of the Jewish people would be interference by Israel in the affairs of the Diaspora.

One suspects that Ben-Gurion also objected to granting the

WZO a status as the "representative of the Jewish people" because by so doing he would grant it a theoretical authority greater than that of the State of Israel. Since Ben-Gurion and all subsequent prime ministers have declared that their first loyalty is to the Jewish people and not to the State of Israel, any organization that they acknowledged as representing the Jewish people would have prior claims on their loyalty and that of all good Zionists.

4. To the extent that the WZO-JA wants any kind of special status within Israel, it has to demonstrate that it is indeed a broadly based organization. This it can only do by broadening its structure to include non-Zionists, who are just as deeply devoted to helping Israel as are the Zionists.

5. The Government of Israel will not bestow any special status or privileges on the WZO outside Israel or limit its own sovereignty by committing itself to consult and coordinate its activities in the Diaspora with the WZO.[46]

It is doubtful, though not impossible, that Ben-Gurion grasped all these points as early as 1950. If so, he stood virtually alone in subscribing to them. By 1952 he had not only converted them into governmental policy, but he had won many over, even within the WZO, to accepting his point of view. This, however, jumps us ahead of the story.

The World Zionist Congress is the supreme authority of the WZO and hence of the JA executive as well. The 23rd Zionist Congress, the first to take place since the establishment of Israel, met in August 1951. Prior to the Congress all the Zionist parties that compose the World Zionist Organization had agreed on the necessity for a Status Law despite objections that Ben-Gurion had raised.[47] The draft resolution submitted to the Congress and agreed to by representatives of Ben-Gurion's own party called upon the Government of Israel to recognize the WZO as "the representative of the Jewish people" within Israel. Consistently however, with Ben-Gurion's position, the draft made no mention of relationships between Israel and the WZO outside the border of the State.[48] Mapai spokesmen were insistent that the proposed Status Law should limit itself to WZO activity in Israel.[49]

Other speakers aligned with opposition parties in Israel addressed themselves to the necessity for WZO "status" in the Diaspora as well as in Israel. A speaker representing the left-wing Mapam accused Ben-Gurion of seeking alternatives to the WZO, which the speaker insisted should be recognized as "the only representative of the State of Israel among the masses of the Jewish people in the Diaspora (Golah)." [50] Emmanuel Neumann, leader of the Zionist Organization of America and aligned with an Israeli opposition party of the Right, also stressed that WZO status must recognize the WZO in its role within the Diaspora. According to Neumann, without such a provision the Status Law would be meaningless.[51]

The Congress resolution, adopted unanimously, reflects a compromise. With respect to WZO status in Israel the resolution stated that:

> The Congress considers it essential that the State of Israel shall grant, through appropriate legislative act, status to the World Zionist Organization as the representative of the Jewish people in all matters relating to organized participation of the Jews of the Diaspora in the development and upbuilding of the country and the rapid absorption of immigrants.

This section occasioned no controversy. This is important to note because, as we shall subsequently see, referring to the WZO as "the representative of the Jewish people" was later to arouse a great storm. In fact, the phrase *representative of the Jewish people* did not even originate with the opposition. The leader of the American section of the JA, subsequent president of the WZO Nahum Goldmann,[52] used it in his speech to the General Council in 1950.[53]

It was the following section, and not the former, that was clearly a compromise proposal:

> In relation to all activities conducted in the interests of the State of Israel within the Diaspora it is essential that the

Government of the State of Israel shall act in consultation and co-ordination with the World Zionist Organization.

Mention was made of the WZO's relationship to Israel in the Diaspora, but in a manner far less compelling than maximalists from opposition parties would have liked.

The AJC did not even wait for the adoption of the final resolution before it issued its first protest. On August 15 Blaustein wrote to Ben-Gurion objecting to the granting of special status to the WZO within Israel unless it was restricted to the Jewish Agency in its resettlement and rehabilitation activity. He reminded Ben-Gurion of the aid that the AJC had given to Israel, in return for which "we have not asked for special status, but have expected and do ask that Israel observe the proper relationship toward Jews in other countries." [54] On August 29 Ben-Gurion replied to Blaustein, agreeing that no monopoly should be granted to WZO outside of Israel to represent Jews living in other countries. But he felt that it was proper to accord the representatives of the Zionist Executive in Jerusalem a special status.[55] On September 4 Blaustein, together with two leading members of the AJC staff, conferred with Abba Eban, Israel's Ambassador to the U.S. Eban in turn communicated with Ben-Gurion, urged him to clarify the situation by cable, and submitted a draft statement for his consideration. Ben-Gurion cabled his reply, which Blaustein termed "satisfactory to us in some respects but not in all." [56] He noted that:

we are disappointed by his failure to state that Israel would consult equally and directly on matters affecting itself and whatever organizations American Jews establish inside or outside the Zionist framework. Instead, Ben-Gurion stated that "such direct relations of the government of Israel with Jewish bodies and organizations will naturally be coordinated with the Jewish Agency." [57]

According to Blaustein, this formulation accords a special status to the JA with regard to work undertaken on behalf of Israel in other countries.

At its October 13-14 Executive Committee meetings the AJC considered three courses of action—to ignore the developments, to publicly condemn Israel and the occurrences at the Congress announcing that these developments had made continued support for Israel impossible, or to express concern, call on Israel to avoid certain actions, and serve notice that AJC's desire to help Israel might be frustrated if Israel persisted in certain activity. The third alternative was adopted and a resolution was passed that not only expressed AJC's opposition to Israel's granting political status in Israel to the WZO but also expressed opposition to granting "any organization any special status . . . outside of Israel." [58]

On October 30 Blaustein again wrote to Ben-Gurion. He stated that:

> we believe that the granting of any kind of special status to the Jewish Agency *outside* of Israel—such as that indicated in the sentence of your cable reading "Such direct relations of the Government of Israel with Jewish bodies and organizations will naturally be coordinated with the Jewish Agency"— would be harmful to Israel as well as to Jewish communities outside of Israel.
>
> Also, as I mentioned in my previous communications to you, the granting by the Knesset of a political or diplomatic status *within* Israel to the Jewish Agency or to the representative of the Zionist Executive in Jerusalem (the designation used in your August 29 letter to me) would carry with it the connotation that Jews throughout the world constitute a political unit of which the Agency or the World Zionist Organization is its representative.[59]

Blaustein's letter is extremely important, since it suggests that at least two months after the Congress had concluded its meetings Ben-Gurion was inclined to honor their request to be given the rights of consultation and coordination with respect to Israeli activity among Diaspora Jewry. Ben-Gurion apparently was more than willing to pay lip service to this request, since he mentions it to Blaustein. Ben-Gurion's subsequent opposition to granting the WZO rights of consultation and coordination

outside Israel was unquestionably what he originally wanted, but
it did represent a change from a position into which he may
very well have been coerced following the Congress resolution.
In that event, there is no reason to doubt that the AJC's strong
protestations against the Congress resolution influenced his
position and reinforced his original inclinations.

From this point on, there are virtually no references to
granting the JA status outside Israel. The fight centered now on
its status within Israel. Ben-Gurion apparently decided to ac-
quiesce to the AJC demand on the latter point as well. On
December 4, 1951, leaders of the JA wrote to Ben-Gurion protesting his decision to omit or amend the opening sentence of a
draft Status Law, which referred to the WZO as "the representative of the Jewish people in all matters relating to organized
participation of the Jews of the Diaspora in the development
and upbuilding of the country." (The wording is identical to
that of the Zionist Congress resolution.) They stated that

> this sentence represents the very basis of the law and without
> it the law has no content. This is the formulation which was
> also adopted in the resolutions of the 23rd. Congress and the
> meetings of the parties which took place before the Congress
> convened. We, therefore, repeat our request to bring the full
> text of the law before the Government, including the above
> sentence, as it was phrased by the Minister of Justice.[60]

The signatories noted that the matter was discussed the previous
day at a meeting of the Jewish Agency executive and that their
letter expressed the unanimous opinion of the members of the
executive.

The December 4 letter apparently had results and the
phrase "representative of the Jewish people" remained, tem-
porarily, in the draft law. In March 1952 Blaustein met with
Eban and Golda Myerson (Meir) in Washington. He persuaded
each of them to cable Ben-Gurion to accept the AJC position
on the JA status.[61] He also met with Sharett and obtained an
agreement that he, Blaustein, would "be afforded the opportunity

to review in advance (as the Foreign Minister agreed) the pertinent portions of any proposed Knesset Act." [62]

His own cable to Ben-Gurion threatened that "if any special status [is] given Jewish Agency . . . [it should] in no way directly or indirectly embody the concept quote as the representative of the Jewish people unquote which would cause strom [*sic*] irreparable unfavorable reaction alienating from Israel many Zionist and non-Zionist friends. . . ." [63]

On March 9, Teddy Kollek, a close associate of Ben-Gurion's then in Washington, assured Blaustein that, from reports he heard, "I do not think there is much to worry about." [64] This was confirmed by a phone call from Eban to Blaustein. Eban reported that Ben-Gurion had called him and asked for Blaustein's views on the wording of a new draft to be proposed to the Knesset. The phrase referring to the WZO as "representative of the Jewish people" had been changed to "authorized Agency operating in Israel on behalf of the Jewish people." Blaustein found the draft basically acceptable but requested that the words *"on behalf of the Jewish people* be omitted.[65] This request, as we shall see, was also honored.

According to Nahum Goldmann, Ben-Gurion was responsive to non-Zionists who argued that the WZO does not represent World Jewry since it only represents Zionists. Ben-Gurion, according to Goldmann, wanted the status to be conferred on an expanded JA. Goldmann, in turn, claimed that he insisted on status for the WZO as presently constituted. In that case, Ben-Gurion said, "We cannot say you are the representatives of the nation. There are Jews whom I need, and they argue that the JA does not represent them." [66] The result, according to Goldmann, was the compromise in which the WZO was not recognized as a representative of the Jewish people but as an "authorized agency" with the right to coordinate the activities of other organizations in Israel.

It should be clear that Ben-Gurion's demand to expand the JA was not a *concession* to non-Zionists, although he might have had the AJC in mind as a party to the expansion.[67] In fact, neither the AJC nor their top leadership were likely to have joined the JA at that time, nor did they ever even hint that they wanted an expanded JA to include themselves. They were far too sensitive to "dual loyalty" charges. Other candidates whom Ben-Gurion might also have had in mind, those whom he might have liked to see in the JA, were leaders of the local Jewish Federations in the U.S.—the large contributors from the local Jewish communities who were already assuming leadership of the UJA, with whom Ben-Gurion and subsequent Prime Ministers established personal relationships and whom Ben-Gurion trusted far more than he trusted American Zionist leaders such as Silver and Neumann. From Ben-Gurion's perspective, these local philanthropists did far more for Israel than the Zionists. They gave far more money, were equally willing to provide political support in the U.S. on behalf of Israel, and were no more opposed to *aliya* than were American Zionist leaders. Therefore, they were more useful than Zionist leaders and they demanded less in return. A handshake, an autographed picture, an invitation to dinner, a testimonial in their honor were all the compensation they sought. Zionists like Silver and Neumann, Ben-Gurion feared, would utilize their position of strength within the WZO to seek to influence Israeli policy. It is most reasonable, therefore, to believe that Ben-Gurion did want to expand the JA not as a concession to non-Zionists but as a way of involving them even further in activity on behalf of Israel and neutralizing the less reliable Zionists.[68] The point of all this, however, is to indicate that to the extent that Ben-Gurion was satisfying a demand of the AJC, it was not so in his insistence that the JA be expanded, but in his insistence that the WZO not be designated as a "representative of the Jewish people."

On March 14, *Davar* announced that an agreement had been reached between the JA and the Government's representatives. According to the report, the JA would undertake to include non-Zionists, and the WZO would be recognized as an "authorized agency . . . to coordinate . . . the activities of other Jewish organizations" operating in Israel.[69]

One cannot help adding that not only did the WZO not get what it asked for, but its designation as an "authorized agency . . . to coordinate . . . the activities of other Jewish organizations" conceded even less to the WZO than had been conceded in a draft that the Government had prepared a year earlier. That draft had designated the WZO as "the representative of the People in all matters relating to the organized participation of the Diaspora in the establishment, development and furthering of the State of Israel." It was this phrase that WZO spokesmen had rejected as being inadequate.[70] In the light of all this it appears that the "agreement" was really a one-sided victory for Ben-Gurion. As for the AJC's intervention, I have already suggested that it was of some consequence, not in forcing the Government to do what it otherwise would not have wanted to do, but in permitting the Government (i.e., Ben-Gurion) to do what it (he) really wanted to do but might not have otherwise been able to do. As we follow the Status Law through to its final enactment we shall see some more evidence of AJC influence.

The Status Law was finally submitted to the Knesset. As might have been anticipated, the opposition parties attacked the law as weakening the WZO and as being contrary to the Congress resolution. Ben-Gurion defended the proposed law and clarified his objections to the Congress resolution. He observed that it is the State of Israel, not the WZO, that is "the new crown, more important and more precious to the people." [71] In expressing his objection to a proposal that Israel consult and coordinate its activities in the Diaspora with the WZO, he noted in language reminiscent of his "exchange of views" with Blaustein two years earlier that Israel would not pass any law on internal matters of Jewish communities in the Diaspora.[72]

Simultaneously, the Zionist General Council was holding its sessions. The proposed bill was attacked there, as well, by Zionists aligned with opposition parties. Nahum Goldmann defended the Draft Law and stressed the necessity for an expanded JA. He argued that the JA could then devote itself to helping Israel politically and economically and allow the Zionist Movement to

devote itself to Zionist activity free from the necessity for ideological compromise. To raise money, he noted, it is necessary "to
give in a little on Zionist ideology." [73]

Goldmann also defended, on principle, the absence of any
mention of the WZO role in the Diaspora. The only major concession he admitted he made was in the "representative" label
to which I have already alluded.

However, Goldmann recommended to members of the Zionist General Council, on behalf of the executive, that they influence their friends in the Knesset to amend the law. [74]

When a bill is presented to the Knesset it undergoes a "first
reading." If it receives an affirmative vote it is passed on to
an appropriate committee, which discusses the bill in detail,
possibly amends sections, and then returns it to the Knesset
plenary for a "second reading," which involves a debate and
separate vote on each article. The bill is then presented in its
entirety for a "third reading."

The Status Law was returned from Knesset Committee for
its second reading in August. The Committee had accepted some
minor changes proposed by the Zionist General Council. [75]

Within the Knesset the opposition concentrated its efforts
on reintroducing the phrase *representative of the Jewish people*
for the WZO rather than the term *authorized agent*. In a surprise
vote, the opposition's amendment was accepted by a vote of 31
to 27. The size of the vote (there are 120 members of the Knesset) suggests that the opposition had a chance majority at the
time of the vote.

The following day the Government withdrew the bill and
Ben-Gurion announced he would resign if the Knesset did not
accept the original wording of the bill. He stressed that "the
Government of Israel decided, without difference of opinion,
that the WZO will not be recognized as the representative of
the Jewish people and the Government attributes great importance to this position." [76] He labeled the amendment as interference in the internal affairs of Diaspora Jewry and added that
"there are organized and important masses of Jews in the world

who are not members of any Zionist organization and despite this they are committed heart and soul to the State of Israel." [77]

WZO leaders were not prepared to fight for what they had already agreed to surrender. The Government immediately introduced a new bill, which was virtually identical to the bill originally introduced in May without opposition from WZO leaders.

The AJC expressed its satisfaction. At the Executive Committee meetings of October 25-26 Blaustein reported that when opposition deputies amended the bill to accord the WZO status that Ben-Gurion assured the AJC would not be granted, he proved his good faith when "on the following day, he withdrew the Bill." [78] Blaustein told the Executive Committee that Ben-Gurion had renewed his assurances that his government would hold out for the bill approximately as originally submitted.

Again one can only conjecture, but it does seem reasonable to suppose that Ben-Gurion might not have been quite so adamant in rejecting the opposition amendment nor have acted quite so drastically in threatening to resign had he not had to consider the pressure from, and obligations that he undertook to non-Zionist organizations and individuals. In his speech on behalf of the new bill, Ben-Gurion stressed the importance of non-Zionists in words that could only have pleased AJC leaders. For example, he said:

> The State of Israel does not assume, and has no right to assume, the authority to determine who is the representative of the Jewish people. . . . Any effort to remove Jews who are not members of the Zionist Organization from the totality of the Jewish people and the totality of direct assistance to the State and direct contact with her—is not only a political mistake but an arbitrary distortion of the Zionist idea.[79]

Bebah Idelson, of Mapai, was much sharper in her objection to labeling the WZO "the representative of the Jewish people." According to Idelson, the WZO was indeed the representative of the Jewish people until the State was established. ". . . The

State of Israel now represents the Jewish people, there is no other representative and none other is possible." [80]

The law was passed as submitted and it would only be anti-climactic to add that Nahum Goldmann expressed his satisfaction.[81] For its part, the AJC hailed the outcome as a great victory. Irving Engel summarized the events as follows:

> Zionist pressures within the Knesset notwithstanding, Israel after formal protest by the AJC, refused to grant the World Zionist Organization the recognition it had been so eagerly seeking as "the representative of the Jewish people the world over." [82]

In January 1953 the AJC "noted with satisfaction the refusal of the government of Israel to grant the WZO recognition as the representative of the Jewish people the world over." [83]

In retrospect, the AJC's victory was a qualified one. First of all, the WZO did receive special recognition. Second, the AJC's achievement was almost purely symbolic. Whether the WZO was a "representative" or an "authorized agent" meant absolutely nothing in the long run. Indeed, a major difficulty in researching the question was that respondents active in the controversy at the time could not recall what it was all about twenty years later. Of course, the AJC did prevent the WZO from being granted status outside Israel. But in this respect, as suggested the AJC got what Ben-Gurion wanted to give them. One might more properly evaluate the outcome as a victory for Ben-Gurion who achieved his objectives due, in part, to AJC support. If one asks, therefore, whether this is a successful instance of Diaspora pressure on formation of Israeli public policy, the answer would be only a qualified yes.

There is perhaps a more important point to be learned from this case. Within the framework of this study, one wonders how to define the WZO. Is it a Diaspora organization, or, if not what is it? In fact, as we have seen, its constituency cuts across Israel and the Diaspora. The problem of locating the WZO within the present framework of analysis only reinforces our understanding of the complexity of Israeli-Diaspora relations. There may be separate Israel and Diaspora interests, but the interrelationships are so intense that it is rare when the two sides can be neatly isolated and aligned one against the other. In this case, Diaspora interests and Israeli interests were aligned against the interests of an organization or an ideology that simply does not lend itself to any simple classification.

ISRAEL'S NATIONALITY LAW

The 1950 Law of Return provides that every Jew has the right to enter Israel as an *oleh* (an immigrant who has the right to reside permanently in Israel). As Ben-Gurion stated when he presented the bill to the Knesset:

> This law lays down, not that the State accords the right of settlement to Jews abroad, but that this right is inherent in every Jew by virtue of his being a Jew if it but be his will to take part in settling the Land. This right preceded the State of Israel; it is that which built the State.[84]

Under the 1952 Nationality Law every *oleh* under the Law of Return automatically becomes an Israel citizen unless he specifically declines citizenship.

The AJC regarded the preferred legal status given to Jews as undemocratic. Apparently the AJC feared that the law, by discriminating between Jews and non-Jews in matters of citizenship, was contrary to its conception of equality before the law and its fight for civil liberties in the U.S. More compelling, in all probability, was the AJC fear that Israel's Nationality Law suggested that Jews have special *national* ties to Israel.

The AJC raised the issue with Israeli officials on a number of occasions. Often there was a rather threatening tone to their proposals. For example, in a letter to Sharett when he was Prime Minister, Blaustein wrote that:

unless something constructive is done in the matter [of the Israel Nationality Law] before an American Jewish Committee Annual Meeting on January 28, 1955, it is more than likely that a resolution critical of Israel will result. This I want to avoid.[85]

The AJC raised the issue more intensely in 1961. In April and May the AJC, disturbed by recent statements and action of Israeli leaders on a number of issues decided to press Prime Minister Ben-Gurion on the Nationality Law as well. Ben Gurion replied, rather abruptly, "We are a sovereign state and make laws according to our needs as we understand them."[8] Israel showed no inclination to respond to AJC threats in 1955 or to its milder protestations in 1961, and the matter was dropped.

ECONOMIC PRESSURES AND ECONOMIC POLICY

In chapter 2 I noted the importance of Diaspora Jewry' contribution to Israel's economy. This contribution comes in the form of outright gifts (primarily through UJA and other institutional campaigns throughout the world), purchases of Israel Bonds, and private investment. In all three cases, however, the large sums that are transferred to Israel come from a relatively small number of individuals. Although the number of non-Jewish investors has grown recently and from 10 to 15 percent of the participants at the 1973 economic conference were non-Jews, the bulk of the money in all three categories comes from a few thousand wealthy Jews throughout the world. The question, therefore, is: To what extent, if any, have these people influenced Israel's policies? Up to this point I have chosen to explore areas of policy where efforts to influence Israel are known. In the area of religious policy, political relations between Israel and the Diaspora, and the status of the WZO and the Nationality Law the question was not whether Diaspora Jewry sought to influence Israeli policy but to what extent Diaspora

Jewry was successful in its efforts. In the present instance, I have chosen to inquire about economic influence, not because examples of such efforts come readily to mind, but because one would anticipate pressures from sources to which Israel is apparently beholden. Furthermore, it is from foreign investors that one traditionally anticipates pressure on public policy.

In this case, one might argue that Israel created the opportunity for the mobilization of such pressures through the convening of (to date), three general economic conferences (1968, 1969, 1973), some 14 specific industry conferences, and the establishment of regional and professional committees. While membership in these conferences and committees is not limited to Jews, and an effort is made to attract non-Jews, the overwhelming majority of participants are Jewish. It is proper, therefore, for any study of Diaspora influence on Israeli policy to inquire into the possible influence of foreign economic contributors and investors, especially since the major contributors and investors are often the same people.[87]

From Israel's point of view, the purpose in organizing these conferences and committees was to encourage a direct contact between foreign and Israeli businessmen and industrialists and to develop closer ties leading to joint ventures in areas of investment, trade, research, and professional training. The notion was that such joint economic conferences and joint committees would benefit the national economy by encouraging foreign investment and by increasing opportunities, knowledge, and markets for Israeli industry. In the process, of course, Israel has institutionalized investor interests and provided a ready channel for the articulation of investor demands. On the other hand, we must note that the joint Israeli-Diaspora nature of these conferences and committees, while strengthening the pressures behind the demands (or recommendations), mitigates the possibility of the evolution of a specific Diaspora interest. In fact, respondents suggested that initiative at the conferences tends to come not from the Diaspora representatives but from the Israelis—often from Government officials for whom the conference recommendations provide support and legitimation.

There is another institutional mechanism for the articulation of economic pressures—the reconstituted Jewish Agency. Since that institution is more fully discussed in a later chapter I only note now that nothing that we will discover about economic pressures in the present discussion needs to be qualified by what the reconstituted Jewish Agency has or has not done.

Economic pressures can be evidenced in three areas:

1. Pressures on broad policy areas.
2. Pressures on specific policy areas or on policy administration and execution.
3. Pressures to grant individual favors and special benefits. I shall discuss each of these areas in turn.

1. Broad Policy Areas. There are two conceptual categories in which pressures in this area can be discussed. First, there is the possibility that economic pressures might be directed toward obtaining noneconomic policy objectives. Second, we can talk about economic and noneconomic pressures directed toward obtaining broad economic policy objectives.

I have already noted in chapter 3 that religious interests have, in certain instances, threatened economic sanctions as a method of securing their goals. These threats were very ineffective, in part because they were used sporadically and only by extremists, and also because they never involved large contributors or investors. Respondents could not cite any instances where the large contributors and investors themselves sought to influence basis noneconomic policy areas. There was a report in early 1972 that "leading Jewish financiers in Europe" voiced their concern "over Israel's seeming diplomatic intransigence." [88] The report quoted one $500,000-a-year contributor as saying that "when we got to Golda . . . we are told in effect to mind our own business." She is quoted by a *Newsweek* respondent as asking him, if he wants to influence Israel's policy, "why don't you settle down here and enter politics?"

Simcha Dinitz, at that time Director of the Prime Minister's Bureau, emphatically denied the story in a letter to *Newsweek*. He claimed that "not a single conversation of this or a similar nature was carried on between a single contributor in Europe or the United States and the Prime Minister." [89] Even if the story were true, and there is no reason to question Dinitz's veracity, the point, as *Newsweek* itself pointed out, was that pressures from contributors had not influenced Israel's foreign policy. Furthermore, even if the *Newsweek* story were true, it would be a unique effort at influencing Israeli policy.

We can erase, therefore, my first conceptual category—the use of economic sanctions by large investors and contributors from the Diaspora to influence Israeli policy in noneconomic areas.

The one area of basic economic policy where some respondents suggested that attempts at influence might have taken place came in the early years of the State. Mapai at that time was seriously committed to socialist principles. The phrase *Socialism in our time* was used in Mapai's election campaign. Yet the Government did not really pursue a socialist policy and one wonders whether the influence of foreign, especially American, Jewish contributors and investors was not a factor.

This question may lend itself to systematic research, but the research necessary to discover the answer to the question goes far beyond the scope of this volume. Here I simply relied on the impressions of respondents who were close to the policymakers of that time. Their opinion was that foreign investors themselves did not seek to change the Government's basic economic policy. The Government itself, in its search for foreign investment, softened its own socialist policies. Within the Government, those more favorable to a free-enterprise system argued against socialist policies and socialist phraseology and sloganeering as injurious to the nation by discouraging investment of foreign capital and the *aliya* of businessmen and industrialists. Parties of the Right attacked the Government's policies as harmful because they did not encourage private investment. But the foreign investors themselves did very little. In other words, the necessity for foreign investment undoubtedly restrained the Government from adopting more leftist policies and slogans, in the opinion of many respondents, but this was not a response to pressures from the investors themselves.

According to a former Israeli ambassador to the U.S., there was no organized effort by the large contributors or investors to tell Israel that it must change its policies. But when the Government went out to find new capital, it turned first to its Jewish friends. In the course of meeting with them, attitudes among Israeli leaders changed. Another respondent involved in governmental investment policy stated that large foreign investors are of the opinion that basic economic policy must be the sole responsibility of the Government itself.

2. *Specific Policy and Policy Administration.* I have lumped policy and administration together, since the two are often inseparable. One of the primary demands, the *leitmotif* of all the economic conferences, as one respondent phrased it, has been the demand for simplification of investment procedures. The slogan that recurs again and again is a "one stop agency for investment." This demand, according to the same respondent, will never be fulfilled so long as Israel remains a democracy. While investor demands, according to the respondent, have resulted in the elimination of a certain amount of overlap, red tape, and duplication, with resultant more efficient bureaucratic procedures, the Government and the country would never tolerate the concentration of sufficient authority in the hands of one individual or agency to enable it to make the host of decisions required to approve an investment project. This is especially true, the respondent stressed, because the investor generally seeks a whole series of government services and often requests special treatment. He is not simply requesting permission to invest money. He wants a plot of land allocated for his project with permission of the Land Authority and/or local authorities. He often wants Government participation or Government loans,

special tax benefits, import licences, and a host of other benefits that require individual decisions. Consequently, the process at its best requires time and the approval of a number of governmental agencies.

Nevertheless, as noted, Israel has been responsive to investor pressure and has introduced some administrative changes.

There are other examples of specific policies that have been recommended by investors and that the Government has adopted.

One example was the recommendation that the Government not be a partner and indeed withdraw from enterprises that have sufficient private capital; that the Government encourage private investment through increased tax benefits; or that military production of a nonsecret nature no longer be allocated exclusively to industrial units under direct army control. However, as noted, these recommendations were made by local as well as foreign investors. In the case of the recommendation regarding military production, for example, pressures from Koor Industries, a major Israeli corporation including chemical, electronic, metal, plastic, cement, and other enterprises and employing six percent of Israel's total industrial manpower, were greater than the pressures of foreign investors.

In other cases as well, according to respondents, it was local businessmen who obtained the support and legitimacy of foreign investors at the economic conferences to press their own demands on the Government. The Law for the Encouragement of Capital Investments no longer discriminates, as it once did, between foreign and local investors. The latter now have the same benefits as the former. Israeli businessmen, therefore, sometimes phrase their demands in terms of encouraging foreign investment when, in fact, any benefits to foreign investors accrue to Israelis as well. Recommendations were often adopted because they buttressed tendencies that already existed within the Government. In some cases they strengthened the hands of the Minister of Finance against pressures from parties of the Left. In other cases, such as the recommendation regarding military production, they strengthened the Treasury and Commerce and Industry Ministries against the Defence Ministry. One suspects that a number of recommendations that came out of the economic conferences were, in fact, initiated by Government officials concerned with investment who sought these recommendations to strengthen their hand in interdepartmental negotiations.

In summary, therefore, the weight and influence of Diaspora Jewry is felt in certain areas of specific economic policy and administrative procedures, but in no case did respondents feel that what was at stake was a specific Diaspora interest or even a specific Jewish interest. Recommendations were accepted not only as a result of pressure but because the Government believed that they were in the best interests of the economy. And they were effectively pressed because at the very outset they had supported from within the Government itself. Diaspora Jewry, in this case as in previous case studies, was more an instrument in the hands of local interests than an independent agent acting in its own behalf.

3. *Special Favors and Benefits.* Investment applications with their requests for special benefits are necessarily treated on an individual basis. Respondents agreed that strictly economic criteria were not the only standards by which the Government decided upon these applications. There was no question that investors who were active in Jewish life, who were leaders of local UJA and Israel Bond campaigns, received favored treatment. Indeed, these special favors were often the subject of newspaper stories. In the course of one year, leaders of the Israel Bond campaign in the U.S., a former leader of the Conference of Presidents of Major American Jewish Organizations, and a group of South African Jewish leaders all received special government favors for their investments.[90] In the latter case, approval was specifically announced "in light of the contributions of the leaders of South African Jewry to the State of Israel." In

other cases, efforts were made to guard the identity and privileges of the benefactors.

CONCLUSION

The classic example of interest-group pressure in public policy formation is that of economic interests. The classic example of foreign pressures in domestic affairs is the example of foreign investors pressuring a government to adopt policies favorable to the investors. Is the Israeli situation any different? Is any special dimension present in the Israeli case in the light of the fact that investors are by and large Jewish? One might posit that, because Israel is so dependent on foreign contributors and investors, and because Israel's basic appeal to them is based on Jewish identities and ties, they would seek to influence Israeli policy beyond the narrow area of their economic concerns. In other words, one might posit that, since foreign contributors and investors have more than economic interests in Israel, they would use their economic leverage to achieve broad economic and even noneconomic policy objectives. Alternatively, one might posit that, because the investors and contributors are attracted to Israel for sentimental reasons, their identification with Israel would constrain them from pressuring for even the more limited economic demands characteristic of foreign investors in other countries. The latter is apparently more correct than the former. Contributors are concerned that their money be utilized efficiently; investors want to make money and are not above utilizing any special ties they might have with Government officials in order to assure themselves of a profit from their investment. But they have not initiated pressure nor sought to influence basic economic policy. Finally, as I have noted, there is no Diaspora economic interest in Israel nor any exercise of economic pressures to achieve policies that Diaspora Jews favor and Israelis oppose.

5

Diaspora Jewry's Influence on Israel's Foreign Policy

To what extent, if any, has Diaspora Jewry influenced Israel's foreign policy? Our primary concern has been with Diaspora pressure, not with the extent to which Israel has, of its own volition, considered the needs or desires of Diaspora Jewry in shaping its foreign policy. However, we must also deal with the latter question because, in the case of foreign policy, it is inseparable from the first. In this chapter, therefore, I will address myself to the broader question of the Jewish and Diaspora component in Israeli foreign policy. Only at the conclusion will I summarize my findings with respect to Diaspora pressure.

Analytically it is important to distinguish not only between pressure *from* Diaspora Jewry and concern *for* Diaspora Jewry but also between Israel's concern for the Diaspora out of its own self-interest (Israeli particularism) and Israel's concern for the Diaspora for the sake of the Diaspora. In practice it is often difficult to make this distinction. That which is good for Diaspora Jewry, other things being equal, is good for Israel. The most obvious example is *aliya*, which I discussed in chapter 1.

Aliya was a *sine qua non* for the viability and security of

Israel, as Ben-Gurion reiterated time and time again. But *aliya* has also served the needs of millions of Jews for whom conditions in their own country of domicile were intolerable and for whom Israel was the only alternative. Thus, for the most part, *aliya* met both Israel's self-interest and the Diaspora's interest. The concern for *aliya*, in turn, influenced Israel's behavior in its international relations and in the U.N.[1] Whether Israel was acting in its own self-interest or the Diaspora's interest is impossible to determine. As we saw in chapter 1, when *aliya* did not serve Israel's interest it was curtailed, but pure self-interest would have dictated a far more selective policy and far greater curtailment. Israel could and did argue that by limiting *aliya* it was serving the needs of *aliya* since only an economically viable country could continue to care for and absorb new immigrants.

A second problem in determining the degree of Israel's sensitivity to the needs of the Diaspora is the fact that Israel may act against the interests or wishes of one Jewish community on behalf of the Jewish interests of another community, or even on behalf of General Jewish principles. Thus, despite telegrams from the Jewish community of Spain, Israel voted against rescinding a previous anti-Spanish resolution in the U.N. on the basis of the fact that Spain had cooperated with the Nazis.[2]

Israel's decision to accept reparations from Germany required it to balance its particularist interests and to some extent the interests of Jews [3] who might benefit from reparations with its loyalty to Jewish memories and Jewish sensitivities.[4] In this case, Diaspora Jewry played a very important role, though not through direct pressure.

The first major step in the exchanges that eventually led to German reparations was taken by the World Jewish Congress in December 1949. Talks were initiated in 1950 and carried on by Dr. Noah Barou of the Congress.[5] The decision of the Israeli Government to seek reparations came in January 1951. However, Israel sought to obtain reparations through the four occupying powers rather than through direct negotiations with the

Germans. The Soviet Union ignored an Israeli note on the subject. France, Great Britain, and the U.S. made it clear that they would not impose obligations on Germany to pay reparations. Hence, if Israel wanted reparations it had to enter into direct negotiations with the Germans.[6]

Israeli leaders feared a public outcry against them should they negotiate directly with Germany.' At this point Nahum Goldmann suggested that Jewish world organizations act on behalf of Israel.[7] Goldmann organized 22 major national and international Jewish organizations on whose behalf he met with Adenauer. At a meeting on December 6, 1951, Goldmann presented Adenaur with Ben-Gurion's condition under which he, Ben-Gurion, would ask the Knesset to approve direct talks with Germany.[8]

But Diaspora Jewry did more than act indirectly on Israel's behalf. The fact that it was Diaspora Jews who established direct contact with Germany helped legitimize Israel's direct contacts. This, at least, was an argument frequently offered by proponents of direct negotiations.[9] According to Goldmann, the reparations agreement is the best example of full Diaspora-Israel cooperation. "Israel would not dare accept reparations without world Jewry," nor would the Government have got a majority in support of its proposal.[10]

On other occasions Israel's self-interest was defined, at least in part, by the desires of Diaspora Jewry. In such cases, it is sometimes difficult to distinguish between *desire* and *pressure*. The outstanding example is Israel's decision to side with the West against the East in the early years of the cold war. There have been those who argued that Israel pursued a pro-Western policy for the sake of the Diaspora. According to Shimon Peres, a leading political figure in Israel, "We want to be friendly with the United States in order to strengthen the link with American Jewry, not the other way around." [11] In 1950, Ben Gurion himself said ". . . in the present conditions prevailing in the world and in the Diaspora, the State of Israel cannot be neutral in the cold war because it means alienating ourselves from the Jewish people, from Jewish communities. . . ."[12] But most observers were of the opinion that the significance of Diaspora Jewry as a factor in Israel's cold war policy was Israel's reliance on American Jewry and its consequent need to demonstrate a Western orientation both to please American Jewry and to utilize it. According to one Israeli diplomat, after the Korean War began:

> We had to make up our mind. . . . The Israeli economy was at its lowest point. Ben Gurion had asked the Soviets for economic aid; it was a feasible expectation at the time, but Moscow's reply was negative. And American Jews were saying, "Playing with Moscow will diminish aid from U.S. Jewry." We had to cut off from one side in order to continue getting aid from America.[13]

Ben-Gurion himself justified his pro-Western orientation by the fact that only in the West does Israel have direct access to Jewry which, in turn, can contribute to the formulation of policy favorable to Israel.[14] Abba Eban expressed similar sentiments.[15]

Israel has always felt that it had a responsibility for the safety and welfare of Diaspora Jewry although, as we shall see, this display of interest sometimes aroused objections from another Jewish community. According to one student of foreign policy, Israel "maintained cordial relations with Peron's Argentina largely out of regard for the half-million Jews living there."[16] It considered it only natural to protest anti-Semitic manifestations wherever they occurred. In 1950 Roumania arrested some forty prominent Zionists and Israel sent a strong note of protest stating that ". . . the persecution of Zionists in any country is bound to impair the friendly relations between that country and Israel and to outrage the feelings of the Jewish People throughout the world."[17] The note aroused no negative reaction from Jews; no Jewish community charged Israel with interference in the internal affairs of another country. Similarly, when Israel protested the treatment of Soviet Jews in the wake of the Doctors' Plot of 1953, there were also no negative reactions from Diaspora Jewry.[18]

A different reaction took place when Israel sent notes to a dozen countries where Jewish sites were daubed with swastika in late 1959. The notes expressed "the sensitivity and awareness of the Government of Israel and the people of Israel to every act that affects Jews in the dispersion." [19]

The Israeli initiative clearly arose out of its sense of responsibility for the welfare of all Jews. Certainly it was of no particular benefit to Israel's foreign relations. It did not help to endear it to the Government to whom the notes were dispatched. It is therefore, an example of Israel's acting on behalf of the needs of world Jewry. The notes, however, occasioned a protest from the American Jewish Committee. Blaustein complained to Ben-Gurion that the Israeli notes "infringed on the autonomy of the Jewish communities concerned." [20]

There is a second instance in which Israel acted on behalf of larger Jewish interests rather than its particularist Israeli interest and aroused apprehension and some dissatisfaction from the Diaspora. In mid-1960 Israeli security agents seized Nazi leader Adolph Eichmann in Argentina, smuggled him out of the country, and brought him to Israel where he was subsequently tried, convicted, and executed for his role in the Nazi murder of millions of Jews. Israel acted in its self-perceived role as a representative of the Jewish people. Policymakers must surely have realized that kidnapping Eichmann from Argentina would not only jeopardize relations with that country but would necessarily raise eyebrows in every foreign ministry in the world. No government takes kindly to the notion of foreign agents kidnapping one of its residents, regardless of the circumstances. Israel apparently was most concerned with the possible effects of its operation on Argentinian Jews but concluded that they would not suffer. [21]

The American Jewish Committee petitioned Foreign Minister Golda Meir to agree to permit Eichmann to be tried either by a German court or by an international tribunal. [22] Other Jewish leaders, concerned about the impact of Israel's act on world opinion, also recommended that Eichmann be tried by an international tribunal rather than by exclusively Israeli judges.[23]

In both the swastika and Eichmann instances Israel risked its self-interest, although the interest risked was not an appreciable one, for the interest of either Diaspora Jewry or what might be called historical Jewish interests. In both cases, however, they met apprehension if not opposition from other segments of Diaspora Jewry. All this indicates how difficult it is to conclude in whose interest Israel does act. It is very hard to find instances where Israel took an appreciable risk in sacrificing its own self-interests for the sake of the Diaspora.

By the same token there are a few instances where Israel clearly sacrificed the Diaspora for its own self-interest. During the mid-1950s, for example, France was Israel's most important ally and its major source of arms. France, in turn, anticipated Israeli support for its North African policies, especially in its war against the Algerian rebels. For those, however, who believed that independence was inevitable, too close a tie to France or the lack of connections to local nationalist forces jeopardized the eventual position of the indigenous Jewish communities. The World Jewish Congress, therefore, sought to maintain relationships with dissident forces in Algeria, Tunisia, and Morocco. The French made their objections known to Israel which, in turn, conveyed its special dissatisfaction to the World Jewish Congress over the latter's discussions with the Algerian rebels then engaged in active warfare against France.[24]

It would appear that Israel was acting exclusively in its own self-interest. But the facts are not entirely clear, nor is it entirely certain that the actions of the World Jewish Congress would have done any good. Israel's argument that Algerian independence would bode evil for the local Jewish population regardless of how friendly the World Jewish Congress would act toward the rebels was certainly vindicated.

The prime example where Israel had to choose between Diaspora interests and its own self-interest is the case of South Africa. Israeli foreign policy in the late 1950s dictated efforts at winning the friendship of the African states. It became obvious by the beginning of the 1960s that part of the price Israel would have to pay for this friendship was a condemnation of South Africa for its *apartheid* policies. While Israel justified her opposition to *apartheid* on moral and even Jewish grounds, her leaders never concealed the fact that her opposition to South Africa, particularly in the United Nations, was also a result of efforts to obtain the friendship of South Africa's Asian and African opponents.[25]

On the other hand, it was clear to Israeli leaders that acting against South Africa would, at the very minimum, create discomfort for South African Jewry. In July 1961, on the occasion of a visit to Israel by the President of Upper Volta, the leaders of both countries issued a joint statement condemning *apartheid*. *Die Transvaler,* a South African paper taken to express the opinions of South African Prime Minister Hendrik Verwoerd, expressed its amazement at the statement, and added: "Has not the time come for Jews in South Africa to do some information work in Jerusalem?" [26] In October, Israel was one of two Western countries who voted to censure South African Foreign Minister Eric Louw for "offensive, fictitious and erroneous statements" in his speech to the General Assembly. Louw, in a broadcast to South Africa appealed for a reaction from South African Jewry.[27]

In November 1962 Israel was the only Western country to vote in favor of sanctions against South Africa. The sanctions included breaking diplomatic ties, closing of ports to South African ships, prohibiting exports to South Africa, and ceasing air ties with South Africa. Prime Minister Verwoerd was quoted as saying:

> I wonder what South African Jewry are going to say about this? Are they still going to send gifts, are they still going to allow their sons to die there, are they still going to build up one area after another? [28]

Meanwhile, as a first step in the implementation of the resolution, Israel replaced its ambassador with a chargé d'affairs.

South African Jews generally felt that "Israel had voted wrongly and the South African government had just cause for grievance." Even the *Zionist Record,* official organ of the South African Zionist Federation, criticized Israel's U.N. vote, although the South African *Jewish Times* defended it.[29] The official position of the local Jewish leadership as reflected in the Board of Deputies was (as it always has been) that the Jewish community *qua* community took no stand on the issue of *apartheid* and that they could not and should not be expected to try to influence Israel's policies.[30] Nevertheless the Board did pass a resolution that "Israel should have joined the other Western nations in abstaining from voting against South Africa." [31]

Israeli policymakers were sensitive to the difficult position in which their decisions had placed South African Jewry. According to Ben-Gurion:

> We knew the Jews there wouldn't suffer very much. The South African Government was angry but not against the Jews there—against Israel.
> If there would have been *pogroms*—if their lives were in danger then we would have abstained.[32]

According to Haim Yahil, who was Director General of the Foreign Ministry during this period:

> On no issue—among those not directly concerning Israel's vital interests—do I remember more discussion than on *Apartheid.* . . . The majority pressed for a strong line on principle; a minority stressed the welfare of South African Jews.[33]

Israel, however, did not break diplomatic relations with South Africa, in part out of its own economic interests but primarily out of consideration for South African Jewry.[34] According to another Foreign Office official, Israel would have broken diplomatic relations except for its concern with South African Jewry.[35]

Israeli policymakers were also aware of the fact that South African Jewry was under pressure to influence Israel.[36] The details of what South African Jewish leaders did or did not do are shrouded in secrecy. According to one student of South African Jewry, both the Zionist Federation and the Board of Deputies decided to make approaches to Israel.[37] Brecher quotes a Foreign Office official as saying: "You can assume that South African Jewry put pressure on Israel, was unhappy with our policy, and that we took it into account."[38] According to a very reliable informant, a delegation of South African leaders came to Israel after they had heard reports that, consistent with its vote in favor of sanctions, Israel intended to discontinue El Al flights to South Africa. The delegation argued that this would, in fact, cut South African Jewry off from Israel. Whether they also threatened or warned Israel that it might alienate South African Jews is not clear. They did return to South Africa with the conviction that they had been instrumental in Israel's decision to continue El Al flights to South Africa.

What can be concluded from all this? Israel was willing to risk the welfare of South African Jewry in pursuit of its particularist interests. But it was a calculated and measured risk. Furthermore, Israel refrained from breaking relations with South Africa and, in one instance, it modified one aspect of its policy under the influence of South African Jewry. Was Israel influenced by "pressure" from the Diaspora or by a concern for the welfare of a Diaspora community? Surely both factors were present.

In the case of South Africa there is a difficulty in arriving at a judgment, but at least most of the facts are clear. In the case of Soviet Jewry even the facts are at issue. It is clear, however, that we are dealing not with pressure from Diaspora Jewry but rather with Israel's sensitivity to Diaspora Jewry's needs. Two charges have been made—first, that Israel moderated its demands on behalf of Soviet Jewry in order to maintain the friendship of the Soviet Union; second, when it did raise demands on behalf of Soviet Jewry, it stressed their right to *aliya* rather than cultural and religious freedom because *aliya* benefited Israel whereas cultural and religious freedom was of no immediate benefit.

The facts are extremely difficult to ascertain. They not only require basic research far beyond those possible within the limitations of this study, but, as we shall see, they do not, by their very nature, lend themselves to disclosure. What I shall do here is catalogue the judgments of a number of observers in order to arrive at some tentative conclusions.

There are a number of sources for the charge that Israel did not do all that it could or should have done on behalf of Soviet Jewry. In chapter 1 I noted the accusations of Louis Shub. Israeli philosopher Eliezer Schweid has made similar charges. According to Schweid, writing in 1968:

> Israel managed the struggle for a change in attitude on the part of the authorities of the Soviet Union toward Soviet Jews in a hesitant manner. The fate of Soviet Jewry hardly was mentioned at the 27th Zionist Congress. And on international platforms, Israel consistently refrained from raising the question in its full form. This arouses one's suspicions that considerations of some particularistic Israeli political application, real or imaginary, may have been given precedence over the weight of obligation and responsibility for Jewry as a whole.[39]

Recent Soviet immigrants to Israel have also been critical of Israel's past policies, which they charge placed Israeli self-interest ahead of Soviet Jewish interests. At a meeting of Israel's Public Committee for Soviet Jewry on January 3, 1973, one new immigrant stated that in 1963 a number of Soviet Jews adopted a plan to publicly renounce their Soviet citizenship. They were discouraged from doing so by an Israeli cultural attaché who met with one of their leaders in Minsk and said that such an act would be embarrassing to Israel.[40]

In a statement signed by 40 members of Kibbutz Chatzerim following a meeting with two recent Soviet immigrants, charges were made that even after 1973 Israel had not really changed its basic policy of not doing anything "to irritate the Russian bear." [41]

Ben-Asher, in his book on Israeli foreign policy, continually stresses the importance of the Diaspora in shaping Israeli foreign policy. He goes so far as to maintain that "the interrelationships between the State and the Diaspora shape Israeli foreign policy and her relations to the nations of the world." [42] It is of significance, therefore, that from his discussion of Israeli-Soviet relations it appears that Israel did not press the question of the rights of Soviet Jews until after Israeli-Soviet tensions became pronounced.[43]

Finally, forces within Israel in the 1960s pressed the Government to a more active policy on behalf of Soviet Jewry. Shimor Peres, relying on his memory rather than on documentation recalls that the Knesset Committee on Foreign Affairs and Security "urged the Government to adopt a more aggressive and open policy on this matter."[44] This suggests that the Government was not so active as it might have been.

Those who deny that Israel neglected the needs of Soviet Jewry in order to secure closer relations to the Soviet Union dismiss these charges. It may be argued that neither Shub nor Schweid, nor any other who has made similar charges, is sensitive to the decision-making premise or basis of Israeli foreign policy. Many recent Soviet immigrants tend to be extremists in foreign policy matters and lack a broad perspective concerning the accomplishments of and possibilities for Israeli activity or behalf of Soviet Jews. As long as Israel maintained normal relations with the Soviet Union it would have been counter productive to publicly accuse it of persecuting Soviet Jews or to denounce it publicly for not permitting Jews to leave. These are tactics of last resort when quiet diplomatic work can no longer be effective precisely because relations between the Governments are tense. Finally, the fact that a Knesset Committee urged the Government to adopt a more active policy is no indication that the Government was not doing all it could. It is always possible to urge the Government to do more, particularly when those doing the urging do not have to execute a policy but can gain public sympathy by their statements.

Israel's primary goal has been to arouse world opinion as to the plight of Soviet Jews. In order to fulfill this function Israel must not appear as the initiator and prime lobbyist or behalf of Soviet Jews. Otherwise, the issue, most effective when presented on a humanitarian basis, will appear as one of political conflict. Israel feels that it can gain far more support for Soviet Jewry if the fight on their behalf is not expressed as an Israeli-Soviet confrontation. As a result, it sometimes appears that Israel is doing less than it ought to on behalf of Soviet Jews.[45]

Assuming that Israel carried on activities within the Soviet Union, encouraging Soviet Jews and assisting them in their resistance and their will to survive, these activities would necessarily be of a secret nature. It is possible that on occasion Israeli representatives discouraged a particular form of protest within the Soviet Union, but this would be a matter of tactics. Perhaps at one time Israel felt that, given the particular conditions then prevailing in the country, militancy on the part of one group of Soviet Jews would unwittingly jeopardize larger and more basic forms of activity.

The potential benefit to Israel from the immigration of a substantial portion of Soviet Jewry is so great that, if only from reasons of narrow self-interest, Israel would be concerned with its encouragement. According to Ben-Gurion, the fate of Soviet Jewry was Israel's main concern in its policy toward the Soviet Union.[46]

Israeli officials were of the opinion that Israel did sacrifice better relations with the Soviet Union for the sake of Soviet Jewry. According to the man who was Director-General of the Foreign Ministry from 1964 to 1967:

Certainly we would be better off in our relations with the Soviets if we did not constantly press for amelioration of the conditions of Soviet Jews. But the imperatives of the situation —the welfare of a major Jewish community demand, in the eyes of Israeli decision-makers, a special effort by Israel.[47]

According to another former Director-General:

the welfare of Soviet Jewry is regarded by "almost everybody" as an Israeli national interest, as well as a vital interest of the

Jewish People. This . . . is the reason for Israel's policy towards the Soviet Union—which alienates Moscow.[48]

International relations authority Nadav Safran felt that Israel's relations with the Soviet Union and her satellites were "soured" in part by their restriction of Jewish immigration and Jewish cultural life.[49] Binyamin Eliav, a Soviet expert who served the Israeli Foreign Ministry in many capacities before his retirement and whose sensitivity and commitment to Judaism and Diaspora Jewry is universally acknowledged, was also of the opinion that Israel did whatever it could for Soviet Jewry.[50]

Was Israel's concern for Soviet Jewry primarily a concern to bring more Jews to Israel or a concern for Jewish survival and religious and cultural freedom in the Soviet Union? Israel's policy has been to demand *aliya* rather than the conditions that might assure a Jewish way of life within the Soviet Union. The issue was brought into sharp focus in the last few years in a debate the leading proponents of which have been Nahun Goldmann on the one side, and former Jewish Agency chairman the late Louis Pincus on the other. According to Goldmann, even under ideal circumstances not all Soviet Jews will leave, and provisions must be made to ensure the possibility of their continuing to live a Jewish life in the Soviet Union. According to Pincus, "Now is not the time to fight for equal rights for Jews in the Soviet Union." He is quoted as saying, "We can't carry on a political struggle on two levels at the same time," and that the only solution for Soviet Jewry was for them to come to Israel. "There is no point in jousting with the Soviet authorities over closing down synagogues or Jewish schools."[51] At the 1973 meetings of the World Jewish Congress he was quoted as again taking issue with Goldmann's recommendation that efforts be made to assure a Jewish life for Jews who chose to remain in the Soviet Union. Pincus observed that most immigrants from Russia say there is no chance of this taking place; by splitting the effort between demands for a Jewish way of life and *aliya*, pressure on the Soviets would weaken.[52]

This is not a new policy. Even when *aliya* was only a trickle based on the principle of "reunion of families," Israeli officials opposed attacking the Soviet Union for closing of synagogues or denying Jews the right to bake *matzo* for Passover. The fear was that to attack the Soviets on these grounds might lead them to discontinue issuing the few permits for immigration to Israel that they allowed.[53]

Proponents of this policy do not feel that it is a sacrifice of Soviet Jews' rights for the sake of Israel's self-interest. Recent Soviet immigrants most critical of Israel for not doing enough on behalf of Soviet Jewry argue that there is no hope for Soviet Jewish life within the Soviet Union and that efforts should be directed only on behalf of *aliya*. *Aliya*, and the hope of *aliya*, is in their opinion the strongest factor in identification and awakening of Soviet Jews. Anything that threatens *aliya* threatens Jewish identification, according to this argument.

The argument does not seem entirely convincing, certainly when applied to the Eastern portions of the Soviet Union or to those parts annexed in the World War II period. One cannot but harbor the suspicion that at least part of the reason that Israel has stressed *aliya* rather than Jewish survival is that the former serves Israel's interest more than the latter. But how would one expect or want Israel to act when confronted by a genuine conflict of interest?

Most Israeli leaders acknowledge the potential conflict between Israeli and Diaspora interests. A few insist upon denying, by definition, such a possibility. No Israeli leader adopts a more simple-minded approach than does former Prime Minister Golda Meir. In the debate over German reparations she justified reparations on the basis of Israel's obligation to Diaspora Jewry. Since there was no place in the world other than Israel where Jews were absolutely safe, she claimed, it was Israel's responsibility to World Jewry to become strong, however possible, in order to be able to help them.[54]

In the Knesset debate over Israel's U.N. vote against South Africa, the opposition parties maintained that Israel had sacrificed Jewish interests to particularist Israeli interests. For ex-

ample, Kalman Kahana charged that Israel had voted in the
U.N. to protect its interest as a state when it should have given
greater weight to the interest of South African Jewry.[55] The
then Foreign Minister Golda Meir replied as follows:

> Kahana says we only concerned ourselves with the State of
> Israel. . . . According to the best of my Jewish understanding
> there is no real conflict between the interests of the People
> and of the State. . . . The strength of the State of Israel is the
> real direct interest of every Jewish settlement in the world.[56]

More subtle in his appreciation of the existence of a conflict of interest, Ben-Gurion was also of the opinion that Israel's
interests come first.

> In questions of international relations we ask ourselves one
> simple question: What is good for Israel? And if it is good,
> all my Jewish feeling and instinct and all my Jewish human
> self-respect tell me: Do that which is good for Israel and
> necessary for her security.[57]

Ben-Gurion subsequently modified this statement somewhat. In
an interview with Michael Brecher he expressed himself in the
following manner:

> It was always my view that we have always to consider the
> interests of Diaspora Jewry—any Jewish community that was
> concerned. . . . If it was a case vital for Israel, and the interests
> of the Jews concerned were different, the vital interests of
> Israel come first—because Israel is vital for world Jewry.[58]

Most other Israeli leaders share the same opinion (in fact, it
would be no exaggeration to say that most Diaspora leaders
share this opinion, although they might quibble over the definition of the term *vital*). Sharett, as Foreign Minister, stressed
the responsibility that Israel had for Diaspora Jewry, but added:

> This is not to say that we can always accept the argument of
> our responsibility as decisive. There were instances where

we knew that a particular act that we were about to undertake would severely hurt the entire Jewish people, and nevertheless we did not hold back.[59]

According to former Prime Minister Levi Eshkol:

> It is difficult to establish a formula as to where Israeli vital
> interests end and the interests of world Jewry prevail. They
> are individual decisions in each case. For example, there is a
> difference between one hundred thousand Jews in South
> Africa and three million in Russia.[60]

Brecher quotes a "Foreign Office veteran" and then Yaacov
Herzog as follows:

> There is a general disposition to take into account Jewish
> interests—as long as Israel's national interests are not sacri-
> ficed. The latter clearly have priority, though Jewish interests
> are sometimes so much to the fore that they dominate.

According to Herzog:

> The "Jewish factor" is always present in the minds of decision-
> makers. Its importance depends on the relative balance of two
> considerations—the degree of danger to local Jewry flowing
> from the act and the importance of the act in terms of Israel's
> national interests. If it came to a crunch, and absolutely
> crucial interests of Israel were at stake, the latter would ob-
> tain, this being considered the ultimate Jewish interest." [61]

Measuring the Diaspora or Jewish component in Israeli
foreign policy in any precise way is impossible. It is very rare
that policymakers deal with absolute alternatives. As we have
seen in the debate over *aliya* in chapter 1 and in a number of
instances in this chapter, policymakers must not only balance
the interests of Diaspora Jewry against Israeli interests, but they
must also determine the relative advantages and disadvantages
to each in the pursuit of a particular policy. The simple juxtaposition of one interest against another can occur only hypo-

thetically. In practice, one must always ask how much of a risk is involved or how great are the advantages and disadvantages to each side. Obviously, however, one's own predispositions about the importance of Jewish values or about Diaspora Jewry are likely to find expression in the balance sheet that is finally drawn up. Furthermore, as I suggested at the outset of this chapter, Diaspora Jewry's strength is itself an Israeli self-interest, even in the narrowest, most particularist sense, so that theoretical distinctions between Diaspora and Israeli interests are difficult to make in practice.[62] Finally, as we saw in the case of South Africa, the line between Diaspora interests and Diaspora pressure is frequently impossible to draw.

What does emerge quite clearly, however, from a survey of Israeli foreign policy decisions in which Jewish interests are involved, is the fact that there was so little direct pressure on Israel.

Perhaps we can better appreciate this phenomenon by asking: What kinds of pressures would we anticipate? Is there a particular Diaspora interest in Israel's foreign policy? A *priori* the only obvious interest is that of each Diaspora community in strengthening friendly ties between its government and the State of Israel. Any tension between Israel and a foreign country necessarily raises the specter of charges of dual loyalty against the Jews of that country and increases the likelihood of anti-semitism.[63] It is therefore in their interest to reduce the tension. One would expect that in so doing they might seek to influence Israel. This anticipation is reinforced by the fact that foreign governments may, in fact, expect their Jewish communities to do so. We have seen that the South African Government pressured South African Jewry, in however subtle a fashion, to change Israel's policy. In the days immediately following Israel's conquest of Sinai in 1956 the U.S. was anxious for an Israeli withdrawal and they asked Zionist leader Abba Hillel Silver to influence Ben-Gurion to withdraw. Silver, however, refused.[64]

There is no question that many American Jews would have been happier with an Israeli withdrawal. Indeed, when Israel invaded Sinai the American Jewish Committee, by its own testimony, "impressed upon Eban the grave public relations issue facing American Jews and urged Israel to mend quickly the rift with the United States." [65] After the fighting stopped, the Committee sought to persuade Israel "to renounce any expansionist aims." [66] Within the Presidents' Conference, B'nai B'rith leader Philip Klutznick and Reform leader Rabbi Maurice Eisendrath were especially critical of Israel. The Presidents' Conference, through the mediation of Abba Eban (then Israeli ambassador to Washington), encouraged Israel to withdraw from Sinai but, according to its founder and then Chairman Nahum Goldmann, there was no pressure on Israel in the sense that "unless you do so and so, we will do thus and so." [67]

Thus, there was some American Jewish pressure on Israel. How much it contributed to Ben-Gurion's decision to withdraw from Sinai is hard to say. Perhaps it was very important, because it reinforced Ben-Gurion's sense of isolation. On the other hand, the pressure itself was really very low key. It was very far from the kind of pressure American Jewry or the Presidents' Conference or even the American Jewish Committee alone might have brought to bear had they been determined to change Israeli policy.[68] Whatever its significance, it was an indication that American Jews were unwilling to support Israel without reservation. Nevertheless, as Goldmann pointed out in his defense of American Jewish behavior during the Sinai affair, they had supported Israel for many years in opposition to American policy in the Middle East.[69] They did so with even greater vigor after 1968, when the Nixon administration refused to supply Israel with the military equipment it requested. Similarly, although South African Jewry was unhappy with Israel's stand, they refused to capitulate to pressure from their own government to withdraw support for Israel. British Jewry opposed their government's anti-Zionist policy in the pre-state period and their policy of increasing coolness to Israel and pro-Arab sympathy since 1970. French Jewry continued to support Israel despite the about face in French foreign policy under De Gaulle. One prominent French Jewish organization sent a delegation to Israel to register its opposition to what it considered Israel's anti-French propaganda; but this was the one exception to the general rule of support from the French Jewish community. According to Yaacov Tsur, veteran Israeli diplomat and Foreign Ministry official, this and South Africa were the only two instances where there were serious attempts by a Jewish community to influence Israel.[70] In an interview with Brecher he noted that "American Jewry tried to modify Israel's policy but they succeeded only in details."[71]

There is a potential conflict of interest between Israel and the Diaspora over Israeli foreign policy. The most remarkable fact in Israel's twenty-seven-year history is that this conflict has found so little expression. Part of the reason rests in the fact that Israel is sensitive to the Diaspora's needs and wishes. Primarily, however, it results from the fact that the Diaspora has asked so little of Israel.

6

The Reconstituted Jewish Agency

The Founding Assembly of the reconstituted Jewish Agency took place in June 1971. The agreement on the reconstitution was approved in February 1970 by the major participants—the Zionist General Council on behalf of the World Zionist Organization and the United Israel Appeal Inc. (UIA), the recipient organization within the United States of funds raised for Israel through the agency of the United Jewish Appeal. Other participants in the reconstituted Jewish Agency (JA) were the major fund-raising agencies for Israel in countries outside the United States. To understand what the reconstituted JA is and, equally important, what it is not, we must briefly review the background of its creation.

BACKGROUND

The WZO-JA Status Law of 1952 envisaged an expanded JA to include individuals and organizations not heretofore members of the WZO. In 1954 Nahum Goldmann invited the American Jewish Committee to a meeting to consider the creation of a permanent framework for cooperation between Zionists and non-

Zionists. Similar invitations were extended to other organizations as well.[1]

In 1957 Goldmann proposed the establishment of an advisory committee or council to the JA on which various organizations would be represented; its purpose would be to advise the JA on budgeting matters. Goldmann anticipated that after two or three years the advisory committee members might become members of an enlarged JA.[2]

What was Goldmann trying to achieve? From these and similar activities during the 1950s and 1960s, as well as from statements he made during this period, it is possible to reconstruct his perception of the problems plaguing the WZO-JA. There were, as Goldmann saw it, two interrelated problems. The organization's prestige was low externally and there was a sense of atrophy internally. Second, the organization had become totally reliant on the State of Israel for the formulation of its political policy. In effect, it was not a politically independent agency. The leading factor responsible for this condition was the organization of the WZO-JA along party lines. Party organization meant that only members of Zionist parties could be members of the WZO. Since most Zionist parties, even in the Diaspora, were oriented toward political parties within Israel, they tended to reflect differences in ideology and personality that were totally irrelevant to many Diaspora Jews. It really meant that there was no place in the WZO for Diaspora Jews who considered themselves friends and supporters of Israel, but were disinterested in joining a local organization oriented toward a particular party within Israel.[3]

A second consequence of the organization of the WZO along party lines was to limit the pool from which WZO-JA leaders could emerge. Obviously, such individuals would have to be party leaders. Even functionaries within the organization were appointed according to party affiliation; while Goldmann never mentioned this publicly, it is more than likely that he shared the opinion of others that the inefficiency, red tape, low prestige, and low morale of the WZO-JA bureaucracy were owing to the fact that its workers were not appointed according to merit.

One device for changing the structure of party control was to reorganize the WZO by national Zionist federations, with which both individuals and parties could affiliate. The fight to establish Zionist federations is an interesting and instructive tale that will not concern us here. The second device was an expansion of the WZO-JA structure to include non-Zionist organizations, which perforce meant nonparty organizations. The inclusion of non-Zionists, it was believed, would increase the numbers and prestige of the organization, serve to weaken party control, and increase the organization's political independence. One of Goldmann's problems, as he saw it, was that he had to weaken party control in the first place, in order to be able to secure the inclusion of nonparty organizations whose affiliation would serve to weaken the parties even further.

Despite the reservations of party leaders, Goldmann at the 24th Zionist Congress in 1956 secured the passage of a resolution inviting non-Zionists to participate in the responsibility for JA work in Israel. As noted, he sought the cooperation of a number of leading Jewish organizations. A few indicated their willingness and did ultimately join the WZO. Goldmann failed to enlist the leading religious organizations in the U.S. although, through the efforts of Louis Pincus, Orthodox, Conservative, and Reform leaders joined the WZO-JA executive on a personal basis. Goldmann also failed to attract the most important and most prestigious nonreligious organizations—Bnai Brith, the American Jewish Committee, or the Council of Jewish Federations and Welfare Funds (CJFWF).[4] Goldmann blames his failure on the parties who approved the initial proposal to invite non-Zionists to participate in the WZO-JA "with reluctance and, far from making the necessary concession, they sabotaged it, consciously or unconsciously." [5]

While Goldmann is no doubt correct in his estimate of the opposition to these proposals, the fact is that the organizations he wished to attract were none too enthusiastic. The American Jewish Committee was reluctant to join and even took strong exception to an expression by the Anglo-Jewish Association of England of its willingness to affiliate.[6] The CJFWF and the Joint Distribution Committee [7] also rejected Goldmann's overtures in the 1950s to formalize relations between their respective organizations and the WZO-JA.[8]

Whereas Goldmann's efforts to expand and broaden the WZO-JA at the political level met with only limited success changes took place in the 1960s that increased American-Jewish participation at the technical level. First of all, CJFWF leaders at the national and local levels were seeking, on at least a modest scale, forms of cooperation with Israel that went beyond just "sending money." They felt that they had knowledge and experience to offer Israel and they sought some framework to express their increased sense of partnership with it.[9]

There were a variety of reasons for this change of attitude Some philanthropic leaders who were once indifferent or even antagonistic to Zionism had turned into enthusiastic sympathizers of Israel; others were searching for new outlets and broader horizons for Jewish activity and were unsatified with the focus of activity that their local community could offer; many Federation leaders were acquiring a new self-image as people responsible for initiating, planning, and coordinating programs at the local level, rather than simply funding ongoing programs, and they transferred this new self-image to their Israeli activities finally, an increased confidence in their own Americanism permitted Federation leaders to allow themselves the luxury of also being involved in the affairs of another country.[10]

A second reason for the increased participation of American fund-raising leaders in WZO-JA activity at the technical level came as a consequence of American tax laws. The Internal Revenue Service of the United States Department of Treasury requires that funds raised in the United States for expenditure outside the U.S. must, in order to qualify for tax exemption, be expended under the supervision of a nongovernmental agency controlled by the American fund-raisers. The organization established in 1960 to meet the recently tightened requirements of th

Treasury Department concerning American tax-exempt organizations operating overseas was the organization today known as the United Israel Appeal Inc. (UIA).[11]

As noted above, virtually every Jewish community in the United States has some form of a Federation or Jewish Welfare Fund. These funds run combined campaigns for local, national, and international Jewish needs. In the last few years roughly three-quarters of this money has gone for international Jewish needs—that is, the money has been transferred from the local Federation and Welfare Fund campaigns to the United Jewish Appeal. The major beneficiaries of UJA funds are the Joint Distribution Committee and the UIA. The latter receives well over two-thirds of the money collected for overseas needs under a rather complicated formula that need not concern us here.

Thus, the bulk of the money collected by Jewish Federation and Welfare funds goes to the UIA. The UIA, in turn, transfers its funds to the JA. However, in accordance with Internal Revenue Service requirements, the UIA cannot simply turn the money over to the JA for the latter to do with it as it wishes. First of all, the IRS requires that the American fund-raising organization actually control the dispersal of funds. For that reason, the JA (i.e., the WZO-JA until the reconstitution of that organization in 1970) was designated as the agent of the UIA. Even this, however, was not sufficient because not all of the old WZO-JA expenditures were tax exempt. For example, much of its activity within the United States, such as encouraging immigration or the organization of Zionist youth groups, was certainly not tax exempt. Consequently the UIA designated the specific programs of the WZO-JA that it was willing to fund and sent a representative to Israel to ensure that funds were being spent in accordance with its mandate.

Thus, as early as 1960, American Jewish fund-raising leaders had, theoretically at least, a large voice in the activities of the WZO-JA. This statement, however, must be qualified. First of all, Zionists were also represented on the UIA.[12] Second, the

UIA did not initiate programs. It merely designated those programs in the WZO-JA budget which it was willing to support. For example, the WZO-JA activities in the United States that were not tax exempt were financed by income from countries outside the U.S. Thus, the fact that the UIA designated those programs it wanted to support had very little impact on WZO-JA programs. It is possible that without UIA supervision more money might have gone to philanthropic enterprises in Israel under party control or more money might have been distributed according to a party key, but the total impact was negligible.[13] What UIA involvement did do, however, was accustom American fund-raising leaders to a deeper sense of participation in WZO-JA programs. The age in which American Jews simply transferred money to Israel had come to an end, although serious institutional and structural recognition of this new relationship was not to come for another decade.

Developments within Israel itself in this period heightened the WZO-JA's sense of crisis and led to a search for allies. As the relative financial contribution of the WZO-JA to Israeli development declined after the first years of the State, the Government assumed partial or full responsibility for more and more of the functions that were heretofore the exclusive domain of the WZO-JA. Proposals to further limit its authority and functions were also voiced in view of the waste, inefficiency, and duplication of effort attributed to the WZO-JA. These voices gained momentum from the development of the Merkaz La'Tfutzot (Center for the Diaspora). The Merkaz La'Tfutzot was an outgrowth of a unit within the Prime Minister's office that functioned between 1961 and 1963 to formalize relationships between Israel and Jewish organizations abroad, to encourage them to initiate and develop programs in Israel, to help service these programs, and to encourage *aliyah*. The unit was expanded into the Merkaz La'Tfutzot and placed under the operating responsibility of the Government-JA Coordinating Committee at the suggestion of Moshe Sharett. Sharett, then chairman of the Jewish Agency executive, hoped that the Merkaz La'Tfutzot would increase the Zionist awareness and orientation of Israelis as well as Diaspora Jews. Sharett also attended to involve the Knesset in its operation.[14]

There were those, however, who saw in the Merkaz La'Tfutzot a possibility of eliminating the JA altogether. In the mid-1960s there were increasing signs of government dissatisfaction with the WZO-JA. For example, at the January 1967 sessions of the Zionist General Council, Prime Minister Levi Eshkol addressed himself to the failure of the Zionist movement to increase immigration from affluent countries and even expand and intensify Zionist education and Jewish cultural activities in the Diaspora. He said:

> As you know, I have never been in favour of abstract debate on the meaning of Zionism and the Zionist Organization's right to exist. I have attached much greater importance to the implementation of its ideas. I would have been wholeheartedly in favour of giving it pride of place in our relations with the Jewish people. But rights imply duties as well. If there is a Charter between us—it obligates both parties to action. I believe the Government of Israel has met and is continuing to meet its obligations to the Movement—if not more. But there is no point in simply drawing attention to the Charter. If it is not backed by deeds, it loses all sense and purpose. The Government must re-examine from time to time its ties and undertakings towards the Zionist Movement on the basis of deeds—or the lack of them.[15]

These must have been frightening words coming from Levi Eshkol who, compared to his predecessor Ben-Gurion, was a staunch friend of the WZO-JA, a contrast to which he alludes in his statement.

Paradoxically, the dramatic increase in the financial contribution of Diaspora Jewry at the time of the Six Day War of 1967 jeopardized rather than buttressed WZO-JA autonomy.[16] Ernest Stock, the UIA representative in Israel for a number of years, pointed out that the first reaction by the Israeli Government was to seek a deeper involvement in the policies and operations of the organization, whose income now constituted " a not inconsiderable portion of the total resources available to the Israeli economy." [17] The Government's decision in 1968 to establish the Ministry of Immigrant Absorption was regarded by some, according to Stock, as the opening wedge of a more thoroughgoing takeover of JA responsibilities.

The immediate threat to WZO-JA autonomy was met with the assistance of CJFWF and UIA leader Max Fisher. Fisher told the Government that the UJA could not continue to function unless the autonomy of the WZO-JA was maintained.[18] These threats to the WZO-JA probably helped secure approval of a proposal at the 27th World Zionist Congress in 1968 authorising the executive to open negotiations with fund-raising and other Jewish organizations with the purpose of formalizing relationships with them. Meanwhile, since the WZO-JA was able to avert a decision to transfer its functions to the Government, the outpouring of funds on behalf of Israel by Diaspora Jewry meant that the WZO-JA controlled a far more substantial budget than it had prior to the Six Day War, that its responsibility for programs within Israel increased,[19] and that the importance of the organization increased concomitantly. In addition, there was a sharp rise in immigration to Israel, which meant additional burdens in the area of *aliya* for which the WZO-JA had always assumed responsibility.

THE RECONSTITUTION OF THE JEWISH AGENCY

The major architect of the reconstituted Jewish Agency was Louis Pincus, Moshe Sharett's successor as chairman of the Jewish Agency executive from Sharett's death in 1965 until his own death in 1973. Pincus's counterpart in the U.S. was Max Fisher, leader of both the UIA and the CJFWF in the crucial period during which consultations took place and an agreement over the new structure was reached.

In retrospect, the decision to expand the JA through fund-raising rather than through other Jewish organizations seems natural enough. First of all, the UIA, as we saw, already had a relationship to the JA and sought a closer one; other organizations had rejected previous overtures. Second, the UIA wanted to be the sole American body represented on the JA. According to Philip Bernstein, CJFWF executive vice-president, "We agreed that the UIA should be the sole instrument (in the U.S.) since it was the sole fund raising group and the JA the sole expenditure group." [20] Third, it was becoming increasingly evident in the late 1960s that leadership and even authority within the American Jewish community was increasingly concentrated in the local federation and welfare agencies—that is, in the constituent councils of the CJFWF rather than in any formal Jewish organization or group of organizations. Certainly, the bulk of very wealthy American Jews from whom most of the contributions to Jewish philanthropy came had greater commitment to the CJFWF or local federations and welfare funds than to any other set of agencies or organizations. The UIA provided an address for the vast majority of those wealthy American Jews who were involved in Jewish philanthropy.

This decision, however, natural as it seems in retrospect, had a number of very important consequences. It meant, first of all, that a very special kind of Jew represented the Diaspora within the JA Structure—either a very wealthy Jew or close to the sources of great wealth. He was also, for reasons I shall discuss below, not politically oriented in either a partisan or even policy-making sense of the term. Pincus, in fact, was putting into effect a lesson that Ben-Gurion himself had learned long ago: the easiest, most comfortable, and least troublesome group of Jews, as far as Israeli policymakers are concerned, is the wealthy "friends of Israel" in the Diaspora.

There was, however, one obstacle to securing a greater involvement of the UIA in an expanded Jewish Agency. The bulk of WZO-JA money from all sources was expended on activity in Israel—primarily immigration and absorption of immigrants, agricultural settlement and, to an increasing extent after 1967, education (including higher education) and social welfare. However, roughly ten percent of the WZO-JA budget was expended on Zionist activity outside Israel—activity that included preparing Jewish youth for immigration to Israel or Zionist information and propaganda. In addition to the tax problems that such activities created, leaders of American Jewish philanthropy may also have had ideological objections,[21] although these objections declined after the Six Day War. But, for tax reasons alone, any structure that involved non-Zionist fund-raisers in closer ties to Israel would have to be one in which Zionist activity in the Diaspora was distinguished from activity within Israel itself. Thus, when Pincus began his discussions with the UIA, it was clear that the JA would have to be detached from the WZO.[22] Under the terms of the agreement, the reconstituted JA undertook responsibility for immigration to and absorption of immigrants in Israel, social welfare and health services in connection with immigration and absorption, education and research, youth care and training, absorption in agricultural settlement, and immigrant housing. The WZO, now a separate organization, was to retain responsibility for organization and public information, encouraging immigration from affluent countries, education in the Diaspora, youth and cultural activities, and the activities of the Jewish National Fund.

The reconstituted JA has three governing bodies. There is an Assembly of 296 members, half of whom are designated by the WZO, 30 percent by the UIA, and 20 percent by national fund-raising agencies on behalf of Israel outside the U.S. The Assembly meets once a year to provide general guidelines for the JA, approve the budget, and elect the Board of Governors. Representation on the Board of Governors (it now has 42 members) is distributed in the same proportion as the Assembly. It meets three times a year to manage the affairs of the JA and elect the all-important Executive. The Executive is structured to give representation to the heads of the operating departments, who are WZO representatives, and to the fund-raising agencies in more or less the same proportion as the other two governing bodies. There are 11 members on the current executive, six of whom are WZO people and five from fund-raising groups of whom four are from the U.S. and one from Great Britain. In addition, there are three associate members who may attend meetings but have no right to vote. All three associate members are professional leaders of fund-raising organizations in the U.S. It comes as a surprise to no one, however, that in the day-to-day operation of the JA, it is the Israelis representing the WZO who administer policy, rather than Diaspora Jews, who determine policy execution.

THE OPERATION OF THE RECONSTITUTED JEWISH AGENCY

The reconstituted JA has enormous potential power. Its resources are vital for the State of Israel.

There are three areas of potential influence. First, the JA has the authority, the legitimate power, to determine policies in that area of responsibility assigned to it under the agreement for reconstitution of the Jewish Agency to which I have already referred. Second, by virtue of the authority and responsibility in such fields as immigrant absorption, housing, social welfare, education, agricultural settlement, and the like, the JA can influence virtually all social and economic policy in Israel, since the exercise of its specific delegation of authority directly affects other policies as well. Finally, by virtue of the importance of the JA to Israel, its leaders have potential influence even over those policies for which they have no responsibility whatsoever. The governing bodies of the JA, or even its individual leaders such as Max Fisher, would surely find an attentive ear in government circles on any issue upon which they might choose to express themselves.

How much influence does the JA actually exercise? I shall organize the discussion around the three areas of potential influence and begin with the broadest of these areas.

Has the JA sought to influence policy outside its area of responsibility? Has it, for example, expressed itself or sought to influence the Government in areas such as foreign policy or religious policy? The answer is an unqualified no.

There is no evidence that even in closed circles JA leaders have in any manner, shape, or form sought to utilize their enormous power to influence Israeli public policy. Of course, no one can say with any assurance that such efforts may not be made in the future; but given the composition of the JA, one would not anticipate such efforts. There is, for example, no comparison in the kinds of criticisms of Israel that emanate from the World Jewish Congress and the kinds of discussions one hears at a meeting of the JA Assembly. Indeed, delegates at the Assembly meeting in 1973 did, from time to time, raise questions or issues outside the specific sphere of JA responsibility, but they were quickly called to order by the session chairman and other delegates.

The second area of potential JA influence is over policies that the JA might influence by virtue of its decisions in policy areas over which it does have direct responsibility. For example, the JA is responsible for immigrant housing. But immigrants are not housed in distinctive structures or isolated areas. Consequently, decisions about location, price, size, quality, quantity, or methods of construction of immigrant housing affect the entire housing market in Israel. If the JA fully exercised its authority to make basic policy decisions with respect to immigrant housing, it would exercise an enormous influence on Israel's housing policy.

The individual most active in JA housing matters is the prominent American builder and Jewish philanthropist Jack Weiler. Weiler chaired the Housing Committee Session at the first Assembly meetings in 1971. He observed that:

> One of the items that was put before the Committee again and again was the question of priorities in housing, as between young couples, individuals with large families, particularly slum dwellers, and of course the new immigrants.[23]

But, he noted, the Committee "felt that it was not sufficiently knowledgeable to make any specific recommendations, at this time, with respect to priorities." [24] He went on to praise the Ministry of Housing for being "seriously concerned about all of these problems, and it intends to do its utmost to relieve the situation in all these areas." [25]

The Committee called financing "the most important area" and recommended establishment of a mortgage loan association to lower interest rates on housing loans and the encouragement of rental housing. The Committee acknowledged the offer of one of its members to advise the Ministry of Housing on the provision of mobile homes in Israel and also held discussions with regard to the construction of modular apartment buildings. The chairman expressed his hope that the Ministry of Housing would take advantage of the knowledge that prominent builders who were represented on the Housing Committee were able to offer to Israel. Finally, the Committee recommended the establishment of a standing Housing Committee to make specific recommendations on housing in Israel.

In summary, the Committee eschewed any role in formulating far-reaching housing policy. It did make recommendations with respect to financing—recommendations that, if carried out, might well have had important consequences for the availability of credit in the Israeli money market. While these recommendations were subsequently repeated, no concrete steps have been taken to implement them.

The third set of recommendations was of a more technical nature, involving recommendations concerning types of housing or construction. These are the kinds of recommendation that have been implemented in one form or another. TACH (Technological Advisory Committee on Housing) was established as a joint committee of the JA Housing Committee and a representative of the Ministry of Housing. Its chairman is Jack Weiler. TACH has brought a number of building experts to Israel for short periods "to work with Israeli builders in developing new methods, introducing new materials, improving the planning process and training middle management personnel—all aimed at shortening the time required to build or to bring down the cost and to provide better housing." [26] TACH also made a series of recommendations to the Ministry of Housing, most of which were accepted.[27] But these suggestions either were of a technical nature (the reduction of duties on certain imported building products or the initiation of long-term design-build contracts), or recommended measures such as long-term land use and availability planning, where the actual planning will remain in the hands of the Government. Weiler himself engaged in a pilot construction project, to demonstrate "how building processes in Israel can be expedited and the costs controlled by proper planning, effective management and the use of new materials [and to] serve as a demonstration of pre-construction difficulties and delays." [28]

In terms of the publicity that the JA accords its Housing Committee, its achievements are those in which the JA takes greatest pride. Without minimizing in any way the important contribution of the JA Housing Committee, its direct influence has been limited to helping effect technical improvements in housing construction and planning. These improvements may have long-term consequences for Israel. There have been those, after all, who argued that the introduction of the stirrup into the West had had the profoundest impact on the development of modern society. But, like the stirrup, any basic policy changes that stem from the Housing Committee's efforts are the result of chance rather than intent.

The third area of potential JA influence has to do with programs for which the JA has direct funding responsibility. One example is higher education in Israel.

In the 1972-73 fiscal year the JA provided 61 percent of the operating budgets of institutions of higher learning in Israel, and the Government provided an additional nine percent. In view of the JA's contributions to Israeli universities, it did not appear unreasonable for them to establish some criteria by which univer-

sities were to receive assistance. In fact, the report prepared
for the delegates to the second Assembly meetings listed some
basic policy questions that those responsible for higher education
in Israel had to answer.[29] They included such questions as:

1. Should higher education be reserved for an intellectual elite
or available to all?
2. Should higher education be based on learning for learning's
sake or should it include technical training?
3. To what extent should there be an expansion of institutions
of higher education?
4. Should the universities provided special programs or do more
than is presently being done to qualify students from Asian and
African origins for entrance?

Ostensibly, any body allocating money to Israeli universities
might want to concern itself with these questions. Certainly it
would have to have some criteria for allocating funds.

The Board of Governors established a permanent committee
on higher education to "help define the criteria for allocations."
Louis Pincus appeared before the Assembly's Committee on
Higher Education at the 1973 meetings to urge the adoption of
a recommendation that the Higher Education Committee of the
Board of Governors be authorized to supervise how the universities spend the money allocated to them. Pincus noted that an
independent committee was about to be established by the
government to make recommendations concerning allocation
criteria, but, Pincus stressed, it was important that the Board of
Governors also be involved in this process through its Committee
on Higher Education.[30]

At this point one delegate voiced his objection to Pincus's
proposal. Diaspora Jewry should only give advice on the allocation of funds, he said, and have no authority. Pincus replied that
if they accepted that point of view, they would not be allowed
to allocate money; that in absorption, health, social welfare, and
other functions, they had to show that they were not just an arm of

the Government. Otherwise, they would not be in conformity with the laws of the United States, Great Britain, and Canada. They would lose their tax exemption. That is why he proposed, he continued, that the Board of Governors be empowered to act on establishing criteria for the allocation of money to institutions of higher education, and added: "You can rest assured that the JA is not going to set itself up against the Government." If our lawyers, he went on, say it is possible, "then we will accept Allon's recommendation (Yigal Allon, Deputy Prime Minister and Minister of Education and Culture) that the independent body which the Government intends to establish to determine allocation criteria will also serve as our advisory committee."

In other words, despite the fact that it is the reconstituted JA and not the Government that funds the lion's share of the cost of higher education in Israel, the JA sought only that degree of policy control that the tax laws of the U.S., Great Britain, and Canada thrust upon it.

This attitude reflects the desires of both the WZO representatives and the fund-raising leaders themselves. Michael Sacher, a member of the JA Executive and leader of the British delegation to the first Assembly, stated that Diaspora fund-raisers must not usurp the role of the Israeli Government. He defined the JA task as follows:

> It is not my view that the Diaspora members of the new Agency should attempt to control the direction in which the monies are spent. But I do believe they have a function in drawing attention to areas which may have been ignored, or to more efficient ways of spending money already in the budget. We abroad cannot have a proper understanding of the main priorities.[31]

The reconstituted JA has acted with utmost restraint in exercising its enormous potential for influence. Representatives of the fund-raising organizations in particular have sought only to help and advise. What will happen if Israel consistently rejects their offers of assistance remains to be seen. It is possible, of course, that the JA will then attempt to exercise its power. What is more likely, however, is that the JA leaders will simply lose interest in the enterprise. But Israel is unlikely to ignore the JA's offer of assistance. As we have seen in the case of housing, the Government has availed itself of this help.

The present UIA representative in Israel, commenting on this phenomenon of Israeli readiness to accept advice, noted that Israelis are more relaxed today about Israel-Diaspora relations than they were in the Ben-Gurion era. They are willing to listen to the Diaspora and they appreciate the fact that Diaspora leaders want to do more than just write checks.[32] The JA meetings have become a focus for exchange of information and discussion of problems of housing, absorption, education, and welfare. Israel recognizes the JA as the address of world Jewry.[33]

As already suggested, the long-run implications of the kind of technical advice and assistance that JA leaders offer should not be minimized. Furthermore, according to a very close observer and participant in these developments, the expertise and know-how that the JA brings to bear on Israel's problems is likely to result in an increase in its influence and authority.[34] Technical, administrative, and bureaucratic improvements have policy implications. Reform in one department, or one ministry, or one set of programs provides an example for others. One should not in any way underestimate the long-run potential influence of the fund-raising leaders. Their impatience with Israeli bureaucracy and many established Israeli procedures has already been felt. But these potentially important consequences do not really flow from any deliberate efforts of the reconstituted JA to shape Israel's public policy.[35]

The other side of the coin is the fact that participation in the JA has probably intensified the Jewish commitment of the non-Zionists. Max Fisher, for example has used the JA forum to urge greater attention to Jewish education and to the problem of Jewish survival in the Diaspora.

CONCLUSIONS

Conversations with delegates to the 1973 Assembly were most enlightening with respect to the question of JA influence over Israeli policy.[36] Who are the delegates to the Assembly? While half represent the WZO and half non-Zionist fund-raising agencies, no conflicts of interest between Zionists and non-Zionists have found expression in any JA meetings. In fact, many of the representatives of the fund-raising agencies, the "non-Zionists," are actually members of Zionist organizations, while to many Diaspora Zionists who represent the WZO, Zionism simply means being especially sympathetic to Israel. Furthermore, the kinds of issues that the reconstituted JA has dealt with do not lend themselves to ideological division.

Nevertheless, among the Diaspora delegates, the non-Zionists (who do not like to be called non-Zionists) set the tone. Since the issues do tend to be concrete and pragmatic, perhaps they feel more competent and comfortable in dealing with them. Some observers, including a WZO representative on the JA executive, felt that the quality of the non-Zionist representatives was higher than that of the WZO people. Finally, it is the non-Zionists who, after all, are paying the bill. While members of Zionist organizations presumably participate in fund-raising campaigns on behalf of Israel, their role and contributions, at least in the United States, are so insignificant as to be a matter of embarrassment to Zionist leaders themselves.

The delegates are all firmly committed to Israel. Their presence at the Assembly or on the Board of Governors is, in a sense, a recognition of their accomplishments and contributions on behalf of Israel. But it is important to understand what the delegates, especially the non-Zionists who set the tone for the deliberations, are not. First of all, they are not ideologists. Their commitment is to the survival and development of Israel as it is today. They believe that their task is to see that the money they provide and the programs for which they are responsible are properly managed. But because they are not ideologists, they have no vision of a different Israel. Lacking such a vision, they are satisfied to accept the basic structure of programs and priorities that the Government of Israel dictates. Because they are not ideologists, they could hardly legitimate too much interference in the internal affairs of another country.

Second, they do not seek personal power. They are not professional politicians whose time and energy are devoted to the search for power. They are pleased at the respect and deference with which they are treated by Israeli leaders. They are flattered by the presence of the Prime Minister and other leading Ministers who come to address them and remain to answer questions and listen to their deliberations. But the last thing they want is more responsibility, which would necessitate greater demands on their time and perhaps on their pockets.

Third, they do not represent group interests. By and large they are fund-raising leaders in their local communities. They will bring the message of Israel and the operation of the JA back to their own communities. But what do these communities want of Israel? What special stakes or interest do the Jews of Detroit, Cleveland, or Philadelphia or, for that matter, Belgium, France, or England have in Israel? There are no special group interests that the delegates represent, therefore no interest that they might seek to achieve by parlaying their potential power over certain areas of the Israeli economy into influence over other areas.

Finally, the vast majority of the delegates do not live in Israel. They do not, therefore, "live" its problems. Precisely for that reason they can always see "the larger picture." They are free of personal bias because basically they are free of personal concerns. Since it is "the larger picture" to which they are oriented, they necessarily defer to the judgment of Israeli leaders, the only ones who can be expected really to know "the larger picture."

In June 1969, the Conference on Human Needs, a forerunner of the JA Assembly, brought together Israelis and leading fund-raisers from the Diaspora to assess Israel's major human needs and to project long-term programs to meet these needs. The president of the CJFWF at that time, Louis Fox, made this interesting statement:

> We have come here to offer a more personal contribution to Israel in terms of thinking, planning and doing. We call it "involvement." Israel's leaders agree that the days have passed for us to be just silent partners. And we agree. Meaningful participation in the progress of Israel will enrich not only Israel—it will enrich our own lives, and will enrich the depth and scope of our own communities.[37]

Irving Blum, CJFWF president in 1972, chaired the Committee on Higher Education at the founding Assembly in 1971. His comments about representatives of Israeli institutions of higher education typify the feeling of JA delegates about Israeli leaders in general. He expressed his confidence that they

> came away with a feeling that our overseas communities have a deep and abiding interest in their problems, and that they are willing and even anxious, to be interpreters of these problems to their constituencies in a most positive and constructive way.
> I earnestly hope that they will assess correctly the overseas communities as an important pool of experience available to them in the future.[38]

To the delegates to the reconstituted JA Assembly, these were very real sentiments, not exercises in rhetoric. By "participation" the delegates from the Diaspora really meant that they have something more than money to contribute to Israel—knowledge and expertise in technical and managerial fields—and they want Israel to avail itself of this competence. The thrust behind the demand for increased involvement and participation from Diaspora Jewry, as reflected in the reconstituted JA, may be so innocent, altruistic, and even naive that the political observer may be easily deceived. But the potential for the exercise of real political influence nonetheless remains.

PART 3

The Nature
of the Relationships

7

The Diaspora Image of Israel

I suggested in chapter 2 that a condition for effective political influence is the desire to exercise such influence. In Part Two, I suggested that Diaspora Jewry does not regard Israel as a suitable object of political influence. To understand more fully the reasons behind this we must now focus on the image of Israel in American Jewish eyes, because it is American Jews who have the greatest potential influence and who have exercised the most effective pressure to date upon Israel.

THE ROLE OF ISRAEL IN AMERICAN JEWISH LIFE

Israel is not only important to American Jews, it represents a basic component of their Jewish identity. Of all issues on the agenda of American Jewish life, concern for Israel elicits the greatest agreement. In a survey of Jewish opinion in San Francisco,[1] a random sample of Jews were asked to express their degree of concern with twenty issues of a general and Jewish nature that face American Jews. The issues about which the highest proportion of respondents felt deep concern (75 percent) was Israel—specifically, U.S. policy toward Israel. The next three issues, in order of importance, were general rather than specifically Jewish issues. Fifth in importance was the condition of Soviet Jews (53 percent expressed concern). The next-highest ranking Jewish issue of importance was of concern to less than half the sample.

The fact, however, that American Jews are concerned about Israel does not mean they are very interested in or informed about Israel itself, much less its policies. This is not surprising in view of the American Jews' self-perception and the role of Israel in that self-perception.

American Jews perceive themselves as a religious group. Elsewhere I have sought to show that this religious identity arises out of the effort to compromise between the two contradictory values characteristic of all Western postemancipation Jewry—the desire for Jewish survival on the one hand, and the desire for acceptance and integration into the general society as individuals and not as Jews on the other.[2] This religious self-definition legitimated Jewish separatism for certain purposes, for example, intermarriage; but it also legitimated the insistence that Jewishness was irrelevant for other purposes, for example, employment or admission into colleges and universities.

In the American Jewish self-perception (as in the self-perception of French or English Jews), differences between American Jews and American gentiles exist in one special realm of life but do not or ought not to extend to others. The realm of national loyalty and national rights is an important example of the latter. Jews insist that their citizenship, their loyalty, and their affection to their state is not colored by their Jewishness. Hence it follows that if they do have special obligations and responsibilities toward Israel, these are not of a political nature. If the Jewish community nevertheless organized itself to assist Israel politically, it did so, at least ostensibly, in the interests of the United States. Such rationalizations have extended even into recent years, when expressions of ethnic self-interest have gained legitimacy, and American Jews might have been more candid in admitting that as Jews they feel special loyalties toward their fellow Jews in Israel—loyalties that find legitimate expression in political as well as philanthropic activity.

This religious self-definition makes the very relationship of American Jews to Israel problematical. For another study a questionnaire was devised to probe the religious ideology of American Jewry and to find what ideological differences, if any, distinguished Orthodox, Conservative, and Reform Jews from each other and from Reconstructionists.[3] The questionnaire was mailed in late 1968 to 130 rabbinical leaders of the major Orthodox, Conservative, and Reform rabbinical organizations. The response rate varied from 62 percent of the Orthodox to 90 percent of the Reform rabbis. In February 1969 the questionnaire was mailed to presidents of all synagogues affiliated with the major Orthodox, Conservative, and Reform congregational bodies. In addition, the questionnaire was mailed to all chapter presidents of a large nondenominational Jewish organization. The rate of return for all but Orthodox synagogue presidents varied from 38 to 42 percent; only 18 percent of the Orthodox synagogue presidents responded.

Some of the items included in the questionnaire pertained to Israel. They were listed in the form of statements with which respondents were asked to express agreement or disagreement. The most interesting response came to the statement that "while there must be a warm fraternal relation between Jews of the USA and Israel, the center of American Jewish life must be *American* Judaism rather than a Jewish culture which has developed or will develop in the State of Israel." Most respondents agreed with this statement.

In other words, American Jewish leaders do not even view Israel as a cultural or ideological center. I suggest that Israel is not any kind of center for American Jews. Rather, concern for Israel and efforts on its behalf increasingly represent the content of American and indeed of Western Judaism. In other words, Israel has become instrumental to one's American Jewish identity.

Israel, and concern for Israel, are preeminently a *symbol* of Jewish identity; support for Israel has become a boundary-defining aspect of membership in the Jewish community.

Support for Israel is an expression of support for Judaism. Israel is not, of course, an empty symbol. The "Israel as a symbol" meaning carries ideological overtones and bears implication about the nature of Jewish identity. In time it may change the very nature of American Jewish identity and undermine its primarily "religious" content. But, for the time being, concern for Israel remains an extension of religious identity.

The notion that Israel is preeminently a religious symbol is reinforced by the fact that identity and attachment to Israel vary with the intensity of the religious identity and attachment of Jews. This phenomenon is true of Diaspora Jews as diverse as the second-and-third-generation American upper-middle-class suburban Jews of Lakeville,[4] the more typical Jews of Chicago,[5] or North African Jews of France.[6] As the author of the study of North African Jews in France notes, "The image of Israel is clouded in a certain mysticism which strikes roots in their religious attitude."[7] The same is true, I suggest, of American Jewry.

If Israel is preeminently a symbol to most American Jews, its image nonetheless differs among various segments of the population. Unfortunately, no real study has been made of Israel's image for American Jews. It is suggested here that two images predominate.

IMAGES OF ISRAEL

The "Exodus" Image

One prevalent image of Israel, especially among younger American Jews, is the "courageous Israeli" as portrayed in Leon Uris's still-popular novel *Exodus*. The Israeli is imagined as tough, hardheaded, courageous, and shrewd. He is something of a superman, albeit in an underdog's clothing. In some peculiar way it is an honor for the American Jew to help him and no surprise if the Israeli does not appear grateful. He makes so many demands on himself that anything others do for him will at best be accepted graciously. Needless to say, one hardly makes demands from the Israeli in return for this help, nor does one seek to influence the policies of a country whose population (certainly whose leadership) comprises individuals of such sterling qualities.

Israel as the "Heim" [8]

A second image, Israel as the "Heim," stands in marked contrast to the first. *Heim* is a Yiddish, as well as German word. Its literal meaning is "home," with all the connotations of warmth, security, and nostalgia that normally surrounds that concept. Its meaning may be captured more accurately if it is translated as "the old home."

To many American Jews, the *heim* prior to World War II was Eastern Europe. To some American Jews, especially those of the younger generation, the concept *heim* has no meaning. But there are others, including some born in the U.S., to whom the *heim* has a meaningful referent. Indeed, sometimes it appears that the further removed the Jew is from Eastern Europe the more lovingly he evokes its memories. Now, what is most remarkable about the *heim*, what makes it really "the old home" is that despite all the love, warmth, and security that it recalls, American Jews do not want to live there. It is really the parents' home. It is the home that the young adult leaves, to which he returns perhaps for a visit, but which he senses that he has in some way outgrown.

Six million Jews were murdered by the Nazis. Jewish life in Eastern Europe was virtually obliterated. As a result, the *heim* disappeared. It took a number of years before the disappearance of the *heim* entered into the consciousness of American Jews. Nor did the consequences of the holocaust affect all Jews in the same way. Many of those who were emotionally affected found a substitute *heim* in Israel.

Now, the characteristic of the *heim*, as noted, is that one does not live there. It is the parents' home, or, in the case of Israel, the surrogate parents' and surrogate grandparents' home. One visits it on occasion, one sends money (without ever having the bad taste to inquire how the money is spent), and one wants very much to feel that life goes on there as it always has—which is why the type of the Jew to whom Israel is *heim* expects and wants all Israelis to be religious regardless of how disinterested he himself may be in religion. This type of Jew is most likely to be indignant at any public criticism of Israel and takes a particular delight in how "old-fashioned" or "quaint" he imagines Israel to be. This is the Jew who is quite certain he would be completely at home in Israel, though he knows very little about the country and makes no special effort to learn anything.

To those who perceive Israel in either the "exodus" or the *heim* image, efforts to influence its policies are inappropriate.

THE SEEKERS OF INFLUENCE

Because Israel is a symbol, its particular policies are not very important to American Jews. The inappropriateness of seeking to influence its policies is reinforced by fear of accusation of dual loyalty. It follows, therefore, that while American Jews do have potential influence on Israeli policy, they will not generally exercise their power. There have been a few such efforts. Until the early 1960s the American Jewish Committee actively sought to influence Israeli policy. The most significant continuing efforts, however, come from American Orthodox Jews.

The question is, why do the Orthodox seek to influence Israel whereas the non-Orthodox, except in unusual circumstances, do not? And what can account for both Orthodox and American Jewish Committee behavior? I will suggest a number of possible answers, not all of which are mutually exclusive. Let us explore the available empirical data that might shed light on the credibility of each of the answers:

1. One possibility is that the Orthodox, like the American Jewish Committee of the 1910s and 50s, are less sympathetic to Israel than the non-Orthodox. The latter are more reluctant to bring pressure to bear, especially since such pressure, even in its mildest form, implies opposition to Israeli policy, thereby tarnishing Israel's image in the United States.

This explanation is inadequate. I have observed above that sympathy with Israel is correlated with religious indentification and activity. Therefore, it should follow that Orthodox Jews who are more "religious" by virtually any standard criteria of religious definition: behavioral, belief, experiential, should be more sympathetic to Israel than other Jews.[9] Of course, there are limits to the correlation between religion and sympathy to Israel. As indicated, within the Orthodox camp itself, some of the most zealously religious are the most hostile to Israel. But even here, the evidence is by no means one-sided. While among the Orthodox themselves there is probably an inverse relationship between religious zealousness and sympathy to Israel as a state, it is by no means clear that the more zealous are less sympathetic to the Land of Israel, or to the religious idea of Zion, than are the modern Orthodox.

Conceptually, one can distinguish between Israel as a state and Israel as Zion. Zion represents the realization of God's promise to the Jews to redeem them from exile, to reunite them in the Land of Israel, and to establish a third commonwealth that will serve as a spiritual center for the entire world. Many Jews, including many Orthodox, feel a special tie to Israel because it is a haven for Jewish oppressed, because it is a symbol of Jewish rebirth, because it is in some way an answer to the holocaust, and because it is evidence of Jewish bravery, strength, and determination, and therefore reflects favorably on Jews everywhere. But among Orthodox Jewry, Israel also lays claim to sympathy and loyalty because it is Zion.[10] Indeed, among traditional religious Jewry in the United States, the crux of the argument over Israel is whether or not it constitutes, from a Divine point of view, a successor or a potential successor to the two previous Jewish commonwealths. Is Israel the fulfillment of God's promises to the Jews, or is it a political entity that happens to exercise hegemony over the territory of Zion and includes within its borders a sizable number of Jews? In the latter case, while some might still feel some special tie to Israel, others might be indifferent, and still others, like the Satmar Rebbe, might feel a special antagonism to the State because they see it as a stumbling block to the reestablishment of Zion as a Jewish commonwealth, an event associated in the minds of religious Jews with the advent of the Messiah.

Whereas the more religiously zealous may be less sympathetic to Israel than the modern Orthodox, it is possible that they are even more sympathetic to Zion or to the Land of Israel which, after all, is associated with the State of Israel. Therefore, no matter how sharp the opposition to the State may be, both Israel and its most fanatical Orthodox opponents share many interests in common. The quality of the anti-Israel attitude of the ultra-Orthodox is expressed in a story about the American Council for Judaism. The Council is the only specifically anti-Israel organization of Jews in the United States. As such, it falls outside the "Community." It is composed of a small number of mostly very wealthy, highly assimilated Reform Jews who fear that Israel creates problems of dual loyalty or raises images of dual loyalty among Americans. Since, in their view, Judaism is only a religion, Israel cannot be a *Jewish* State and cannot make any claims on the loyalty of American Jews. The Council was formed in the 1940s and sought to enlist a prominent Orthodox rabbi who was known for his opposition to the creation of a Jewish State. The rabbi refused to join, however, and is reported to have stated: "For you, Zionism is too much; for me, it is not enough." [11]

Even if we fail to distinguish between Israel and Zion and simply label all those who oppose the State as being unsympathetic to Israel, modern Orthodox Jews still tend to be more sympathetic to Israel than the non-Orthodox. According to a 1945 survey by the Elmo Roper Organization, which compared pro-

and anti-Jewish State opinion among Jews, 87 percent of the Orthodox, 83 percent of the Conservative, and 72 percent of the Reform were pro-state, whereas six percent of the Orthodox, 10 percent of the Conservative, and 20 percent of the Reform were anti-State.[12] Roper did not distinguish among types of Orthodox Jews and, presumably, some non-Zionist Orthodox were included in his sample.

In a questionnaire mailed to 100 Orthodox, 100 Conservative, and 100 Reform rabbis in the mid 1950s, Orthodox rabbis were far more positive about Israel's importance and far more ready to identify personally with Israel than were Conservative or Reform rabbis.[13]

In the more comprehensive study already referred to, the attitudes of Orthodox, Conservative, and Reform rabbis, and of synagogue presidents and leaders in a prominent secular organization, were tested.[14] Respondents were asked to express their agreement or disagreement with a series of statements, among which were the following:

a. While there must be a warm fraternal relation between Jews of the USA and Israel, the center of American Jewish life must be *American* Judaism rather than a Jewish culture that has developed or will develop in the State of Israel.
b. Israel should become the spiritual center of World Jewry.
c. A Jew who really wants to do what Judaism requires of him should move to Israel.

With respect to each of these questions, the rank order of responses remained the same. The Orthodox, whether rabbis, synagogue presidents, or leaders within a secular Jewish organization, were more sympathetic to Israel than their counterparts of the Conservative and Reform movements.

Each of the three available studies reports the same results. Orthodox Jews are more closely identified with Israel than non-Orthodox. Consequently, the greater willingness of Orthodox Jews to intervene in Israeli policy can hardly be explained by their lesser sympathy with Israel.

2. An alternative explanation for Orthodox efforts to influence Israeli policy is the opposite of the first. Since the Orthodox are more closely identified with Israel, they have more of an interest in its policies and they are prepared to expend greater energy and resources in influencing that policy.

This explanation is inadequate because it does not account for such efforts as those of the American Jewish Committee to influence Israeli policy in the 1940s and 50s. The Committee was then just emerging from its former hostility to the creation of a Jewish State. It was certainly less closely identified with Israel than a host of other secular Jewish organizations, such as B'nai B'rith or the American Jewish Congress, which made no similar efforts to influence Israeli policy.

3. It would appear that neither sympathy and identity with nor lack of sympathy and absence of identity with Israel accounts for efforts by American Jewish groups to influence Israeli policy. A third explanation is based on organizational style. Perhaps, it may be argued, many American Jews and groups of Jews would like to influence Israel's policies. But to do so requires great effort. It requires that one be informed about what Israeli policies really are and where the points of access to decision-making exist. It requires expenditure of time, effort, and money that could be devoted to other objectives. Perhaps, therefore, while many American Jewish organizations have policy preferences with respect to Israel, only a few seek to express them. What distinguishes the Orthodox or the American Jewish Committee is not their identification with Israel but their identification with their own policies. In the case of the Orthodox, there is the sense of religious urgency or religious command associated with policies to which they are committed. The Orthodox, unlike virtually every other Diaspora group, have a clear image of what Israel should be like and a sense of religious obligation to translate that image into specific policies. In the case of the American Jewish Committee, it is organizational self-respect. The Committee is distinguished from other American Jewish organizations

in terms of its organizational interests, in terms of its constituency, and, perhaps even more, in terms of its style. Its own self-image is a basic component of that style. The Committee fights hard for what it wants, harder than other organizations, because its self-image demands that it get what it wants.

Diaspora Jewry in general and the American Jewish Community in particular are organized without the normal political instruments for conflict resolution. There is no constituency that can express policy preferences or organizational preferences in an election; there is no single decision-making mechanism that can arbitrate among conflicting groups; there are no instruments of raw power that one group can utilize against another to bring about an acknowledged victory. In such circumstances, a great deal of authority and status rests on reputation. It is as though each organization says, "If there *were* some instrument for really determining who was stronger, we would come out the strongest." For organizations that are concerned with their status in the Jewish community and whose reputation in the non-Jewish community rests on their alleged leadership within the Jewish community, the price of failure to achieve one's goals is very high.

The American Jewish Committee is especially vulnerable to failure because its own particular legitimacy rests on its elitist status. Some organizations can legitimate themselves in terms of their mass membership. The very fact that so many American Jews are affiliated with them legitimates what they try to do. Other organizations legitimate themselves in terms of their goals. Even if they fail to achieve their goals, they legitimate themselves with self-assurances that they are doing what is right. But the Committee is a relatively small organization, whose specific goals have tended to be flexible and whose style has been characterized by an absence of ideological fervor. The Committee's claim to status is that as *the* organization of the American Jewish elite, it stands aloof from a great deal of the nitty gritty of Jewish life, interceding only when its voice is necessary to resolve great issues. Its own crucial position in the general and Jewish community, however, permits it to succeed when it does finally intervene. What it cannot afford to do is intervene and lose.

The creation of the Jewish State was an embarrassment to the American Jewish Committee. Individually, most of its leadership and probably most of its membership had already come around to the idea of supporting a Jewish State. This was already in evidence by the time the U.N. adopted its partition plan in November of 1947. But in organizational terms the creation of Israel posed a great problem. The creation of Israel was *the* major event of Jewish history in two thousand years, and American Jews had played an active part in the success of that event. But in its public image the American Jewish Committee, the ostensible elite of that community, had been a relatively passive bystander. The Committee, therefore, had to develop some relationship to Israel. It would have done little good for it simply to have jumped on the pro-Israel bandwagon. To have done that would have meant to acknowledge the bankruptcy of its past policies. Indeed, the Committee did finally jump on the pro-Israel bandwagon along with virtually every other American Jewish organization. But before it did that, it felt it had to extract some concession from Israel. It had, as it were, to face up to Israel as an equal, to win some victory against it, to wring some concession from it, to accomplish what no other Diaspora organization would have the temerity, much less the ability, to do. The Committee, therefore, intervened in the early 1950s, demanding from Ben-Gurion a statement on the status of American Jews in the eyes of Israel, demanding what amounted to a virtual retraction of Zionist dogma on the part of the state.

4. A final explanation to account for the efforts by some groups to exercise influence is the importance that these groups attach not so much to their own policies as to those of Israel.

As indicated earlier, most American Jews perceive their relationship to Israel as a symbol of their Jewish identity. While this symbol is not devoid of ideological implication, and while it is not a matter of total indifference to them as to what Israel says or does, the boundaries of American Jewry's indifference are very wide. The relationship between American Jews and Israel, expressed primarily through philanthropic activity, is analogous to the relationship of most American Jews to a synagogue. The relationship is expressed there primarily through affiliation, in itself a rather formal act apparently devoid of any great meaning, but in reality of great significance. What is there about the synagogue that most Jews seem to think is so important? They don't attend synagogue services very often and they are fairly ignorant about what takes place there. If and when they do attend the services, the stress is on the act of attendance rather than on what they do once they get there. The most important aspect in the American Jew's relationship to the synagogue service is his knowledge that services take place —that they exist. What would most arouse the congregant would be if the synagogue closed its doors, if it ceased to function, if the average synagogue member had no place *not* to go to. Like the synagogue service itself, American Jews hardly pay attention to Israel's policies because these have little to do with the basis of their attachment to Israel.

Under what circumstances will American Jews seek to influence Israeli policy? Only when these policies have consequences for them that they simply cannot overlook. The case of American investors illustrates this point. They have, from time to time, sought to obtain more favorable conditions for their investments in Israel. It is interesting that they never organized thmselves for this purpose. There is no organization of foreign investors established to pressure the Israeli government to create a more favorable investment climate. This is, no doubt, because the great majority of American investors in Israel are Jewish and, like other Jews, they do not believe that efforts to influence Israeli policy are really legitimate or proper. But as businessmen, their stake in Israel's economic policy is too immediate for them simply to ignore the possibility of influence. Consequently, they do make such efforts; but these tend to be specific, directed to a particular business, to exacting concessions in a particular case, rather than any attempt to change the overall economic policy of the government.

It might be argued that the specific strategy has some chance of success while the attempt at overall change will fail. Perhaps. On the other hand, the payoff from a victory of the latter strategy would be much greater. The significant fact is that it has never been attempted. The efforts at change that have already been made suggest that attempts to influence Israeli policy are proportional to the importance that Israeli policy has for the American Jew.

As a general rule, it may be concluded that American Jews will attempt to influence Israeli policy if that policy affects the American Jews' status in America or if it affects the status of Israel as a Jewish symbol.

Examples of the first type of policy might be of three kinds. First, there might be foreign-policy conflicts between Israel and America. These might raise problems of dual loyalty for American Jews. In the past, as we have seen, American Jews have tended to side with Israel, believing, however, that they were also acting in America's best interests. The one exception was the Sinai invasion, where conflict was most severe and where Israel also behaved in a manner contrary to American Jewish expectations. A second example might be Israeli domestic policies that violate the rights or liberties that American Jews are anxious to protect for themselves. If Israeli policies toward the Arab minorities were repressive, for example, one might anticipate the intervention of Diaspora Jewry. The American Jewish Committee opposed a proposed constitutional provision providing that the President of Israel must be a Jew, and one reason they opposed the Nationality Law, which conferred Israeli nationality on every Jew settling in Israel, was that it distinguished between Jews and non-Jews. This last case also provide a third example illustrative of Israeli policies that might affect the status of American Jews in America, namely any policy or statement that implied that Israel *laid claim to the* political loyalty or allegiance of American Jews.

The AJC, as we know, sought an authoritative statement that would deny Israel's right to political claims on American Jewry. The *quid pro quo* involved in such a statement was the abnegation of American Jewry's right to intervene in Israel's political affairs, a concept that may or may not have been on the minds of the parties to the agreement at the time it was reached. Why was it that the AJC alone made these demands, when they were consistent with what all of American Jewry wanted? There were, as we saw in chapter 4, answers peculiar to the particular case. There was a great deal of tension at that time between the AJC and other major Jewish organizations, including the Zionists, who suspected the former of still harboring hostility to a Jewish state. But, in more general terms, the AJC went it alone, because it was far more sensitive to charges of dual loyalty and to the political consequences of Israel on American Jewry than was any other organization except the American Council for Judaism. (The Council solved its problems by denying the existence of Israel as a Jewish symbol.) But, as isolated as the Committee was at that particular time, it never would have succeeded in obtaining the statement it did if Israel had believed that the statement was contrary to the wishes of American, and indeed of world Jewry.

The second type of policy likely to arouse the intervention of American Jewry would be if Israel did something that affected its symbolic status. If, for example, there were significant voices in Israel seeking to erase the Jewish component of Israel, thereby undermining the state as a symbol of Jewish identity, one might anticipate either the active intervention of American Jewish groups in Israeli policy and/or the turning away from Israel by American Jews in their search for new symbols. American Jews might act under either one of these conditions because they would feel that Israeli policies did have consequences for them. In the cases where American Jews have sought to influence Israel, it has been precisely for these reasons.

Orthodox efforts to influence Israel exemplify, at least partially, the second condition for American Jewish efforts at influence: Israeli activity affecting its symbolic status. Israel has meaning to American Jewry because it is a Jewish State. But to Orthodox Jews, the content of Judaism is far more specific than it is to the non-Orthodox. Of all the groups in Jewish life, the definition of Judaism, its form of expression, and its basis, are clearest to the Orthodox. Not only does Judaism find expression primarily in religious acts, symbols, and beliefs, but these acts, symbols, and beliefs, as far as the Orthodox are concerned, are highly formalized, specific, and unambiguous. Consequently, it is the Orthodox segment of American Jewry that is most sensitive and quick to act in instances where it sees that the symbolic meaning of Israel as a Jewish state might be affected. In this respect, it is not for the sake of or on behalf of religion that Orthodoxy acts, but rather for the sake of preserving Israel as a symbol of Jewish identity, a symbol that would erode for the Orthodox if the Jewish (read religious; read Orthodox) character of the State were destroyed.

This is not the only reason that the Orthodox are most active in efforts to influence Israeli policy. Furthermore, it does not account for the efforts of the Orthodox extremists, who do not see Israel as a symbol of Jewish identity. They are catalyzed not only by their sense of identity with Jews of similar persuasion in Israel, but also by their identification with the Land of Israel, with Zion, which makes whatever happens to their peers in Israel of special interest to them, greater no doubt than their identification with their peers in London, where another band of extremists also resides.[15]

Other Orthodox Jews also have close ties with the Orthodox in Israel and feel a sense of identity with them. As in the case of the zealots, efforts by American Orthodox to influence Israeli policy often spring from the initiative of their peers in Israel.

I have suggested that efforts by the Orthodox and the American Jewish Committee, or other scattered attempts to influence Israeli policy, are the exception. By and large, American, indeed world Jewry, does not utilize the resources at its disposal to intervene in Israeli policy-making. The major reason for this is that, given the nature and meaning that Israel has for Diaspora

Jewry, such exercises of influence are irrelevant and fall outside the boundaries of legitimate activity.

This means that other Israeli policies, even those which do effect the Diaspora, do not elicit Diaspora intervention. One might anticipate that Diaspora leaders would be more sensitive to instances where Israel placed her own needs before those of the Diaspora. But this has not been the case. American Jewry did not identify with South African Jewry or Soviet Jewry, for example, more than with Israel. American Jewry has never sought to pressure Israel to do more for other Jewries; on the contrary, it has let Israel take the lead in deciding what it could or could not, should or should not do on behalf of world Jewry.

Second, Diaspora leaders have, with a few exceptions, never been sensitive to Israel's acting out any universalistic Jewish ethic. Diaspora leaders have never exercised their judgment as to the appropriateness of Israel's behavior in accordance with any standard of universal morality. On the contrary, those Diaspora leaders most closely identified with Israel have sometimes been most willing to accommodate their own moral principles to particularist Israeli needs. Thus, it was the President of the Zionist Organization of America who appealed to American Jews to support Johnson's policies in Vietnam,[16] and it was the South African Zionists who were less reluctant to support the South African Nationalists, because of the Nationalist Party's friendship with Israel.[17]

There was a period when a few voices within the Zionist camp pressed for a greater role for Diaspora Jewry in shaping Israeli policy. Paradoxically, the most radical voice of all was that of an Israeli citizen, Meir Grossman, a member of the JA Executive and a former associate of Zev Jabotinsky.

Grossman stressed the necessity for interrelationships and mutual influence between the State and the Jewish people. He argued that the 12 million Jews of the Diaspora were all potential citizens of Israel and hence had the right to influence Israel's policies.[18] Indeed, he even accused world Jewry of avoiding their responsibility by not pressing Israel to adopt certain policies in the field of education.[19] The religious Zionists expressed support for Grossman's position and, as might be expected, Mapai adamantly opposed it. Less radically, American Zionist leader Abba Hillel Silver threatened that if world Jewry were not satisfied with what Israel did, they would lessen their support for Israel. He felt that Zionists had the right to be informed and consulted by Israel on its decisions.[20]

But Diaspora Zionists never really pressed their demands for an independent role because they were unwilling to accept the responsibility for their decisions and because they constantly feared dual loyalty charges. When Jewish leaders met in Jerusalem in January of 1969 at the invitation of the Prime Minister, many of them accused Israeli public relations of ineptitude. Irving Kane, then President of the American Israel Public Affairs Committee, which is the chief lobby for American Jews on behalf of Israel, was asked by an Israeli reporter if he felt that his or other Jewish organizations should at least be advised in advance of Israeli plans so that they could prepare for their public relations job. His reaction was reported as follows:

> Kane shudders. "Heaven forbid—it would put us in an impossible position to have knowledge that Israel was not passing on to the State Department." [21]

Diaspora Zionists have, with few exceptions, been quite willing to accept Israeli dictation on what is best for Israel and what is best for the Diaspora. Indeed, one member of the Zionist Executive argued that this concern for Israel's wishes was so great that it obviated the need for such instruments as the double *shekel* [22] to insure Israel's preponderance of representation within the Zionist organization. When proponents of the system argued that it was justified since the Congress dealt with matters affecting the lives of Israeli citizens, Zvi Herman, a member of the Zionist Executive, stated that on matters of security and foreign policy, only the Israeli government makes decision. He then added:

Will we decide on questions of education, social welfare, security, taxation? Even in those spheres which on the face of it have remained within the competence of the Zionist movement, is any decision reached without first of all being submitted to the Coordinating Board or without obtaining the approval of the Government? and if the Government says a single word: We do not want this project! Will the Zionist Movement attempt to implement it?[23]

In 1954 Grossman proposed to extend the authority of the WZO Public Relations Department to inform the Government of the aims and desires of the Zionist movement and to apply "to the appropriate political factors concerned when Zionist interests urgently demand such steps."[24] In response, Berl Locker, chairman of the Jerusalem Executive, stated:

The sponsors of this resolution apparently do not recognize the fact that a sovereign state is in existence and in relation to it we are not sovereign. We have not even got the competence to deal with this question, and for this reason I propose that we adjourn this debate.[25]

When a motion dealing with the Anglo-Transjordan treaty of 1948 was introduced, Nahum Goldmann, then President of the World Zionist Organization, declared that the resolution

must be rejected . . . without debate, since, if the Zionist Organization decides to make declarations, and to offer advice about political policies [it] will negate the possibility from the standpoint of the State of Israel of the existence of the Zionist Organization. . . . We must support the policy which the sovereign State of Israel decides upon. The State is sovereign in regard to the Zionist Organization and not only in regard to the Arab States.[26]

The outcome of such a resolution, he argued, would be "severe friction with the State of Israel," and it would "transform the nature of cooperation with the Zionist Organization."[27]

Zionist leaders no longer argue for a greater voice in Israeli policy. Critics of Israeli-Diaspora relations today tend, as we shall see, to come from outside the Zionist leadership establishment.

8

The Israeli Image
of Diaspora Jewry

The restraint that Diaspora Jewry exercises is a partial explanation for its lack of influence over Israeli policy. Another part of the explanation rests on Israel's view of the Diaspora—a view that denies legitimacy to Diaspora influence.

Israel is one of the most ideological of the developed nations of the world. Israelis believe that the State was created as an act of their own will and as a consequence of their ideology. There is nothing especially unique in believing that one's nation-state was created by the will of its founding fathers. But Israelis not only believe that they created their State by an act of will, they also believe that in so doing they were acting out the consequences of their ideology—Zionism. Israelis, especially those who form the governmental elite, believe that an individual (or a state) through his own efforts may so structure his environment as to achieve his goals. Since Israel's efforts were an outcome of its ideology, ideology assumes enormous significance. Ideology leads to volition plus activity, and the volition and activity of one party may in the final analysis be all that is needed to achieve one's objectives.

The exigencies of statehood, economic difficulties, and international complications have moderated these beliefs to some extent, although with respect to security they appear to have reinforced them. Nonetheless, Israeli leaders are still more ideologically oriented than leaders of most Western countries. Therefore, images and concepts formed in the early development of the Zionist movement and sharpened during the formative years of struggle preceding the establishment of the State still carry policy overtones and consequences.

The core concept of Zionism as Israeli leaders understand it was and is the ingathering of the Jewish people in the Land of Israel. Early Zionist thinkers paid relatively scant attention to relationships that would ensue between a future Jewish State and Jews who chose to remain in the Diaspora. Indeed, many thinkers did not even foresee the possibility of a Diaspora after the creation of a state. But their images of Diaspora Jewry had a direct bearing on how the national elite viewed the Diaspora after 1948. My initial concern in this chapter will be to trace the images of the Diaspora as they were reflected in the writings of the most influential Zionist writers and leaders. However, I will concentrate only on those ideologues who were influential in Eretz Yisrael (the Land of Israel).[1] Ahad Ha'am (1856–1927), for example, was probably the most influential Zionist thinker in the world, but he left little impact on the settlers of Eretz Yisrael.

Like his intellectual adversary Simon Dubnow (1860–1941), Ahad Ha'am, assumed that a majority of Jews would always live in the Diaspora. Like Dubnow, he categorized modern political Zionism as the reaction of modern, assimilated, Western Jews who, rejected by Gentile society, came to the realization that assimilation was not a solution to the Jewish problem, and, in their ignorance of Judaism, despaired of its creative survival in the Diaspora.[2] Ahad Ha'am rejected the Zionist classification of Jews into Zionists and assimilationists.[3] Indeed, he expressed himself as more closely identified with those like Dubnow who

sought a renaissance of Jewish peoplehood in the Diaspora than
with the Zionists, whose sole attachment to Judaism rested on
their desire to create a Jewish State.[4] Ahad Ha'am differed
from Dubnow and the "Diaspora nationalists" only in his belief
that creation of a national center in Eretz Yisrael was the only
way to rebuild Jewish life in the Diaspora and that accomplish-
ing this task was of the highest priority.[5]

Ahad Ha'am's theories turned Zionism into a means for
strengthening Jewish life in the Diaspora. It is not surprising,
therefore, that he exercised little influence among the settlers of
Eretz Yisrael.

A man whose activity and thought left a great impact on the
early Zionists, regardless of where they lived, was Theodore
Herzl (1860–1904), the founder of political Zionism. Herzl was
concerned with Diaspora Jewry only as an instrument to achieve
the purposes of Zionism. Nevertheless, his writings indirectly
reflect an image of Diaspora Jewry. Herzl never doubted that
once a Jewish State was established, the masses of Jews,
oppressed as they were by anti-Semitism and economic hardship,
would migrate there. The Jewish homeland, in Herzl's formulation, was the solution "for those Jews who cannot or will not
assimilate." [6] According to Herzl, the creation of a Jewish homeland and the mass immigration that would ensue would resolve
the problem of anti-Semitism and ease the path for those Jews
who wished to remain in the Diaspora and assimilate.[7]

In his later speeches and writings, responding in part to
pressures within the World Zionist Organization, Herzl acknowledged that raising the spiritual level of the Jewish people
within the Diaspora itself was a legitimate Zionist activity.[8] But
this activity was conceived of as preceding the creation of a
Jewish State. After acquiring a homeland, Zionism would still
have the task of achieving the moral and spiritual perfection of
the people,[9] but this task would lie presumably within the
Jewish State itself. In other words, once the political goals of
Zionism were achieved, Herzl really saw no future role for
Diaspora Jewry. Those who remained in the Diaspora of their

own free will were those who demonstrated their desire to assimilate. Given Herzl's rather exclusive understanding of Judaism in national terms, nonnationals could hardly be expected to remain Jewish in the long run.

Herzl's leadership was recognized by the factions and parties of the Zionist world that were already developing during his lifetime. These factions gained ascendancy after his death and divided the Zionist Organization along ideological rather than geographic lines. Labor Zionism, the Zionist-Socialist Movement, achieved preeminence within the World Zionist Organization only in the 1930s, but it dominated the major Jewish political institutions of Eretz Yisrael from the time of their inception in the wake of World War I and the British conquest of the land. It was Labor Zionism that forged the primary cultural and educational institutions in Eretz Yisrael. Only the religious institutions remained outside the Labor Zionist orbit of influence.

Two writers whose activity and thought exercised great influence over the early settlers were Joseph Hayim Brenner (1881–1921) and Aaron David Gordon (1856–1922). Brenner, virtually unknown outside Israel, made an enormous impact on the Labor Zionists and early pioneers.[10]

Both Brenner and Gordon drew sharp distinctions between the Jews of the Diaspora, the Galut Jew who is the Jew of the past, and the new Jew of Eretz Yisrael. For Brenner, "We, the new Jews, have nothing to do with Judaism." [11] In his view, Eretz Yisrael provided an opportunity for the Jew to remake himself.

> Our function now is to recognize and admit our meanness since the beginning of history to the present day, all the faults in our character, and then to rise and start all over again.[12]

According to a historian of the Yishuv, Israel Kolatt, the impact of Brenner and others like him

> led to placing the Jewish revival in Eretz Yisrael as diametrically opposed to the *gola*. [Diaspora] Labor versus parasitism,

self defense versus submission. This dichotomy exerted a powerful influence on education in Eretz Yisrael.[13]

Unlike Brenner, Gordon affirmed the Jewish past. But he too juxtaposed the Diaspora Jew and the new Jew. Gordon's key to individual and national renaissance was manual labor. Its neglect had turned the Diaspora Jew into an economic and spiritual parasite.[14] To Gordon, *Galut* (literally "exile") was a condition of mind and a style of life as much as a political status. He contrasted the Galut and Galut style with everything he hoped would be achieved in Eretz Yisrael. In his own words, "Whoever seeks national rebirth and a full life as a Jew must give up the life of the Galut." [15] He demanded "a complete revolution in our Galut notions and attitudes and in our Galut view of life." [16] The Galut Jew, he believed, was a personality type, "unnatural, defective, splintered." [17] The new Jew would be entirely different from the Diaspora Jew in his personality, in his attitude toward manual labor, in his attitude toward other peoples and toward nature, and in his capacity to sense and appreciate his unity with natural life. Therefore, says Gordon,

what we seek to establish in Palestine is a new, recreated Jewish people, not a mere colony of Diaspora Jewry, not a continuation of Diaspora Jewish life in a new form.[18]

Whereas Gordon, unlike other Zionist thinkers, envisaged the continuation of the Diaspora, these Jewish communities were to be "colonies" of Jewish Palestine, the "mother country." [19]

It is little wonder that the leaders of Israel, schooled in the thought of people like Brenner and Gordon, would not welcome the influence of Diaspora Jewry and might even consider that submission to its influence would be a betrayal of their own ideology. How, then, did the political leaders of Israel see the relationship between Israel and the Diaspora?

Berl Katznelson (1887–1944) was the preeminent ideologist-leader of the dominant wing of Labor Zionism until his death in 1944. It was Katznelson rather than Ben-Gurion who delivered the keynote addresses at various labor conferences. In addition, as founder, and editor until his death, of *Davar*, the daily paper of the General Federation of Labor, Katznelson must be ranked second only to Ben Gurion as the foremost educator of the labor movement and of the nation's political elite. Walter Laqueur, author of the most recent history of Zionism, calls him:

> the intellectual and moral preceptor of his generation . . . an accomplished speaker who carried his audience with him by the strength of his conviction . . . and his transparent honesty, he was accepted as the teacher of his own generation and exerted great influence on the following one.[20]

There were, of course, Zionist labor parties outside Eretz Yisrael, and Katznelson addressed himself to the question of relationships between these parties and the federation of Jewish workers in Eretz Yisrael (the Histadrut). In a speech delivered in 1924, Katznelson responded to proposals that a joint committee of labor Zionists from Eretz Yisrael and the Diaspora should take responsibility for the Histadrut. Katznelson said:

> We believe in and desire mutual influence between Israel and the Diaspora but we do not recognize in the least that the influence must be expressed in granting prerogatives or control functions, or leadership to any groups outside Eretz Yisrael.[21]

Direct influence, he asserted, would come only after *aliya*. Then, through social, ideological, and political interaction, the way would be open to the new immigrants to influence the Histadrut.[22]

Katznelson apparently did not feel that this in any way contradicted his call for an international Jewish workers' organization to assist in constructing a workers' society in Israel. Indeed, as Katznelson saw it, such an organization would strengthen the ties between the Histadrut and Jewish workers abroad and, through its practical work, would serve as an educational instrument (i.e., a one-way channel of influence) of the Histadrut.[23] In other speeches and writings, Katznelson made clear that strengthening the ties between Jews in Eretz Yisrael and the Diaspora was necessary in order to insure the leadership of Israelis over the Diaspora and educate Jews toward *aliya*.[24]

In greeting the publication of an American Labor Zionist newspaper, Katznelson wrote that he welcomed publication "of *your* paper," which would "enable *us* to influence the masses of Jews to assist in the construction of a Jewish socialist country (emphasis added)." [25]

Katznelson did recognize the physical dependence of Eretz Yisrael on Diaspora Jewry. This, he felt, led to the unfortunate development of a Zionist orientation that stressed philanthropy rather than *aliya*. It was the task of Eretz Yisrael to become independent of Diaspora Jewry, indeed to eradicate the Diaspora and by inference to leave only one definition of Zionism—*aliya*.[26] Concern for the Diaspora, therefore, especially for its youth, was concern for self. "What is today Diaspora will tomorrow or the next day be the *Yishuv* [the Jewish settlement in Eretz Yisrael in the pre-State period], the Histadrut." [27]

The preeminent educator of Israeli Jews was, however, not Berl Katznelson, but rather David Ben-Gurion (1886–1973). Ben-Gurion held a commanding position in the affairs of Eretz Yisrael for over fifty years. As early as the founding conference of the local Poale Zion party in 1906,[28] he had argued for the centrality of Eretz Yisrael and for those who had settled there. In a speech at the May 1950 Zionist General Council meetings, Ben-Gurion recounted a debate that took place forty years earlier at a meeting of the International Zionist Socialist Movement—the Poale Zion. The movement had established a Fund for Israeli Workers. Ben-Gurion recalled how he and Ben-Zvi, the two delegates from Eretz Yisrael, argued that the control of the Fund must be in the hands of the workers of Eretz Yisrael. "Our comrades from abroad saw in this idea a dangerous heresy and a betrayal of our movement's international ties." But Ben-Gurion maintained that only the settlers in Eretz Yisrael understood their own needs.[29]

As Ben-Gurion played an increasingly central and finally

dominant role in Eretz Yisrael, his views on Israel-Diaspora relations became the dominant policies of the State. In 1910, he joined Yitzchak Ben-Zvi, later to become Israel's second president, in editing *Ha'Adut*, the Poale Zion periodical. He was a founder and Secretary General of the Histadrut from the time of its formation in 1921 until 1935. He served as chairman of the executive of the Jewish Agency from 1935 to 1948 and as Prime Minister of Israel (with a short interim) from 1948 to 1963. Ben-Gurion was a prolific writer and speaker. As the prime leader of the Jewish people in Israel, he saw a special obligation to transmit his own ideals and ideology to his followers, especially the youth. Furthermore, unlike other settlers in Eretz Yisrael, Ben-Gurion wrote and spoke extensively on Diaspora Jewry and the relationships between the Diaspora and Israel. The thinking of Israelis today, especially of its leaders, bears his stamp more than that of any other individual.[30]

For Ben-Gurion, as for most of Israel's leaders, a Jewish State was never an end in itself, at least ideologically. "The cardinal aim of our State is the redemption of the people of Israel, the In-gathering of the Exiles," [31] Ben-Gurion declared. Indeed, the value of ingathering the exiles, that is, the concentration of the Jewish people in Eretz Yisrael, dictated the creation of an instrumentality in the form of the State. Ben-Gurion testified that in 1937 he arrived at the conclusion that the British government would not continue to adhere faithfully to the mandate

and therefore, the fate of *aliya*—that is, the return of Jews to their country and development of an independent Jewish economy—depends entirely from now on, on the establishment of a Jewish state . . . not as an ultimate end but as an instrument, and perhaps, the only instrument for realizing the vision of national redemption.[32]

Ben-Gurion constantly reiterated that not only would he be unsatisfied with merely achieving a Jewish State, he would not even be satisfied with a Jewish majority in Palestine if there would be any limitation imposed on the right of Jews to immigrate there.[33]

For Ben-Gurion, Zionism meant the concentration of all Jews in Eretz Yisrael. Elsewhere, however, he defined Israel's purpose in more universalistic terms. Its ultimate purpose was to be

> a model people and a model state . . . our historic goal is a new society built on freedom, equality, mutual assistance, and love of humanity; in other words, a society without exploitation, discrimination, enslavement, the domination of man by man, the violation of conscience, and tyranny.[34]

He declared that the goals of the State "could be defined in two short sentences. In-gathering of the exiles. 'Love thy neighbor as thyself.'"[35]

Where does Diaspora Jewry fit in? The Jewish State had been created for Diaspora Jewry, and their place, in turn, is in Israel. But Diaspora Jewry did not come. In his speeches and writings in the 1950s, certain ambiguities appear in Ben-Gurion's assessment of Diaspora Jews. On the one hand, he was deeply disappointed in them. This disappointment is expressed most sharply in his evaluation of the Zionist leadership in the Diaspora. Ben-Gurion belittled them. He judged the Zionist organization as no better and no worse than the many non-Zionist Jewish organizations that were friendly to the State. Furthermore, according to Ben-Gurion, there were no differences between Zionists, non-Zionists, and anti-Zionists in terms of their integration within the society wherein they reside.[36] By not coming to Israel, Zionists not only betrayed the goals of Zionism as Ben-Gurion defined them, they also denied the State the greatest assistance they could render. For the building of Israel, said Ben-Gurion, can only be done in Israel:

> In New York and Miami, in London and in Paris, one cannot participate in the building of Israel. . . . Without Jews in the land, all help of other kinds will not avail. *The Land will be built only by her residents.*[37]

Furthermore:

Israel can have no security without immigration. The population of Egypt alone numbers twenty-three million. *Aliya* is not
only the redemption of Jews from physical or spiritual extinc-
tion in the Diaspora and the supreme historic mission of the
State of Israel; it is of paramount importance for our security.[38]

But despite his continued call for *aliya*, his stress on Israel's
need for *aliya*, and his expression of disappointment with Diaspora Jewry for not responding to his call, Ben-Gurion paid increasing attention in the 1950s to Diaspora Jewry as an ongoing
community with an existence independent of its ties to Eretz
Yisrael. He noted the fact that world Jewry could render great
service to Israel even if it remained in the Diaspora. Without
ever absolving the Zionist organization of its sins, he looked to
the continued existence of Diaspora Jewry. Thus he remarked
that world Jewry is Israel's only faithful ally [39] and, referring
specifically to American Jewry, "serves as a link and a bridge
between Israel and America." [40] However, according to Ben-
Gurion world Jewry was also dependent on Israel for its survival as a Jewish community. Its identification with Israel, along
with Israel's ethical, cultural, and political leadership, provided
the Diaspora with its key to survival.[41]

Thus, toward the end of his public career, Ben-Gurion
developed a greater interest and concern with Diaspora Jewry's
survival. Indeed, preserving Diaspora Jewry from assimilation
became a third goal of Israel, along with its two messianic
ideals—ingathering the exiles and being a "light to the nations."[42]
Large-scale *aliya* now became a long-term process; the more
immediate task was to strengthen Jewish life in the Diaspora.[43]
This too, however, required the strengthening of the ties between
Israel and Jews abroad.

In 1953, the lifelong Zionist and distinguished publicist and
author Maurice Samuel met with a group of Israeli leaders. He
commented as follows on their image of Diaspora Jewry:

These highly intelligent men were concerned with a single
idea, the development of Israel. They thought of Jews every-

where else in the world as material for Israel, *and as nothing else.*[44]

While this was, no doubt, a fair characterization of Israeli leaders at that time, Ben-Gurion as noted, did subsequently adopt a less provincially Israeli orientation to the Diaspora. Nevertheless, a second observation of Samuel's remained true of Ben-Gurion in his later career as well:

> it was taken for granted that American Jewry as a Jewry had nothing to teach Palestine Jewry, and never would have. It could provide human material, money, and political influence, but insofar as it remained itself, it had no spiritual value for Palestine and Israel.[45]

Samuel went on to add that American Jewry tended to accept this evaluation, a fact noted in the preceding chapter.

A consequence of this image of Diaspora Jewry was that despite everything that Diaspora Jews might do for Israel, their interference in the formation of Israeli policy was unthinkable. Their opinion might carry some moral weight, but religious Zionists in the Diaspora could not oblige Israel to act in any specific manner on religious matters, or Labor Zionists on workers' matters, or General Zionists on educational or economic matters.[46] Indeed, Ben-Gurion even questioned the *moral* right of Diaspora Zionists to adopt policy positions vis-à-vis Israeli affairs. Addressing himself to religious Zionists, he noted that Judaism requires one to live in Israel and speak the "holy language." Since religious Zionists in America do not observe these commandments, they have no moral right to require Israelis to observe other commandments that they happen to accept and Israelis do not. He went on to say:

> Diaspora Zionists in general and American Zionists in particular will be making a grave mistake if instead of participating in general, unifying and basic aspects connected to the upbuilding of the State and the realization of Zionism

—i.e., the demands created by increased *aliya,* settlement, security and Hebrew culture—if instead of this, they participate in those aspects which separate and divide, which are matters of controversy among the citizens of Israel.[47]

What Ben-Gurion is saying is that Diaspora Jews should remain silent on those issues which are controversial within Israel. Diaspora Jews must not only refrain from taking sides against Israel, they must not even take sides with one party or another within Israel. What is left for them is to speak out in support of those issues upon which the people of Israel are themselves united.

The State, according to Ben-Gurion, is sovereign, and only its citizens can determine its laws or the structure of its government.[48] There were, he notes, Zionist "maximalists" who argued that the State of Israel is composed not only of Jews living there but of all the Jews in the world, and Zionists from all over the world should, therefore, be represented in the Israeli parliament and Government.[49] This, he says, would destroy the sovereignty of the State. Just as the State cannot compel foreign citizens to pay taxes or serve in its army, so they, in turn, cannot compel the citizens of Israel in matters affecting their personal lives, domestic or foreign policy, or questions of war and peace.[50]

But Ben-Gurion's desire to limit Diaspora Jewry's intervention in Israeli affairs extended not only to matters such as lawmaking or foreign policy, where, one might say, Diaspora Jewry had neither the same stakes and investment as other Israelis nor the necessity to face the consequences of their decisions; it extended also to matters where Diaspora Jewry had the greater investment and made the greater contribution. Ben-Gurion himself discussed a political controversy that arose in 1948 over control of the United Jewish Appeal in America. On one side were the American Zionists, led by Abba Hillel Silver; on the other side were a group of non-Zionists, led by Henry Montor and Henry Morgenthau, Jr. Ben-Gurion and his party supported the non-Zionist group; indeed, they swung the balance in its favor. Part of the reason for Ben-Gurion's support was that the non-Zionists accepted the proposition that only Israel should have a voice in the expenditure of funds collected for Israel.[51]

As I have noted, Ben-Gurion was conscious of Israel's obligations to Diaspora Jewry. Although in his opinion foreign policy had to rest entirely within the Government's authority, nevertheless, "in light of the fact that there are masses of Diaspora Jews, the State of Israel, in addition to political, strategic, and economic calculations, must also consider the interests of the masses of Jews in foreign lands." [52] A basic aspect of Israeli foreign policy, said Ben-Gurion, is the offering of assistance and defense to Diaspora Jews who require it.[53] But this itself is tempered by Ben-Gurion's definition of Diaspora Jewry's interests:

> It was always my view that we have *always* to consider the *interests* of Diaspora Jewry—any Jewish community that was concerned. But there is one crucial distinction—not what *they* think are their interests, but what *we* regarded as their interests. If it was a case vital for Israel, and the interests of the Jews concerned were different, the vital interests of Israel came first—because Israel is vital for world Jewry.[54]

And finally:

> In considering international relations, we must ask one simple question: What is good for Israel? And what is good for Israel is good for the entire Jewish people . . . and whatever is good for Israel falls within the scope of the injunction bequeathed to us by the victims of the holocaust.[55]

Israel's first Minister of Foreign Affairs and second Prime Minister, Moshe Sharett, was often thought to be more sympathetic and understanding of Diaspora Jewry than Ben-Gurion. The differences may have been more of style than of content. It was his estimate that Diaspora Jewry needs Israel because it unifies the Jewish community. Dismissing the role of religion in unifying the Jewish people (religion was too static), Sharett asserted that only Israel provided a challenge to the idealism of Jewish youth and provided them with the opportunity for enthusiasm. In addition, Israel's survival was crucial to the survival of Diaspora Jews because Israel was their most precious possession and they could not imagine their existence as Jews without it. Therefore, he argued, Diaspora Jews must do everything to defend and strengthen Israel. Their reward would be that "they fulfilled their holy and supreme obligation," [56] an obligation that they must undertake not only for Israel's, but for their own sake as well.

Israel's responsibilities, in turn, were quite modest. The State was simply obligated to remain loyal to its original vision and not act as if it were, or believe that it was self-sufficient, nor isolate itself from world Jewry.[57] How little this really demanded of Israel is evident in Sharett's conclusion. Israel's first obligation, he noted, is to her own security. While the Diaspora might expect special consideration to be given to their needs or their views,

> the decisions as to how [Israel] should behave in one instance or another must be left to the competent authorities. In no event can there be any limitation on the sovereign right of Israel to determine its policies.[58]

Both Ben-Gurion and Sharett minimized the right of Diaspora Jewry to have a voice in Israel's policies. But they did recognize the moral weight of Diaspora opinion. (Even here, as we have seen, Ben-Gurion had reservations.) A test of how much consideration Israel was willing to give to the opinion of Diaspora Jewry—indeed, of its willingness even to tolerate criticism from Diaspora Jewry, much less respond positively to such criticism—came during the tenure of Israel's third Prime Minister, Levi Eshkol.

To understand the background of what occurred, one must recall that, prior to the Six Day War, Israel had been suffering from an economic recession, the Government's popularity was at a low ebb, and many of the most dynamic forces in the

country were organized in an opposition party, Rafi. Rafi's
nominal leader was Ben-Gurion (who had resigned from his
own Mapai party), and its effective leaders were two of the
most widely admired personalities of Israel's "younger" generation, Moshe Dayan and Shimon Peres. Admittedly, the Israeli
Government was probably especially sensitive to criticism.
Nevertheless, the events of March 1967 are, I believe, paradig-
mas of the real relationships between Israel and Diaspora Jewry
in the political realm.

The weekly *Jewish Observer and Middle East Review* was
the official organ of the Zionist Federation of Great Britain and
Ireland. Its then editor, Jon Kimche, was and is a well-known
writer on Israel and Middle Eastern affairs. Kimche was believed
to have had ties to Rafi and to have met with Rafi leader Shimon
Peres in February of 1967. Nevertheless, as the events unfolded,
Peres's influence over Kimche, or Kimche's ties to Rafi, never
became the issue.

In the March 3 issue of the weekly, the editor, in a signed
article, called for the resignation of Israeli Justice Minister
Yaacov Shapiro for his role in allegedly suppressing free speech
in Israel.[59] The same issue of the paper carried an article citing
widespread unemployment in Israel.[60] Kimche prepared another
article on unemployment for the March 10 issue. When the
editorial committee insisted that the article be withdrawn,
Kimche refused and claimed unreasonable censorship instigated
by the Prime Minister of Israel. The March 10 issue did not
appear, but Kimche did submit his article to *The Times*, which
published it along with Kimche's accusations of censorship.[61]
Kimche was dismissed as editor.

Whether Kimche was or was not dismissed because of
Eshkol's intervention, or on the basis of instructions brought by
Deputy Defense Minister Zvi Dinstein on a special trip to Lon-
don, is a matter of dispute and not relevant to present purposes.
What is relevant and is not a matter of dispute is that the
Israeli Ambassador in London was instructed by Eshkol to con-
vey to the Zionist Federation the concern of Israel with regard

to the paper's demand that Justice Minister Shapiro resign.[62] There is no question that the Government of Israel showed great sensitivity to criticism that it interpreted as interference in its affairs, even when expressed by a longtime friend of Israel.[63] Eshkol referred to this matter in a Knesset debate. He had, he said, with the Government's knowledge, instructed the Ambassador in London to inform the Zionist Federation of the Government's displeasure about the article calling for Shapiro's resignation. He coupled Kimche's demands with a statement by Jacques Torczyner, President of the Zionist Organization of America, that criticized Israel for responding too quickly and too strongly to border raids from Arab terrorists along the Jordanian border.[64] All of this, said Eshkol, was unreasonable interference in Israel's affairs.

Israel's image of the Diaspora and of Diaspora-Israeli relations denies legitimacy to any efforts by the Diaspora to shape Israeli policy. In the minds of many Israeli leaders, acceptance of such influence would be virtually tantamount to a betrayal of Israel's mission and purpose. This, coupled with the Diaspora's own perception of Israel (discussed in chapter 7) neutralizes to a great extent the political resources that Diaspora Jewry possesses to influence Israeli policy.

None of this, however, least of all the Kimche incident, should imply that Israel does not consider the needs of Diaspora Jewry in formulating its policies. Israel, as we have seen, is concerned with the physical and material condition of Diaspora Jewry and, increasingly, with its spiritual and cultural well-being as well. What Israel jealously guards for itself, however, is the right to determine what are or are not the Diaspora's real needs and real interests. It goes without saying, therefore, that it certainly will not provide opportunities for the Diaspora to exercise its voice in determining the real needs and real interests of Israel.

9

Israel and the Diaspora: Political Influence

THE LIMITED INFLUENCE OF DIASPORA JEWRY

Throughout this volume I have defined *influence* in a special way: the exercise of power, through direct or indirect threats of sanctions or promises of rewards, by one party over another party, causing the second party to act in a manner it would not otherwise act.

Diaspora Jewry exercises very little influence over Israeli public policy. It is not true to suggest that it exercises no influence. In religious policy, foreign policy, policy toward the WZO, even economic policy, we have seen examples of the Diaspora's exercising influence. But it is fair to say that in the sum total of factors that constitute influences on the sum total of Israeli policies, Diaspora influence is slight.

On the surface, this is a surprising conclusion, because the potential political resources that the Diaspora can bring to bear on Israel are enormous. It is true that there is no one political community that can be called the Diaspora. Diaspora Jews do not perceive a distinctive Diaspora interest. It is also true that not all Diaspora communities—whether considered as national communities, or as subcommunities (organizations or sets of organizations) within the national community—have enormous political resources. But there are at least a few communities that do possess these resources, whose sheer size, financial contributions to Israel, and the relative influence they exercise within their own countries (the latter being the most important factor)[1] provide them with enormous potential influence. First and foremost in this respect is the Jewish community of the United States.

In the course of this study, I have suggested a number of explanations for the absence of Diaspora influence. I summarize them here under three major headings.

1. Limited Efforts at Influence. Israel, as noted, is not viewed as a suitable object of influence. As far as most of Diaspora Jewry is concerned, Israel represents Judaism. Support for Israel is an affirmation of one's Judaism. Israel is, therefore, extremely important to Diaspora Jewry. But its image of Israel and its relationship to Israel are devoid of political implications. Absent, for the most part, from the Diaspora's image of Israel is the vision of a different Israel. Orthodox Jewry has such an image, and this is one reason that it has been the least reticent in bringing pressure to bear. But to most of Diaspora Jewry, Israel is functional as it exists today. American Jews, for example, give little or no thought to an alternative social or political system because the particular social or political system is not important to them. If the social system were grossly inequitable, if there were wide-scale discrimination or exploitation or abridgement of freedom, if Israeli foreign policy were suddenly to become anti-American, it would cause acute embarrassment to American Jewry, which is concerned within the U.S. itself with issues of social equality, minority rights, and support of their country in foreign affairs. But short of such radical departures from the status quo, Diaspora Jewry is relatively unconcerned with Israeli policy.

The early Zionists had a vision of the state that they sought to create. They did not all agree. But they all had their notion of what Israel would be like. To some, it was to be built upon traditional Jewish law; to others, it was to be a spiritual center of Jewish culture and civilization; to others, it was to serve as an example to the world of how a modern state could function in accordance with principles of social justice, equality, and liberty. To almost all, the vision included a universal dimension. Israel, by exemplifying their particularist vision, would also become "a light unto the nations."

The creation of the State and the exigencies of its fight for survival have dimmed the vision Jews once had of Israel. This dimming has been caused by other factors as well. The truth is that whereas Diaspora Jews now share the classical Zionist dream of a Jewish homeland, they have no Zionist vision. Israel perhaps has a particularist Jewish meaning to Diaspora Jewry. Israel is important to the Diaspora for its Jewish survival. But Israel has no universalist meaning to most Diaspora Jews. It is not integrally related to whatever variety of visions Diaspora Jews may have of a different kind of world, of a different kind of society, of a different kind of social order. Hence, the Diaspora is not driven to press Israel into doing anything very different from what it is doing today.

Related to this is a second factor. Diaspora Jewry has very few special interests in Israeli policy-formation. The investment of interest and the stakes that Diaspora Jews have in Israel are not related to specific policies that Israel pursues. Whenever the stakes have been high enough, as with Israel's attitude toward South Africa for South African Jewry or with religious policy for Orthodox groups, or as with Israel's relations with the World Zionist Organization for the American Jewish Committee, Diaspora communities did seek to influence Israeli policymakers.

Third the commitments and loyalties of Diaspora Jews to their own countries of residence raise the issue of propriety and legitimacy in any intervention in the internal affairs of another country.

Finally, the enormous sympathy for Israel among Diaspora Jews makes them reluctant to exercise the sanctions within their power. This is a partial explanation for Reform Jewry's reticence in pressing harder to secure equal rights in Israel. It even serves to explain the behavior of the most outspoken Diaspora leader, a man who was at one time the preeminent political leader of Diaspora Jewry—Nahum Goldmann. Goldmann became increasingly critical of Israel in the late 1950s. He had powerful friends among American Jews. Yet he never sought to utilize his position to pressure Israel. In his own words, "I just made speeches." [2] Goldmann is of the opinion that even if he had invoked other pressures, he would have failed. But the fact is that he was too committed to Israel to experiment with sanctions.

2. *Israeli Unwillingness to Legitimate Diaspora Influence.* I have noted that Diaspora influence has no legitimacy in the Israeli political mentality. This is less true today than in the past. On the other hand, the absence of legitimacy was more important in the past, when Diaspora pressures were stronger and Israel was weaker and more susceptible to them. The statement is less true of some segments within the Israeli political structure than of others. But, as a general rule, the Israeli self-image, and the juxtaposition of this image against that of the Diaspora Jew, deny a legitimacy to Diaspora influence that even foreign governments have. This alone is not sufficient to explain the lack of Diaspora pressure (in the past more than the present) on issues where one might have assumed a far greater sensitivity to the expression of Diaspora values.

3. *The Absence of Political Instruments for Channeling Diaspora Pressure.* Diaspora Jewry is not organized for the expression of its political interests within Israel. Only one organization reflecting Diaspora interests—the World Zionist Organization-Jewish Agency—was incorporated, however tenuously, into the Israeli political structure. Even this organization was, in fact, dominated by Israelis. Furthermore, organization of the World Zionist

Organization along political-party rather than national lines in-troduced cross-cutting cleavages within that organization and prevented the formation of a Diaspora, as opposed to an Israeli interest. Nevertheless, one did find on occasion an expression of Diaspora interests—for example, in the debate between Ameri-cans and Israelis about the obligation of Zionists to immigrate to Israel, or the debate over selective immigration of North Africans.

The reorganization of the World Zionist Organization along territorial (Zionist Federation) rather than party lines has in-creased the potential for the expression of particular Diaspora interests. But the reconstitution of the Jewish Agency and its separation from the World Zionist Organization have also re-duced the latter's area of authority within the Israeli political structure. Both the Jewish Agency and the World Zionist Organ-ization are still potential sources for channeling Diaspora in-terests into the Israeli political system. Neither, however, is an intricate part of that system. They operate from outside it rather than from within it. They confront the Israeli Government *qua* Government rather than as participants in the political policymaking process. An exception to this is the standing Com-mittees of the Jewish Agency. However, up till now, they have functioned at the level of technical, rather than political policy-formation.

Other organizations at the international and national level— the World Jewish Congress, B'nai B'rith, the Conference of Presidents of Major American Jewish Organizations, or the American Jewish Committee—have even less access to the Israeli political system.

Nevertheless, one cannot disregard the fact that there are differences of sensitivity to the Diaspora from different parts of the system. Within the Government, the Foreign Ministry has regular channels for conveying information concerning the Diaspora. Indeed, as noted, one function of Israel's foreign representatives is to represent Israel to local Jewry and to convey information back to Israel concerning developments within the Diaspora. In addition, there is an adviser to the Foreign Minister for Diaspora affairs. The Foreign Minister, in turn, informs the Prime Minister and the Government about Diaspora Jewry. In the case of the U.S., former Prime Minister Golda Meir had her own ties; and while she might have consulted with Israel's representative in Washington, she was likely to arrive at conclusions based on independent sources of information.[3] Both the Foreign Office and the Prime Minister's office are sensitive to the Diaspora. The Ministry of Defense tends to see the relationship with Diaspora Jewry as less central to Israeli affairs.[4]

Among the political parties, the religious parties are the only ones that actively encourage the intervention of Diaspora Jewry. Consequently, they are also more sensitive to Diaspora demands, although the National Religious Party, as we have seen, has rarely found this to be much of a limitation. The Independent Liberals are sensitive to the demands of Conservative and Reform Jewry and, as we saw, their leader, Moshe Kol, initiated a meeting with Reform Jewish leaders in order to assist them. The Liberal Party, formerly the General Zionists, was at one time very closely associated with the Zionist Organization of America (ZOA), although the latter tended to reflect the policies of the former rather than vice versa. In general, opposition parties have often charged the Government with insensitivity to the Diaspora. But one suspects that this is more often than not convenient political rhetoric, rather than the reflection of some basic ideological position. Even Moshe Dayan, when he led the opposition party, Rafi, charged the Government with insufficient openness to Diaspora criticism. (Left-wing Mapam could be found, on occasion, defending American General Zionists against Ben-Gurion in the 1950s!)

Having noted all this, I return to the basic point that, with the exception of American Orthodoxy, Diaspora Jews have no regular channel within the mainstream of the Israeli political system for conveying their interests and demands.

DIASPORA DISSATISFACTION WITH ISRAELI-DIASPORA RELATIONS

Within the context of the Diaspora's widespread and enthusiastic support for Israel, voices expressing dissatisfaction with Israeli-Diaspora relations have increased in number and tone in the last few years. I do not refer to the voices of the New Left—the Jewish antagonists of Israel. They are simply unhappy with Israel and with Jewish support for Israel. Nor are these the voices of the rank and file of Diaspora Jewry. Rather, they are the voices of some Diaspora leaders who, for a variety of reasons (to which I shall return) have expressed their dissatisfaction with the nature of Israeli-Diaspora relations.

Their criticism takes two forms, which I would argue are really two sides of the same coin. They complain that the Diaspora is overcommitted to Israel; that it gives too much money to Israel at the expense of its own welfare and educational needs;[5] that Israel is too prone to interfere in Diaspora affairs by telling Diaspora Jews what they should or should not do;[6] and that Diaspora concern for Israel and the centrality of Israel in Diaspora affairs may come at the price of a weakened Diaspora.[7]

This criticism suggests that Diaspora Jewry relies too much upon Israel or is too involved with Israel,[8] implying that this comes at the expense of the Diaspora's own well-being.

Other complaints have to do with the absence of Diaspora involvement in Israel. In late 1972, the Conference of Presidents of Major American Jewish Organizations (a roof organization representing the Presidents of the Major American Jewish organizations) met in Israel. According to the press, those present said that they "wanted to play a more active role in criticizing defects in Israeli society, but implied that Israeli leaders were not willing to listen to criticism."[9] In an address before the annual meetings of the American Jewish Committee in May 1971, William Frankel, editor of the *Jewish Chronicle*, also stressed the necessity for some forum of Diaspora Jews that would advise Israeli leaders on Israeli policy that directly affected Diaspora Jewry. This opinion was echoed in a paper by American Jewish leader Philip Klutznick, who suggested that there is a necessity for consultations between Diaspora leaders and Israel since "decisions made by the State of Israel affect the condition of all world Jewry." [10] He raised the specter of a civil war within world Jewry.

One might argue that the two sets of criticism are mutually exclusive, one group demanding greater autonomy for the Diaspora and another insisting on the creation of some forum which, if anything, would increase Israeli-Diaspora interdependence. But both reflect a dissatisfaction with the present balance of power between Israel and the Diaspora. In fact, Israeli recognition of and respect for Diaspora autonomy is more likely to be a by-product of closer ties than simply a result of a unilateral decision by Israel to be less involved in the Diaspora. The latter condition is likely to arise only from real disinterest by each side in the affairs of the other—a condition that the critics themselves probably agree would be disastrous for world Jewry. What they really want is what Jack Neusner has termed "a mature relationship," [11] a relationship likely to emerge only from a structure of interdependence different from that presently prevailing, not from a greater sense of autonomy and independence.

THE DIFFICULTY OF THE PROPOSED SOLUTIONS

The Diaspora cannot force Israel to a greater sensitivity nor can it even "pressure" it to undertake basic changes against its will. The ball is firmly in Israel's court. What can, and what should Israel do?

It can choose to ignore the problem, perhaps confining itself to rebutting charges by its critics. The late Louis Pincus spent considerable energy in the few months before he died answering the critics.[12] Instead of summarizing his major points, I have incorporated them into a rebuttal, sharper than any Israeli has yet offered. Perhaps this rebuttal might seem unjustly harsh and only exacerbate the tensions. But I permit myself such a reply because my sympathy is with the critics' sense of unease rather than with the self-satisfaction that is characteristic of Israelis. Here, then, might be Israel's reply to the criticisms of some Diaspora leaders:

1. Without regard to the nature of the criticism, it might be well first to consider its source. The critics certainly do not reflect the mass of Jewish public opinion in the Diaspora, not even the opinion of Jewry in the affluent countries. Much of the criticism comes from rabbis and institutional or organizational leaders whose position of importance in the Diaspora, especially the American Jewish community, has been displaced by the centrality that Israel has assumed in the eyes of most Jews. Many of the critics are people who are really on the fringes of power and prestige and who may be frustrated by new developments in Jewish life that have denied them greater power and prestige—critics who, to borrow a sociological concept, are "downwardly mobile" in terms of their prestige.

2. Part of the reason that Israel has assumed an important role in Diaspora decision-making is that the Diaspora leadership is itself of such second-rate quality. One need not be inordinately sensitive to "heroic" qualities to appreciate that Israeli representatives in the major Western countries are generally individuals of greater knowledge, understanding, wisdom, articulateness, and sensitivity than are the Diaspora leaders themselves. It is no wonder that so many Diaspora Jews are prepared to take their cues from them rather than from the indigenous leadership.

3. Assuming that Israel did agree to consult regularly with a forum of Diaspora leaders, who would be represented on this forum? The leaders of Jewish organizations? No one could seriously argue that such individuals are representatives of Dias-

pora Jewries' wishes or needs. There are no "representative leaders" of the Diaspora. If Jews could vote for their leaders, is there any question that Yitzchak Rabin or Moshe Dayan or Abba Eban would get more votes than the paper leadership of Diaspora Jewry?

There are structural problems in addition to the question of representation. These include the problem of the scope and nature of the forum's authority. Should this forum of Diaspora leaders deal with all Israeli policy—tax laws? foreign policy? How are areas of authority to be delimited? Clearly, some matters ought to be left entirely to Israelis. But how does one determine the forum's scope of authority and responsibility when it is so easy to demonstrate that decisions in one policy area affect others? However impossible it is to resolve the problem of "scope" in a theoretical sense, it is no doubt possible to do so pragmatically. A more serious question is one of the "nature" of the forum's authority.

Is the forum to be a purely consultative and advisory body, or is it to be a decision-making body? If only consultative— then Israel does not need it. It continually consults with Diaspora leaders, and there are a number of forums (the reconstituted Jewish Agency, the World Jewish Congress, COJO, and the World Zionist Organization) where Diaspora and Israeli leaders meet and where the latter can hear the opinion of the former. But if the forum is to bind Israeli leaders, then one may well ask what justice there is in nonresidents having binding power over the decisions of a foreign country and, realistically, whether Diaspora leaders want such authority or, given the law of their own countries, whether they could legally exercise such authority.

Finally, there is no one Diaspora interest. Any forum of Diaspora leaders is far more likely to pit one Diaspora interest against another.

4. It is not necessarily true that Diaspora leaders are more attuned to, aware of, or sympathetic to Diaspora Jewry's needs

than are Israeli leaders themselves. No Jew is a greater "lover of the Jewish people" merely bcause he chooses to remain in the Diaspora. Despite all the criticism one may justly invoke against Israelis for placing their Israeli identity ahead of their Jewish identity, no one familiar with Israelis and American and Western European Jews could seriously argue that the Americans and Europeans are more concerned with the Jewish people than are the Israelis. This is true of rank-and-file Jews as well as of their leaders. Since a significant proportion of Diaspora Jewry would not be represented in such a forum—for example, the Jews of the Soviet Union—and other groups, such as the wealthy and the intellectuals, are likely to be overrepresented (the former because they are the joiners, the latter because of the deference of Diaspora Jewry to intellectuals), the question is whether any forum of Diaspora leaders can be trusted to better represent the mass of unrepresented Jews than Israeli leaders themselves.

5. The flow of money to Israel "at the expense of Diaspora institutions" reflects the wishes of the contributors themselves. In fact, the relative distribution of funds between Israel and the Diaspora is as autonomous a Diaspora decision as one can imagine. The greatest reservation that the fund-raisers represented in the reconstituted Jewish Agency have about the expenditure of their money is the share that goes to the World Zionist Organization for expenditure in the Diaspora. That money is spent on education and cultural programs, about which some of the critics express concern.

6. Israel, and support for Israel, are the central expression of Jewish identity today. Israel is the center of Jewish life because Diaspora Jews find no other form of expression so Jewishly meaningful to them. It is a mistake to assume that if Diaspora Jews worked less, contributed less, or were less interested in Israel, they would work harder for, contribute more to, or be more concerned with some other Jewish institution or project.

7. There is a real crisis of survival confronting Diaspora Jewry in the West. But voices from within the Jewish establishment rather than from Israel confer a legitimacy on life patterns inimical to survival. It is not Israeli leaders who tell Diaspora Jewry that philanthropy is just as important as attending synagogues or maintaining the ritual tradition; this was said by an American communal and fund-raising leader in 1965. He maintained that contributions to local Jewish hospitals or Israel or any other Jewish philanthropy was the equivalent of performing Jewish ritual commandments. The statement was reported in the Anglo-Jewish press. No outraged voices were raised from the Jewish establishment against this distortion of Jewish values. It is not the Israel establishment that condones intermarriage or argues that Judaism must accommodate itself to young couples who insist on intermarrying; this is said by a portion of the American Reform rabbinate. Israelis do not argue that day school education is undemocratic, or that it is wrong to seek Government support for Jewish schools since that would violate principles of church-state separation, which apparently are more important than insuring adequate Jewish education to those who want it. It was most of the American Jewish establishment who raised these arguments, at least until recently.

Israeli representatives abroad are urged to attend synagogues, to send their own children to day schools (they even get a special allowance for this purpose), and to respect Jewish tradition. One may argue that not every Israeli representative abroad does so. There are many "ugly Israelis." In at least one instance, an Israeli consul sent his children to a private Protestant school in a city that has a Jewish day school. But the thrust of the Foreign Ministry policy is that Israeli representatives abroad are responsible for knowing and observing the basic amenities of the Jewish tradition. It was the Israeli Prime Minister who argued in 1970 that a law had to be amended (the "Who is a Jew?" controversy), because it might otherwise encourage intermarriage in the Diaspora. Israeli leaders are highly sensitive to the dangers of assimilation, and they have devoted major efforts in recent years to supporting Jewish education in the Diaspora.

The point of all this is that, on the one hand, the American Jewish establishment includes elements whose activity encourages assimilation. Israel, on the other hand, is sensitive to and anxious about Diaspora survival. Thus, quite apart from the fact that activity on behalf of Israel is itself a barrier against assimilation, the Jewish establishment in the United States, for example, is no more concerned about, or is a better representative of survivalist forces in Jewish life than is Israel.

8. Israeli representatives, one must admit, may not always have adopted the proper tones in speaking to the Diaspora. They may sometimes have appeared abrasive and inconsiderate. But in the last analysis, faced with enormous threats, its leaders cannot afford to be sanguine about its security situation. If Israelis, sometimes put parochial interests above universal ones, if they tended to favor Nixon or worry about the consequences to themselves of American Jewish opposition to the war in Vietnam, they are hardly to be blamed. Why should Israelis refrain from pointing out their self-interest to Diaspora Jewry, any more than Diaspora Jewry should refrain from pointing out its own self-interest to Israel? In the last analysis, even Israel's harshest critics do not suggest that Israeli representatives did more than advise American Jewry—and in a severely restrained manner at that—about their position on Nixon or Vietnam. One suspects that what really disturbed the critics in this case was not that Israel tried to pressure American Jewry, for it did not do so, but that Israel did not share the peculiar politically liberal proclivities of the majority of the American Jewish establishment.

A PERSONAL CONCLUSION

The problem of Israel-Diaspora relations today must be recognized for what it is. It is the problem of a few people, some of whom live in Israel, others of whom live in the Diaspora, but all of whom are, for various reasons, unhappy with the present state of Israel-Diaspora relations. They represent a very small percentage of Jews.

I happen to be a part of that small group, but this must not blind me to the unrepresentative character of my sentiments. I could argue persuasively that the present state of Israeli-Diaspora relations is of the nature of a "temporary honeymoon" and that unless certain actions are taken the relations will in the long run lead to serious estrangement. But I am less concerned about the future prospects of Israel-Diaspora relations than I am about the current state of these relations. It is the latter concern that leads me to suggest a new pattern of Diaspora involvement in Israel.

The problem of Israeli-Diaspora relations is not a problem of political representation. It is, rather, the far more difficult problem of political values and political responsibility. Israel can afford to ignore its Diaspora critics as unrepresentative, their criticism as unfounded, and their proposals as inept and impractical. It cannot afford to ignore the problem of Israeli-Diaspora relations if it is to remain true to the political values upon which the State was established. The problem, as I see it, is that Israel is becoming untrue to itself. Diaspora Jewry has a corrective role to play and I believe that some Diaspora Jews have sensed this.

The founders of Israel never viewed the State as an end in itself. The State was an instrument—primarily, an instrument for "ingathering the exiles." The State, in other words, was to be an instrument to serve the Jewish people.[13] Ben-Gurion continually stressed a second function of Israel—to be a "light unto the nations." Whether the fulfillment of this universalist mission is or is not also the realization of a particularly Jewish value is relatively unimportant. My own inclinations are to believe that it is. Ben-Gurion also believed that it was. The phrase, after all, is a biblical one. Ben-Gurion's referent, however, may or may not have a particularly Jewish content. The point is that the State is fulfilling its function of being a "light unto the nations" when its conduct expresses the moral values of justice, mercy, and righteousness. The religious Jew may argue that it can achieve the expression of these values only by conducting itself in accordance with traditional Jewish law. But even for the religious Jew, being a "light unto the nations" is the consequence of Israel's conduct—that is, if the State conducts itself according to Jewish law, it will reflect principles of justice, mercy, and righteousness, and it will thereby be a "light unto the nations." From this perspective, traditional Jewish law becomes an instrument. Ben-Gurion regarded the instrument as ineffective. Whether he was right or wrong does not concern me here. At this point, I am far more concerned with the fact that Israel seems to have lost sight of the two basic values that justified and legitimized its creation—serving the Jewish people and becoming an exemplary state.

It seems to me that these are the core values and criteria by which Israeli policy ought to be guided and judged. Obviously, these are not sufficient policy guidelines. First of all, situations may arise where the application of one value must come at the expense of the other. (Theoretically, the decision whether or not to challenge South Africa for its *apartheid* policy might have been such an example. In reality, it was not the principle of service to Jews versus ethical conduct that led to indecision, but rather service to Jews versus Israel's self-interest). Second, these values do not by themselves necessarily tell the policymakers what decisions to reach in every given situation. They are not specific enough. Reasonable men will argue whether or not accepting German reparations was a service to the Jewish people. Finally, other values, even if of secondary importance, must also be considered. Economic prosperity is an independent value that may be less important than serving the Jewish people or behaving in a morally exemplary way, but it is still a legitimate value. But what is one to do when just a little bit of self service, just a little violation in the spirit of a trade agreement might bring a great deal of economic prosperity? Is Israel obligated to make economic sacrifices for the sake of marginal benefits that might accrue to Diaspora Jews? Was Israel, in other words, obligated to build its ships in French shipyards because French Jewry asked it to do so, if it could build the ships elsewhere more economically?

Israel's core political values, however inadequate for deciding what precisely must be done, do provide a criterion for judging, in a very general way, the legitimacy of what was done. The judgmental role is not one that only the Diaspora may exercise. Israelis have a greater right to exercise this role because it is they who bear the burden of fulfilling the basic values. But it is also a role that they are less well equipped to fulfill precisely because the burden is upon them. It is only natural that two processes should take place among Israelis. First of all, confronted with their immediate needs for survival plus a myriad of other values—personal welfare, economic prosperity, and the like—Israelis are likely to forget the higher values to which their State is ostensibly dedicated. Second, they are likely to turn the State into an end in itself—to sanctify, as it were, the means. Americans, including American Jews, express a loyalty and love for their country, not because of America's mission or function, but because it is their country. Frenchmen, Englishmen, and Russians do the same. Why should Israelis be any different? One anticipates an Israeli national feeling no different in essence from American, British, French, or Russian national feeling. One may find this more or less unfortunate, depending upon one's universalistic cosmopolitan propensities, but it would be unrealistic not to expect it.

It is, therefore, important for the Diaspora to exercise a judgmental role, however restrained and circumspect it ought to be, in doing so. This is a necessary corrective to the natural tendencies inherent in Israelis to ignore, pay only lip service to, or rationalize away the basic values upon which the State was established.

A judgmental or critical role is the most appropriate political role for Diaspora Jewry, which cannot hope to become involved in the decision-making process. Decisions must be made by those who can be held accountable for them—by those directly or indirectly responsible to a free electorate. Decisions must be made by those who also assume the consequences for these decisions. There is no reason why Israel ought not to consult this or that Diaspora community, this or that individual, these or those leadership groups. It does so even now. But the decisions must be made by Israelis within the Israeli political system. Diaspora Jewry is not an integral part of that system; it cannot expect to be part of that system, nor should it be. But Diaspora Jewry's wishes must be part of the decision-making premises upon which the policymakers arrive at their choices.

To some extent, this is already true. Israel does take account of the impact of its decisions upon the Diaspora. But there is no reason for the Diaspora not to play a more active role as well. Israelis ought to assume that they must answer to Diaspora Jewry in a far more critical sense than is true today. Israel must sense that Diaspora Jewry is concerned primarily with whether or not Israeli policies are in accord with the two major values upon which the State was created, which serve as the basis for Diaspora Jewry's attachment to it. Diaspora Jewry has a right to insist that its involvement in Israeli life, which Israel itself has invited, focus upon the expression of these two primary values. For example, Diaspora Jewry contributes funds to higher education in Israel; Diaspora Jews have a right to ask how higher education expresses the values of service to the Jewish people or creation of an ethically exemplary State. This very insistence on accountability to the Diaspora for the fulfillment of these values will serve to reinforce them in the Israeli consciousness. But there is also no reason for Diaspora Jewry not to undertake active educational and cultural programs in Israel along the same lines. There is no reason why Diaspora organizations ought not to initiate activities within Israel that reflect their own concerns with Judaism, Jews, and the ethical imperatives in, for example, Jewish-Arab relations.

The problem, of course, is that not only has Israel become

less faithful to the basic political values upon which it was founded, but the Diaspora does not stress these values in its image of Israel. Israel has become instrumental to the Diaspora as well as to Israel. Israel, as I suggested in earlier chapters, has become functional for Jewish survival in purely symbolic terms. Consequently, there is a tendency to reify the symbols and forget the instrumental intention of Israel's establishment. Furthermore, through its reward system, Israel, consciously or unconsciously, has promoted a leadership group that tends to accept Israel as it is, rather than Israel as it should be. An article in the Israeli daily *Ha'Aretz* made the point in the sharpest terms:

> For Israel, interested primarily in mobilizing contributions and political pressure, it is more comfortable to make arrangements with the Montors, Schwartzes and Friedmans [professional leaders, past and present, of the campaigns to mobilize funds for Israel in the United States] than with the Silvers, Klutznicks or Soloveitchiks [American Jewish leaders with significant constituencies, who have been critical of Israel despite their basic sympathy to the State]. For twenty years, the blessings of Ben-Gurion, Eshkol or Sapir became the certificate of legitimacy to community leadership.[14]

This may change. One hopes so. A new foundation for Israeli-Diaspora relations based upon criticism and self-criticism in the context of the mutually accepted values of Israeli society may cause greater discomfort, but in the last analysis will provide greater prospects for a long term relationship. Not only will this help maintain Israel's Jewish identity, but it should also bring the more sensitive spirits in Diaspora Jewry to Israel, to help insure that the State continues to express the kinds of values to which they are committed and to participate in the process of their expression. Finally, it will eliminate the dangerous dichotomy of universalism-particularism which, I have suggested, is destructive of Jewish identity. The Diaspora Jew's responsibility to Israel will now, in fact, also become his responsibility to see to it that Israel acts as a "light unto the nations." The Diaspora Jew will no longer have to balance his particularist Jewish obligations to Israel with the universalist ethical obligations to which he is also committed.

Most Jews in the Diaspora and in Israel do not feel this way about Israel or about Israeli-Diaspora relations. But this is no reason for those who share a different perspective and vision, in both Israel and the Diaspora, not to act.

Notes

CHAPTER ONE

1. Very little has been written on the subject of political relationships between Israel and the Diaspora. The one very excellent discussion of the topic that touches on a number of aspects also covered in this volume is the chapter "Israel and the Diaspora" in Ben Halpern, *The Idea of the Jewish State* (Cambridge, Mass.: Harvard University Press, 1961).

2. David Easton, *The Political System* (New York: Alfred A. Knopf, 1953), p. 129.

3. The full exchange of views is reported in Morris Fine, ed., *American Jewish Year Book 1952* (Philadelphia: Jewish Publication Society, 1952), p. 565.

4. S. Castro, "Current Status of European Jewry," Address to the International Conference of Jewish Communal Services, Amsterdam, August 17, 1972 (Paris: European Council of Jewish Community Services, 1972).

5. See, for example, Walter Eytan, *The First Ten Years: A Diplomatic History of Israel* (New York: Simon and Schuster, 1958), pp. 199–200.

6. See the discussion in this chapter and in the chapter on Foreign Policy.

7. *Natanel Lorch, Ha'Nahar Nalokhesh: Al Peru V'Yisrael* (Tel Aviv: Ministry of Defense, 1969), p. 132. Such experiences are commonplace in Latin America. See, for example, Michael Brecher, *The Foreign Policy System of Israel* (London: Oxford University Press, 1972), p. 241; but similar instances have occurred even in France. Yaacov Tsur, *Yoman Paris* (Tel Aviv: Am Oved, 1968), pp. 54–55.

8. Eytan, p. 193.

9. As a matter of fact Eytan relates that King George VI once

startled the chief rabbi of the Commonwealth by mentioning that he had the day before received "your Ambassador," meaning the Ambassador of Israel in London. *Ibid.*

10. *Ha'Aretz,* April 16, 1973, p. 9.

11. *Ibid.,* April 29, 1973, p. 2.

12. *The Economist* 183 (May 11, 1957): 498.

13. *New York Times,* Sept. 11, 1966, p. 4.

14. *American Jewish Year Book, 1952,* p. 567.

15. The question is discussed in Alex Bein, *Theodore Herzl,* trans. Maurice Samuel (Philadelphia: Jewish Publication Society, 1941), pp. 383–91.

16. *Ibid.,* p. 384.

17. *Ibid.,* p. 387.

18. *Ibid.,* pp. 387–88.

19. Herzl's testimony is instructive (Royal Commission on Alien Immigration, *Minutes of Evidence taken before the Royal Commission on Alien Immigration* [London: Wyman and Sons, 1903], 2: 211–21). Herzl reiterated his objection to restrictive immigration, but he did argue that increased immigration was inevitable because of Jewish persecution in Eastern Europe. He further argued that "if the number of immigrants grows, I think you will get anti-Semitic feeling" (p. 213) and that the two proposals to alleviate the situation, dispersing the immigrants in different parts of England or assimilating them, were morally wrong and impractical. Therefore, he argued, the only solution was to "divert the stream of immigration" (p. 212) to "a home . . . which will be legally recognized as Jewish" (p. 213). When he maintained that the charity presently distributed by English Jews to immigrants was also wasteful and that his advice to English Jewry would be to "unite your forces and find out the right place" he was asked:

Question: "Find out the right place for what?"
Answer: "For settling."
Question: "You want a system of settling, probably away from this country?"
Answer: "Yes." (p. 214)

Herzl testified honestly and judiciously. Nevertheless, the sum total of his testimony must have been of comfort to those who favored restricting immigration.

20. Raphael Patai, ed. *The Complete Diaries of Theodor Herzl,* trans. Harry Zohn, vol. 4 (New York: The Herzl Press 1960): 1562.

21. Bein, p. 448.

22. Patai, p. 1525.

23. *Ibid.,* p. 1526.

24. *Ibid.*

25. *Ibid.,* p. 1538.

26. World Jewish Congress, *Unity in Dispersion: A History of the*

World Jewish Congress (New York: World Jewish Congress, 1948), p. 17.

27. *Ibid.*, p. 15–16.

28. Moshe Gottlieb, "The Anti-Nazi Boycott Movement in the American Jewish Community, 1933–1941," Brandeis University doctoral dissertation, 1967). The Jewish agency at that time, while dominated by the World Zionist Organization, included some prominent non-Zionists as well.

29. *Ibid.*, p. 127.

30. *Ibid.*

31. Quoted in David Yisraeli, "The Third Reich and the Transfer Agreement," *Journal of Contemporary History*, 6, no. 2 (1971): 132.

32. *Ibid.*

33. Yigal Ilam, *Mavo L'Historia Tzionit Acheret* (Tel Aviv: Lewin-Epstein, 1972), p. 122.

34. *Ibid.*

35. *Ibid.*, p. 110.

36. Halpern, p. 47.

37. *Ibid.*, pp. 353–55.

38. Chaim Weizmann, *Trial and Error* (New York: Harper and Brothers, 1949), pp. 300–301.

39. Ilam, pp. 110–11.

40. Joseph B. Schechtman, "The Frozen Stampede," *Midstream* 6 (Summer 1960): 66–67.

41. *Ibid.*, p. 69.

42. *Ibid.*, p. 70.

43. *Session of the Zionist General Council, July 21–29, 1954* (Jerusalem: Organization Department of the Zionist Executive, n.d.), pp. 122–23.

44. *Ibid.*

45. *Session of the Zionist General Council, August 23–31, 1955* (Jerusalem: Organization Department of the Zionist Executive, n.d.), pp. 10–11. (Pages cited are from the Hebrew transcript.)

46. *Ibid.*, p. 50.

47. *The Twenty-Fourth Zionist Congress April 24–May 7, 1956* (Jerusalem: The World Zionist Organization, 1957), p. 447.

48. *Session of the Zionist General Council, August 23–31, 1955* (Hebrew version), pp. 43–44, 47.

49. *Ibid.*, p. 81.

50. *Ibid.*, p. 83.

51. Louis Shub, "The Diaspora Factor in Israel's Foreign Policy," *Judaism* 15 (Summer 1966): 293.

52. *Ibid.*, p. 295.

53. *Ha'Olam* (August 26, 1948), p. 669.

54. William Frankel, "The State of World Jewry," Address to the Annual Meeting of the American Jewish Committee, Waldorf Astoria, New York, May 16, 1971. (I am indebted to Mr. Frankel for a copy of the text of his address.)

CHAPTER TWO

1. This point has been made by a number of observers. See, for example, Ben Halpern, *The Idea of the Jewish State* (Cambridge: Harvard University Press, 1961), p. 242.

2. Milton Himmelfarb, "McGovern and the Jews," *Commentary* 54 (September 1972): 48.

3. Richard G. Hirsch, "Ordination address delivered at the Hebrew Union College-Jewish Institute of Religion," Cincinnati, June 3, 1972 (mimeo), p. 6A. I am grateful to Rabbi Hirsch for a copy of his address.

4. *COJO Report,* The Plenary Session of World Conference of Jewish Organizations, July 1971 (mimeo), p. 27.

5. Charles S. Liebman, *The Ambivalent American Jew* (Philadelphia: Jewish Publication Society, 1973), chap. 4.

6. Arnold Mandel, "The Jews in Western Europe Today," in Morris Fine and Milton Himmelfarb, eds., *American Jewish Year Book 1967* (Philadelphia: Jewish Publication Society, 1967), pp. 27–28.

7. Samuel Castro, "Current Status of European Jewry," Address to the International Conference of Jewish Communal Service, August 17, 1972 (Paris: European Council of Jewish Community Services [mimeo], 1972), p. 9.

8. Bernard Wasserstein, "Jewish Identification Among Students at Oxford," *The Jewish Journal of Sociology* 13 (December 1971): 150.

9. Allie Dubb, "The South African Jewish Student and His Jewishness," *Jewish Affairs* 25 (July 1970): 91.

10. Chaim Avni, *Yahadut Argentina* (Jerusalem: Hebrew University, Institute of Contemporary Jewry, 1972), p. 103.

11. "The Law of Status of the World Zionist Organisation-Jewish Agency for Israel, 1952," Sec. 5.

12. Michael Brecher, *The Foreign Policy System of Israel* (London: Oxford University Press, 1972), p. 573; based on Nadav Halevi and Ruth Klinov-Malul, *The Economic Development of Israel* (New York: Praeger, 1968), tables in Appendix.

13. David Krivine, "The Jewish Partnership in Israel's Industry," *The Jerusalem Post* "Weekend Magazine," October 24, 1969, p. 4.

14. Ministry of Finance, "Perut HaHachnasot MiMosdot V'Irgunim" (mimeo). In fact, over $250,000,000 was raised for Israel in the various United Jewish Appeal and other campaigns, but part of that money goes, for example, to payment of prior loans.

15. Fine and Himmelfarb, eds., *American Jewish Year Book 1971,* p. 189.

16. Avraham Barkai, "HaMashkia MiChul," *Al HaMishmar* (weekly supplement), August 8, 1972, p. 9. Barkai bases himself on *The Bank of Israel Report, 1971,* p. 65. The figure of $383 million

for Net Private Transfers also comes from Barkai, whose source is
the same report.
    17. Interview with Yeshayahu Stoper, Investment Authority, Min-
istry of Commerce and Industry, October 19, 1972.
    18. In preparation for the Economic Conference of May 1973, the
treasury department sent four pairs of representatives to the U.S.
and Europe

> to establish contacts with wealthy *Jewish* businessmen who have
> not yet invested in Israel and to persuade them to attend the
> Conference in Jerusalem. The job of persuasion in each locality
> will be done with the assistance of *Jewish* businessmen who
> already have business in the country. (*Ha Aretz* [October 16,
> 1972], p. 13; emphasis added).

    19. Barkai, citing the 1971 *Bank of Israel Report*.
    20. Israel Government Tourist Corporation, *Tourist Survey*
(Annual Report published by the Israel Government Tourist Corpora-
tion).
    21. *Ha'Aretz*, May 2, 1972, p. 6.
    22. *Ha'Aretz* "Weekly Supplement," May 12, 1972, p. 8.
    23. Brecher, p. 39.
    24. Israel Kolatt, "Changing Relations Between Israel and the
Diaspora." *Study Circle on Diaspora Jewry*, Series 6–7 (Jerusalem:
The Institute of Contemporary Jewry, The Hebrew University, 1968–
69), pp. 17–18.
    25. Elsewhere I have argued that whereas the proposition that
Israel is dependent on the Diaspora may be true, it is inappropriate
as the source for an ideology of interdependence. Charles S. Liebman,
"American Students in Israel and Israel-Diaspora Relations," *Unity
and Dispersion*, 12 (1971): 66–67.
    26. Figures for individual countries were gathered from *The
Jewish Communities of the World* (London: Institute of Jewish
Affairs, World Jewish Congress, 3d rev. ed., 1971).

CHAPTER THREE

    1. Interview with Yaacov Herzog, December 1970.
    2. On the basic divisions of American Orthodoxy, see Charles S.
Liebman, "Orthodoxy In American Jewish Life," Morris Fine and
Milton Himmelfarb, eds., *American Jewish Year Book* 1965 (Phil-
adelphia: Jewish Publication Society, 1965), pp. 21–97.
    3. In 1949 there were four religious parties: Mizrachi, Hapoel
Hamizrachi, Agudath Israel, and Poalei Agudath Israel. The four
parties offered a combined list of candidates in the first Knesset
elections under the name of the Religious Front.
    4. On the public effort by the Mizrachi, see Ha'Merkaz Ha'Olami
Shel Mizrachi, *Din V'Kheshbon 1949–1955* Jerusalem: Ha'Merkaz
Ha'Olami, 1955), pp. 65–66.

5 *Ha'Tzofe,* January 10, 1950, p. 4.

6. *Ibid,* January 23, 1950, p. 1.

7. *Ibid.,* February 7, 1950, p. 1.

8. *Din V'Kheshbon Shel Vaadat Ha'Khakira B'Inyenei Ha'Khinuch B'Makhanot Ha'Olim* (Jerusalem: n.p., May 9, 1950), p. 5.

9. *Ibid.*

10. *Ibid.,* p. 101.

11. *Ibid.,* p. 102.

12. *Ibid.,* p. 105.

13. *Ibid.,* p. 106.

14. *Ibid.,* p. 107.

15. *Ibid.,* pp. 104–5.

16. *Ibid.,* p. 11.

17. *Ibid.,* pp. 12–13.

18. *Ibid.,* pp. 13–14, 24–25.

19. *Ibid.,* pp. 111–12.

20. Ha'Merkaz Ha'Olami, p. 69.

21. At a meeting of the Merkaz Olami of Mizrachi, together with their Knesset representatives, in early December 1949, a motion to organize a public committee to assist the Religious Front in the education controversy was adopted. "Pressure and public opinion are liable to help us." *Bet Meir Archives* 31/1, Minutes of the Meeting of the Merkaz Olami, No. 23.

22. *Ibid.* Report of Leon Gellman, March 12, 1950.

23. *Ibid.,* 32/1. Letter from Leon Gellman to Israel Rosenberg, March 4, 1950.

24. *Bet Meir Archives.* Minutes of the meeting of the Merkaz Olami, No. 41, January 13, 1950. See also the remarks of Rabbi Zev Gold: "We must tell our friends there in America that they must carry on concentrated activity."

25. *Ibid.,* 32/1. Cable of January 22, 1950.

26. *Ha'Tzofe,* August 4, 1953, p. 2.

27. In December 1952, the Union informed the Merkaz Olami of its decision that religious ministers must resign from the government in the event of a government decision in favor of any form of national service for women. *Bet Meir Archives,* 32/1. Letter from Meir Cohen, executive director of the Union of Orthodox Rabbis, to the Merkaz Olami n.d.

28. According to the General Secretary of Agudath Israel of America, "Our organization was not as influential and well-organized in those days as we are today, and it, therefore, took a few months until the campaign gained momentum." Letter from Joseph Friedenson to the author, July 27, 1973.

29. In a letter from Leon Gellman to Pinchas Churgin of April 6, 1951, there is an implication that Churgin did not oppose the draft. *Bet Meir Archives,* 32/1.

30. *Ibid.* Letter from Mordecai Kirshblum to Bezalel Bazak, August 21, 1953.

31. *Ibid.*

32. *Ibid.* Letter from Mordecai Kirshblum to Bezalel Bazak, August 31, 1953.

33. For example, on December 29, Rabbi Zev Gold, a Mizrachi leader and a rabbinical figure known and respected in the Union of Orthodox Rabbi circles, cabled the Union asking them to postpone a meeting of rabbis that they had called to discuss the problems of religion in Israel with obvious reference to the National Service Law. He stated that such a meeting would be harmful to religious interests within Israel and to negotiations then taking place within the Government. *Ibid.*, cable from Zev Gold to the Union of Orthodox Rabbis, December 29, 1953.

34. See *Der Tog-Morgan Journal* and the *Forwards,* the two major Yiddish dailies in the U.S., of January 8, 1954, with interviews of Leon Gellman. Gellman, then visiting the U.S., noted that "during the 40 years I lived in the U.S., I never heard as many criticisms against Israel as I managed to hear now during eight weeks." In an information bulletin published by the Mercaz Olami for Mizrachi leaders throughout the world, the editors note that "Agudah is conducting a poisonous campaign in the Diaspora and especially in the U.S." *Bet Meir Archives,* 31/1, "Information to the Leaders of the Movement in the Diaspora," January 16, 1954.

35. The demonstration was discussed in all the Israeli papers and it received front-page coverage in the *New York Times* and *Herald Tribune.*

36. *Bet Meir Archives,* 32/1, quoted in a letter from Bezalel Bazak to Aaron Potashnik, March 24, 1954.

37. *Jewish Chronicle,* February 12, 1954, p. 1.

38. *Divrei HaKnesset,* February 14, 1954, pp. 922–23.

39. *Bet Meir Archives,* 31/1. The letter is reproduced in a mimeo memorandum intended for circulation to Mizrachi leaders in the Diaspora. The memorandum itself is dated February 16, 1954.

40. *Ibid.*

41. *Jewish Chronicle,* February 16, 1954, p. 32.

42. This is implied in a cable from a prominent New York Orthodox rabbi, Herbert Goldstein, to the Chief Rabbi. Goldstein takes the credit for averting the demonstration but one assumes that he cabled this information to the Chief Rabbi in response to the latter's request. *Bet Meir Archives,* 32/1, copy of cable from Herbert Goldstein to Herzog, n.d. Judging from the context, it must have been sent around February 15.

43. *Ibid.*, Letter from Bezalel Bazak to Mordecai Kirshblum, February 21, 1954.

44. *Ibid.*, 31/1.

45. *Ibid.*, 32/1. The *Archives* contain only a copy of the cable without a date. However, from a letter from Bazak to Kirshblum of April 10, 1954, it would appear that the cable was sent around April 7.

46. *Ha'Aretz,* May 15, 1963, p. 18.

47. *Ibid.,* May 27, 1963, p. 3.

48. *Bet Meir Archives,* 32/1. Letter from Yitzchak Goldschlag of the Mercaz Olami to Mordecai Kirshblum, June 12, 1963.

49. *Ibid.* Letter from Mordecai Kirshblum to Yitzchak Goldschlag, June 20, 1962.

50. *Maariv,* July 31, 1963, p. 1.

51. *Ha'Aretz,* August 19, 1963, p. 1.

52. *Ibid.,* August 28, 1963, p. 2.

53. *RCA Files.* Press Release on Zim Line, n.d.

54. *RCA Files.* Letter from the Chairman and Co-Chairman of the RCA Israel Commission to all members of the RCA concerning the *Shalom* issue, September 16, 1963.

55. *Bet Meir Archives,* 32/1. Letter from Mordecai Kirshblum to Bezalel Cohen, September 25, 1963. See also his letter to Prime Minister Levi Eshkol of November 19, 1963, where he notes that the *Shalom* issue has united all religious Jewry, from Neturei Karta to the religious Zionists.

56. For example, the Merkaz Olami cabled the American Mizrachi that Moshe Sharett, then Chairman of the Jewish Agency Executive, was coming to America and urged that a delegation of Mizrachi and the RCA meet with him on the *Shalom* matter. *Ibid.,* cable from Bezalel Cohen to Mordecai Kirshblum, November 28, 1963. Sharett subsequently expressed his objection to two kitchens. (See, for example, the statement found in Pinchas Ferber, ed., *L'Parashat Ha'Kashrut B'Oniyat Ha'Degel Ha'Yisraelit Shalom* (Tel Aviv: Information Department of the NRP, 1964), p. 41.

57. *Ha'Aretz,* December 23, 1963, p. 8.

58. Ferber, pp. 49–52.

59. *Bet Meir Archives,* 32/1. Letter from Joseph Dov Soloveitchik to Yitzchak Goldschlag. The date cannot be ascertained, but the letter was apparently mailed in December of 1963 or early in January of 1964.

60. On the efforts to "cool it," see, for example, the letters of Bezalel Cohen to Mordecai Kirshblum of December 27, 1963, and Kirshblum's letter to Yitzchak Goldschlag, December 30, 1963, and to Bezalel Cohen of January 3, 1964, all in *Bet Meir Archives,* 32/1. On January 1, 1964, Tel-Aviv Chief Rabbi and later Israeli Chief Rabbi Isar Yehuda Unterman denied that the Israeli rabbinate was issuing any threats or prohibitions of travel on Zim lines. *Ha'Aretz,* January 2, 1964, p. 5. As a matter of fact, Unterman upheld Nissim's "threat" to cancel all kashrut certification on Zim ships, but his tone was far more conciliatory than Nissim's and was an obvious effort to defuse the issue.

61. *Ha'Aretz,* January 8, 1964, p. 8.

62. On the rumor that the NRP had been ready for some compromise a year earlier, see *ibid,* February 28, 1964, p. 2.

63. *Ibid.*, January 8, 1964, p. 5.

64. *Ibid.*, February 28, 1964, p. 2.

65. *Ibid.*, January 8, 1964, p. 8.

66. *Ibid.*, p. 5.

67. *Ibid.*, February 7, 1964, p. 1.

68. Interviews with Moshe Kroneh, March 1972, and Avraham Harman, February 1971, and letter from Y. Giladi, July 22, 1973.

69. *Ha'Aretz*, February 28, 1964, p. 2.

70. On the background to appointment of the Committee, its recommendations, and the final proposal of the government to the Knesset, see Yitzchak Rafael, "Baayat Nitukhei Metim," *Givilin* 25 (September 1966): 69–79.

71. *Ha'Aretz*, June 29, 1965, p. 5 and December 12, 1965, p. 4.

72. Interview with Samson Weiss, executive director, and Joseph Karasick, president of the Union of Orthodox Jewish Congregations of America, January 1971, and Ephraim Sturm, executive vice-president of Young Israel, June 1972. Representatives of Rabbi Moses Feinstein and the Lubavitcher Rebbe also urged Young Israel to join the battle to amend the law.

73. In January 1967 Hershel Schachter, then president of the Religious Zionists of America, wrote to Bezalel Cohen, acting chairman of the Mercaz Olami, about the autopsy question:

> as loyal members of the Conference of Orthodox Presidents, it has been demanded of us, and will be demanded in the coming days to express an opinion, to sign notices to the press, etc., and . . . we will have to adopt a clear position. Therefore, we must receive full information as events develop . . . we never want to oppose a clear stand of our movement . . . but, since we have no other source of information, we receive our impressions from the press and even from *Ha'Tzofe* [the NRP daily] and may easily be deceived. (*Bet Meir Archives,* 32/1. Letter from Hershel Schachter to Bezalel Cohen, January 5, 1967.)

74. See, for example, *ibid.,* letter from Schachter to Minister of Religion Zerach Wahrhaftig, of April 11, 1967. Schachter wrote that the public views the Zionist camp as too compromising "and when a burning issue such as this *post mortem* arises, where the most moderate and even the various Reformists and secularists identify with the opposition to it, we lose our opportunity and possibility to appear before the general public as the brave fighters and defenders of values which have become sanctified to us." Schachter was responding to Wahrhaftig's letter to him of April 4, 1967, in which the minister of religion expressed his opposition to demonstrations and the use of threats by the NRP to leave the government.

75. Association of Orthodox Jewish Scientists, *Policy Statement* (mimeo) dated January 29, 1967. Material pertaining to the activity of the Jewish Scientists and the Union of Orthodox Jewish Congregations of America was provided by former UOJCA executive vice-

president Dr. Samson Weiss. This material is hereafter referred to as *UOJCA Files*. However, it should be clear that the material was selected by an official of the UOJCA, not by the author. Dr. Weiss did, however, claim that he provided *all* the material in the UOJCA files relating to efforts to influence Israeli policy.

76. *UOJCA Files*.

77. *Ibid.*, letters of February 8, 1967, April 18, 1967, October 16, 1968, and September 6, 1969. In the letter of April 18, for example, the UOJCA writes ". . . unless Hadassah will put its foot down and find the courage and backbone to stand up and insist on dramatic changes, we can look forward to a situation which will wreak havoc on all we deem sacred and significant."

78. Referred to in the UOJCA letter of April 18, 1967.

79. Interview with Joseph Friedenson, General Secretary of Agudath Israel of America, August 1972.

80. Conversation with Dr. Yitzchak Levi, pathologist at Hadassah Hospital, September 1971.

81. *Bet Meir Archives,* 32/1. Letter from Zerach Wahrhaftig to Hershel Schacter, April 4, 1967.

82. *Ibid.* Letter from Hershel Schachter to Bezalel Cohen, April 10, 1967.

83. The text of the cable is cited in *Inside Israel,* "The Recurrent Issue of Autopsies in Israel," a mimeographed sheet published by the American Jewish Committee in Israel, n.d. The story on the cable is reported in the *Tog-Morgen Journal,* April 7, 1967, p. 1.

84. *Bet Meir Archives,* 32/1. Letter from Hershel Schachter to Bezalel Cohen, April 10, 1967.

85. *Tog-Morgen Journal,* April 10, 1967, p. 1.

86. *Ibid.,* also April 7, 1967, p. 1.

87. Joseph Soloveitchik and Rafael Soloveitchik are cousins, but whereas the former, as noted, is the leading spiritual figure with whom the religious Zionists in the U.S. identify themselves, Rafael Soloveitchik is very much in the camp of Israeli non-Zionists.

88. *Tog-Morgen Journal,* April 11, 1967, p. 1.

89. *Ha'Aretz,* April 27, 1967, p. 7.

90. A delegation of the Rabbinical Council of America met with various parties to the dispute, including a group of Israeli doctors (interview with Israel Klavan, June 1972). The president of the UOJCA also met with Levi Eshkol (interview with Samson Weiss, January 1971), and the Orthodox Scientist wrote directly to him on May 5, 1967 (*UOJCA Files*).

91. A survey of events, including mention of the 1967 incident, is found in *Ha'Aretz,* June 29, 1969, p. 5.

92. *RCA Files*.

93. *Ha'Aretz,* June 29, 1969, p. 5.

94. *Ibid.,* June 13, 1969, p. 4.

95. Interview with Rabbi Simon Dolgin, March 1971. Rabbi Dolgin became Director General of the Ministry of Religion.

96. Interview with Rabbi Israel Klavin, June 1962.
97. Israel Information Services, *Background Note*, "Post Mortem Examinations in Israel" (Consulate General of Israel, New York City, June 1969).
98. *Ha'Aretz*, June 29, 1965, p. 5 and December 5, 1965, p. 4. At a meeting of hospital representatives in March 1968, opposition was expressed to any changes in the 1953 law. See Appendix A to *Gizat Ha'Zahav shel Mechkar Ha'Gviyot* (Jerusalem: Committee for Safeguarding Human Dignity, n.d.).
99. The following paragraphs, which serve as background to the discussion of the more recent controversy, are drawn from my article "Who Is Jewish in Israel?", *The American Zionist* 61 (Dec. 1970): 27–31.
100. The coverage in the American press was sufficient to arouse Orthodox leaders. They feared that any decision by Israel to recognize a distinction in Jewish identity between religion and *leom* would encourage intermarriage and eventual assimilation. It would legitimate the argument of a Jew that he could marry a non-Jew and there would be no need for the non-Jew to convert to Judaism since he or she might become Jewish by other criteria. It would also legitimate total dissociation from religious standards of behavior by one who might argue that he was still a good Jew by some other standard. Since even many secularists in Israel, not to mention religious leaders in the Diaspora, were of the opinion that the Jewish religion was the major barrier to assimilation, Israel's behavior was felt to be a contributory element to assimilation. (Interviews with Norman Lamm, December 1970, and Samson Weiss, January 1971).

Orthodox leaders in both the U.S. and Great Britain immediately cabled their dismay to Prime Minister Golda Meir at the Supreme Court decision and their hope that the Knesset would change the law (*UOJCA Files*). The Lubavitcher *Rebbe* (leader of the largest and best-organized worldwide movement of *hasidim* and a man of great importance even outside his own circle of followers) and Rabbi Joseph Soloveitchik also encouraged their supporters to act on behalf of a change in the law. Max Stern, an Orthodox Jew prominent in Jewish philanthropic circles, distributed articles to other Jewish philanthropic leaders on the need to amend the law, in the expectation that they would bring the matter to the attention of Israeli representatives and would indicate their support for a change in the law. (Interview with Norman Lamm. Lamm, a leading modern Orthodox rabbi and one of the outstanding intellectuals in the Orthodox rabbinate, believes that all of this activity had some impact. My own impression is different.)
101. Interview with Rabbi Ralph Simon (June 1973) and Rabbi Richard Hirsch (May 1972). Simon was present at the meeting in his capacity as the president of the organization of American Conservative rabbis, and Hirsch in his capacity as director of the Israel Commission of the international organization of Reform Judaism. A

local Reform rabbi, Tuvia Ben-Horin was also present at the meetings.
102. Kol is leader of the anticlerical Independent Liberal party.
Although a small party holding only four or five seats in the Knesset,
they are consistently members of the Coalition because their middle-
of-the-roadish, slightly Left-of-center views on most economic issues
are not far from those of the Labor party, and their anticlerical views
make them a convenient balance to the Labor party's other perennial
partner, the NRP.

103. According to one report, NRP leader Moshe Shapiro and the
minister of justice agreed that non-Orthodox conversions performed
within Israel would not be recognized (Benjamin Kreitman, "Who Is
a Jew?", *Conservative Judaism* 24 [Summer 1970]: 25). I do not
know Kreitman's source, but all the facts concerning the negotiations
preceding the submission of the bill to the Knesset indicate it must
be true.

104. Interview with NRP Knesset member Zevulun Hammer,
February 1970, immediately after the crucial Knesset vote.

105. Telephone interview with Rabbi Joseph Wilenkin, August
1962.

106. The ad appeared in the English-language daily and the two
afternoon dailies, which are also the two papers with the largest
circulation.

107. Newspaper clippings on the mass meetings, protests, and
texts of cables are taken from the *Religious Zionist Archives* in Mosad
Harav Kook, Folder No. 239. Page references to newspaper reports
were occasionally missing. Reports of various protest meetings
appeared in: *Jewish Press,* January 14, 1972, p. 2; *Forwards,* January
28, 1972, n.p.; *Forwards,* February 25, 1972, n.p.

108. Menachem Rubinsky, leader of Agudath Israel's youth
organization in the U.S. (interview, August 1972), claimed that his
associates organized a letter-writing campaign to *The Jerusalem Post,*
the Israeli English-language daily, as well as to the Anglo-Jewish
press. Joseph Friedenson of Agudath Israel (interview, August 1972)
also reported on the letter-writing campaign of his organization. The
Committee for Jewish Survival (interview with Joseph Wilenkin,
August 1972) claimed that his group was instrumental in sending
10,000 telegrams to the prime minister, and Rabbi Abraham Gross
(interview, August 1972), was also active in organizing a letter-
writing campaign to Israeli officials.

Among the letters written to the prime minister were a number
that asserted that unless the law were changed, both contributions
to Israel and *aliya* would suffer. (Copies of a number of letters were
supplied by the Israeli Committee to amend the law—Ha'tnuah
L'Maan Shlemut Ha'am. The Israeli Committee also succeeded in
obtaining a news story in *Maariv,* Israel's largest daily, describing the
content of some of the letters, (*Maariv,* December 19, 1971). One
letter, for example, stated:

Many of my congregants who have been contemplating Aliyah now have second thoughts, for they question whether the chances of their children marrying a Gentile will be increased in Israel since the Jew is no longer defined by traditional Halachic interpretation. To be honest, I am unable to respond to them without some misgivings and apprehension. . . . This past year we have raised over $260,000 in Israeli Bonds, and I find that more and more of my congregants are disturbed, disillusioned and angered by the possible results of a law that fails to recognize the traditional definition of a Jew.

Another letter was signed by both the rabbi of a congregation and the chairman of his congregation's Israel Bond drive. They wrote:

Religious leaders want *giyur ka-halakha* [conversion in accordance with Jewish law]. The Government of Israel has blurred this issue. This act of the government has made it difficult for us. We have just conducted our Yom Kippur Appeal. In view of the government's stand, some people refrained from participating . . . other synagogues and organizations are meeting the same problem.

The Lubavitcher *Rebbe* spoke and wrote continuously on the issue in a manner that sometimes bordered on hysteria. Egypt's war of attrition against Israel took place during this period and in a pamphlet distributed to his followers in Israel the *Rebbe* suggested that Israeli soldiers were dying along the Suez Canal because Israel had granted the status of Jew to those who were not authentically Jewish.

A petition to the government of Israel was signed by a number of English rabbis, though, significantly, not by Chief Rabbi Jacobovits.

109. Rabbis Moshe Feinstein and Yaakov Kamenetsky, leaders of the non-Zionist religious world, met with the Prime Minister to discuss this issue when she visited the U.S. (Interview with Joseph Friedenson, August 1972).

110. Four American rabbis met with the prime minister in Israel and presented her with a petition signed by over 1,000 American rabbis. Interestingly, they sought the interview through the intervention of the American embassy in Israel—an act that did not endear them to or increase respect for them in the eyes of the Israelis involved. (Interview with Eli Mizrachi, Assistant Director General of the Prime Minister's office, March 1972).

111. Interview with Rabbi Yehuda Feldi, leader of the Israeli Committee, March 1972, and Rabbi Abraham Gross, August 1972.

112. The Union of Orthodox Rabbis demanded that the NRP resign from the Government to protest the Government's definition of Who Is a Jew (*Jewish Press,* Nov. 19, 1971, p. 3 and March 3, 1972, p. 27; *Forwards,* May 23, 172, n.p.).

The Union of Orthodox Rabbis also organized a telegram campaign to pressure the NRP to leave the Government. They provided seven alternative texts of telegrams to be sent to Israel (*Religious Zionist Archives,* Folder No. 239).

113. Rabbi Moshe Feinstein addressed a public letter to the NRP, demanding that they "stand firm with all those who are faithful to Torah. . . . If they vote, G-d forbid, to recognize any other form of conversion, and even if they merely remain silent and abstain from voting, we shall be forced to completely condemn the National Religious Party in Israel" (*Jewish Press,* July 14, 1972, p. 10).

114. A leader of the Merkaz Olami, for example, reported that there was hardly a meeting that took place in the U.S. in which the NRP was not asked why it refused to obey the decisions of the chief rabbinate and did not either insist that the Law of Return be amended or else leave the Government. He noted that for the last half year an active campaign was conducted in the Diaspora against the NRP and its representatives in the Government (*Ha'Tzofe,* April 14, 1972, p. 1. *Maariv,* March 21, 1972, p. 2 reported on a series of demonstrations organized by the Committee for Jewish Survival against NRP Minister Burg, who, as we shall see, was sent to the U.S. to explain the NRP position).

115. For example, see *Ha'Aretz,* June 6, 1972, p. 3, and August 3, 1972, p. 3.

116. *Jewish Press,* April 7, 1972, p. 23.

117. Interview with Ephraim Sturm, August 1972.

118. Interview with Richard Hirsch, May 1972.

119. *Statement Opposing Revision In the Law of Return* (mimeo), April 1972. I am indebted to the Rabbinical Assembly of America for providing me with a copy of the *Statement.* There was some opposition to the statement within the Conservative movement. Interviews with Rabbis Richard Hirsch (May 1972) and Rabbi Bernard Segal (August 1972). The latter, executive director of the Conservative Synagogue organization, felt that his movement had no objection to amending the law to provide that conversions must be in accordance with Jewish law. He objected only to this phrase as a political instrument to exclude non-Orthodox rabbis. Those conversions performed by Conservative rabbis in accordance with Jewish law should be validated, he felt, while all others would be invalid. Bernard Mandelbaum, past president of the Jewish Theological Seminary of America, also represents the traditionalist wing within Conservative Judaism. In a letter to *The Jerusalem Post,* July 1972, he wrote of the "tragic" fact that the Conservative movement had joined hands with the Reform movement. "In a matter of this importance in defining 'Who is a Jew' the Conservative Movement stands for the *halachic* position, in contrast to the Reform Movement." However, the views of Mandelbaum and Segal are no longer representative of even the leadership, much less the rank and file of the Conservative movement.

120. *Ha'Tzofe,* April 14, 1972, p. 1.

121. Interview with Moshe Kroneh, March 1972. The NRP counterattack did meet with some success. The Religious Zionists of

America issued an elaborate defense of the NRP's position in a press release dated July 13, 1972, in which they explained why that party refused to support Agudath Israel's amendment. The president of the Rabbinical Council of America also defended the NRP against detractors, a defense that ultimately involved him in a rather harsh exchange with the Young Israel.

122. Interview with Moshe Kroneh.

123. See, for example, the ad in *Ha'Aretz,* June 29, 1973, p. 3, including an attack on Burg, signed by the Committee for Jewish Survival.

124. For example, one prominent American Orthodox rabbi noted that former NRY leader Moshe Shapiro would call the president of the Rabbinical Council of America (RCA) or Rabbi Soloveitchik and ask for help. Rabbi Soloveitchik would ask the RCA executive director to convene the organisation's Israel Commission, which theoretically determines the organisation's policy but like all other RCA organs is very much under Rabbi Soloveitchik's influence (Interview with Emanuel Rackman, April 1971). According to another leading American Orthodox rabbi, cables from Israel would give American Orthodoxy a signal as to the seriousness of the issue. "We count cables and look at the names of the signers." Key signators would be NRP leaders or the chief rabbis. Cable recipients were Rabbi Soloveitchik, other heads of American Yeshivot, and the leadership of the RCA and the UOJCA; generally a consensus among Orthodox organizations would develop around whether or not to enter the conflict, but Rabbi Soloveitchik's opinion was often critical (Interview with Norman Lamm, December 1970). Individuals such as the Lubavitcher *Rebbe* or Rabbi Moshe Feinstein, a leader within the nonreligious Zionist world, could also influence the religious Zionist groups. The non-Zionists are influenced by the Israeli Yeshiva world (Interview with Ephraim Sturm, June 1972).

125. Interview with Rabbi Israel Klavan, June 1972.

126. A number of respondents volunteered this term.

127. On occasion Israeli religious politicians even invited American Orthodoxy to extend its pressure to internal party matters as well. *Bet Meir Archives,* 32/1 contain cables and letters from 1950 and 1963 in this regard.

128. Interview with Eli Mizrachi, March 1972. A leader of an Orthodox organization noted that his group sent cables on every issue. He termed it "an exercise in futility" besides being "very expensive."

129. Interview with Emanuel Rackman, April 1971.

130. Interview with Yaacov Herzog, December 1970.

131. Interview with former Israeli consul Chaim Zohar, October 1970.

132. Interview with Rabbi Stanley Wagner, executive vice-president of the RZA, August 1972.

133. Interview with Avraham Avichei, November 1970.

134. Interview with Ephraim Sturm, June 1972.

135. Interview with Avraham Harmon, February 1971.

136. American Jewish Committee, *In Vigilant Brotherhood* (New York: Institute of Human Relations, n.d.), pp. 50–51.

137. Interview with the former Israeli Ambassador to France, Yaacov Tsur, July 1971. See also Yaacov Tsur, *Yoman Paris* (Tel Aviv: Am Oved, 1968), p. 92.

138. The respondent asked that he not be quoted. His information was firsthand.

139. For example, former Jewish Theological Seminary leader Louis Finkelstein, the preeminent leader of Conservative Judaism until his retirement in 1971, objected to mixed seating of the sexes in Conservative synagogues in Israel.

140. Rabbinical Assembly of America, *Proceedings of the Rabbinical Assembly,* 1964 (New York: Rabbinical Assembly of America, 1964), p. 97.

141. *Ha'Aretz,* June 2, 1963, p. 3.

142. For the background of the case and presentation of the Orthodox point of view, see *Maariv,* Feb. 2, 1964, p. 3.

143. *The Jerusalem Post,* Feb. 17, 1964, p. 6.

144. *Marriv,* Feb. 20, 1964, p. 1 and Rabbinical Assembly.

145. Letter from Rabbi Wolfe Kelman to the author, May 18, 1973.

146. In 1964 they issued a joint statement with them opposing constraints on missionary activity (in fact, the statement was drafted by a Conservative leader), but this did not involve the status of Conservative and Reform Judaism in Israel. The statement was also signed by Jewish secular organizations in the U.S.

147. *Ha'Aretz,* October 1, 1968, p. 15. The demands are quoted in "A Statement to the Prime Minister of Israel" on the occasion of the Convention of the Central Conference of American Rabbis, Jerusalem, March 10, 1970.

148. The details of the incident that follows were related by Rabbi Ezra Spicehandler, in an interview, May 1972.

149. Interview with Ezra Spicehandler.

CHAPTER FOUR

1. On the recognition of the AJC importance, see Abba Eban's remarks in Foreign Office, *Kinus Tzivey Yisrael, July 17–23, 1950* (Jerusalem: Foreign Office [mimeo], 1950), p. 78.

2. *Encyclopedia Judaica,* 10: 27.

3. Naomi W. Cohen, *Not Free to Desist: The American Jewish Committee 1906–1960* (Philadelphia: Jewish Publication Society, 1972), p. 294.

4. *Ibid.*

5. *Ibid.,* pp. 298ff. and Nahum Goldmann, *The Autobiography*

of Nahum Goldmann: Sixty Years of Jewish Life (New York: Holt, Rinehart and Winston, 1969), pp. 234–35.

6. Irving Engel, "Report of the Executive Committee: Highlights of 1949," Morris Fine, ed., *American Jewish Year Book 1951* (Philadelphia: Jewish Publication Society, 1951), p. 527.

7. *AJC Files,* Executive Committee Meeting—Minutes, October 16–17, 1948.

8. "The Report of the Executive Committee of the American Jewish Committee," *American Jewish Year Book 1950,* p. 554.

9. *Ibid.*

10. Engel, p. 528, and *AJC Files, Executive Committee Meetings,* May 7–8, 1949.

11. *AJC Files,* Executive Committee Meeting—Minutes, May 7–8, 1949.

12. *Ibid.* Administrative Committee Meeting—Minutes, Oct. 4, 1949.

13. *Ibid.*

14. *Ibid.* Letter from Joseph M. Proskauer to Ben-Gurion, Oct. 5, 1949. (The letter was not written on AJC letterhead.)

15. *Ibid.* Executive Committee Meeting, October 22–23, 1949.

16. *Ibid.,* Mike Shulman, "American Jewish Committee Blackmails Israel, AJC Leader Charges," *Jewish Weekly Times,* April 6, 1950.

17. *Ibid.,* Executive Committee Meeting—Minutes, April 29–30, 1950.

18. *Ibid.,* Letter from Jacob Blaustein to AJC Members, May 26, 1950.

19. Foreign Office, pp. 78–79.

20. Cohen, pp. 311–12.

21. The full "exchange of views" is found in *American Jewish Year Book 1952,* pp. 564–68.

22. *Ibid.*

23. *AJC Files.* Letter from Simon Segal to Dr. John Slawson, August 23, 1950.

24. Twenty-Third World Zionist Congress (1951), *Stenographic Report* (Hebrew) (Jerusalem: Zionist Executive, 1951), p. 17.

25. *Sessions of the Zionist General Council, May 7–15, 1952* (Jerusalem: Jewish Agency, n.d.), p. 11.

26. *Ibid.*

27. *Ibid.,* p. 72.

28. *AJC Files,* Letter from John Slawson to Herbert Ehrman, Feb. 29, 1960.

29. *Ibid.,* letter from Jacob Blaustein to David Ben-Gurion, Dec. 5, 1960, marked "Personal and Confidential."

30. *Ibid.,* memorandum to the Executive Board, Dec. 19, 1960.

31. Cohen, p. 314.

32. *Ibid.*

33. *AJC Files.* Message conveyed by Harman on behalf of Ben-Gurion to Jacob Blaustein, Jan. 17, 1961.

34. The American Jewish Committee, *In Vigilant Brotherhood* (New York: Institute of Human Relations, n.d.). The full text is found on pages 69–70.

35. *Ibid.*

36. *Ibid.*

37. *Ibid.*, p. 59.

38. Quoted in Bertram Gold, "Who Speaks for the Jews?". text of an address delivered to the 1972 annual AJC meeting in New York City.

39. The incident is reported in World Jewish Congress, *Press Survey*, No. 3444 (Oct. 27, 1972) in an item from the Oct. 26, 1972, issue of the *Jerusalem Post.*

40. The JA, when first organized in 1929, included non-Zionists, but they had ceased their participation by the beginning of World War II. In the period under discussion the WZO and the JA were, therefore, the same organization and the JA executive was the WZO executive. During this period, the JA executive was divided into an American section, located in New York, under the chairmanship of Nahum Goldmann, and a Jerusalem section under the chairmanship of Berl Locker. Since there was no president of the WZO at the time (Goldmann was elected to the office in 1956), Locker and Goldmann were the two formal leaders of the WZO. In 1970 the JA was reorganized and a number of major structural changes separating the JA and the WZO took place. These are discussed in chapter 6.

41. In responding to a draft Status Law that the Government had prepared as early as April 1951, Dr. Joshua Freudenheim, legal adviser to the JA executive, contrasted the Government draft with his own and found the former less adequate. He noted that the Government draft conferred authority on the WZO in limited spheres only, and thereby distorted "the primary aim of the granting of legal status, to raise the prestige of the WZO relative to other bodies operating in the Jewish world and to expand its influence and power of attraction." *Zionist Archives*, S5/T1125, "Notes on the Government's Proposed Law Concerning the World Zionist Organization."

42. There were also Israeli non-Zionists such as the representatives of the Communist party and Agudat Israel who voiced their position on these issues. Both adopted distinctive positions stemming partly from their ideology but more immediately from the fact that they were not represented within the WZO. Their weight was so slight that I have chosen to ignore them.

43. *Ha'Artez*, May 16, 1950, pp. 1–2.

44. *Ibid.*, May 18, 1950, p. 2.

45. *Divrei HaKnesset*, May 6, 1952, p. 1924 and Nov. 5, 1952, p. 60.

46. These points are to be found in Ben-Gurion's speeches before

the Zionist General Council session of April 1950 and reprinted in *Molad* 5 (May 1950): 67–76 and *Divrei HaKnesset*, May 5, 1952, pp. 1886–90; May 6, 1952, pp. 1919–27; and Nov. 5, 1952, pp. 56–61.

47. Ben-Gurion's objections are reflected in cables and correspondence between New York and Jerusalem in which, as one correspondent notes, ". . . the request for a State recognition has now become a matter of contention. *Zionist Archives* S5/T1125. But Ben-Gurion was unable to carry his own party, which supported a resolution more favorable to the WZO than a previous draft, which had been prepared at Ben-Gurion's request by the Ministry of Justice. According to Nahum Goldmann, in a decisive meeting of Mapai the party supported Goldmann's position in favor of a Status Law and insisted that Ben-Gurion withdraw his objection (Interview, October 1970).

48. *Ha'Aretz*, August 23, 1951, p. 1.

49. Twenty-Third World Zionist Congress, *Stenographic Report* (Jerusalem: Zionist Executive, 1951), pp. 143–44.

50. *Ibid.*, p. 59.

51. *Ibid.*, p. 95.

52. Goldmann, though not a member of the dominant Mapai party, was, in this period, closely identified with its policies.

53. The General Council, also known as the Actions Committee, is the supreme governing body of the WZO in the interval between World Zionist Congresses. At the 1950 meetings Goldmann said:

it is necessary to determine that Zionism represents organized Jewry, and that if others cooperate it can only be through this channel. Everything must go through the Zionist Movement as the sole authorized representative of the Jewish people in its work in Israel. *Sessions of the Zionist General Council, April 19–25, 1950* (Jerusalem: The Zionist Executive, 1950), p. 25.

54. *AJC Files,* Executive Committee Meeting, October 13–14, 1951. The minutes contain the text of Blaustein's letter to Ben-Gurion and a summary of the subsequent exchanges.

55. *Ibid.*

56. *Ibid.*

57. *Ibid.*

58. *Ibid.*

59. *Ibid.*, letter from Blaustein to Ben-Gurion, Oct. 30, 1951.

60. *Zionist Archives,* letter from Goldmann and Locker to Ben-Gurion Dec. 4, 1951.

61. *AJC Files,* letter from Jacob Blaustein to John Slawson, March 3, 1952.

62. *Ibid.*, letter from Jacob Blaustein to Abba Eban, March 3, 1952.

63. *Ibid.*, cable from Jacob Blaustein to David Ben-Gurion, March 3, 1952.

64. *Ibid.*, letter from Teddy Kollek to Jacob Blaustein, March 9, 1952.

65. *Ibid.*, letter from Graydon Snyder (on behalf of Blaustein) to John Slawson, March 13, 1952.

66. *Sessions of the Zionist General Council, May 7–15, 1952*, p. 123.

67. Morris Boukstein (interview, March 1973) believed that Ben-Gurion thought that Blaustein would join an expanded JA.

68. This explanation strikes me as the most reasonable one. Eliyahu Elath, Israeli Ambassador to the U.S. from 1948 to 1950, was also of the opinion that when Ben-Gurion spoke of an expanded JA he had U.S. Jewish Federation leaders in mind (interview with Elath, Feb. 19, 1973). On the other hand, it is possible that Ben-Gurion was closer to Goldmann's notion of including non-Zionist organizations rather than large contributors. In fact, the two possibilities are not mutually exclusive.

69. *Davar*, March 14, 1952, p. 1.

70. "Notes on the Government's Proposed Law. . . ."

71. *Divrei HaKnesset*, May 6, 1952, p. 1923.

72. *Ibid.*, p. 1925.

73. *Sessions of the Zionist General Council, May 7–15, 1952*, p. 18.

74. *Ibid.*, p. 124. He suggested, for example, that the Council seek to secure an amendment providing that the Government must consult with the JA executive before it undertakes any activity among Diaspora Jewry. *Zionist Archives* S5/T1125 ("Extracts from the Discussions of the Zionist General Council on the Status of the Zionist Organization").

It is difficult to explain Goldman's about-face other than by the possibility that he wished to protect his reputation for independence and defend himself against the charges that he had surrendered completely to Ben-Gurion. In any event, the Council appointed a subcommittee to formulate specific amendments to the Status Law as proposed by the Government in the Knesset. The subcommittee, in turn, did not request any amendment on the question of WZO "status" abroad. It did propose some minor technical changes. For present purposes, the only recommendation of interest was a very minor change in language softening somewhat the thrust of the recommendation within the Status Law itself for an expanded JA. That is, the Status Law itself could not expand the JA. It merely recommended it. What the Zionist General Council subcommittee did was to request that the language of the recommendation be softened to provide more flexibility to the WZO. In fact, the changes were minor. Indeed, if one had not been told to begin with that this was the intent of the subcommittee's recommendation, one could hardly deduce it from the actual wording.

(The various documents are found in the *Zionist Archives* S41/1321. In a letter dated May 26, 1952, from the Organization

Department of the Executive to Dr. I. Schwartzbart [*Zionist Archives*, S5/T1126] the writer says that the General Council proposed that the Knesset "delete its recommendation for an expanded JA in the Status Law." According to the author of the letter, whose name cannot be ascertained, "the committee of the Zionist General Council which dealt with this matter was not on the whole in favor of the proposition to enlarge the Jewish Agency through the joining of non-Zionists; some members rejected it outright, others did not like to have it, as it were, forced upon the Zionist Organization by the Government.")

However, as I have indicated, the General Council did not request the Knesset to delete this recommendation. It proposed changes that ostensibly softened the recommendation.

75. Committee chairman Moshe Unna downplayed the whole idea of an expanded JA. According to the chairman, "if the WZO decides to broaden its base, with the agreement of the Government" then the new body will benefit from the status now being conferred on the WZO (*Divrei HaKnesset*, August 11, 1952, p. 2866). The chairman's language suggested that the matter lie entirely in the hands of the WZO, which was under no pressure to make any structural changes whatsoever. The language of the bill, however, was more forthright.

76. *Ha'Aretz*, August 13, 1952, p. 1.

77. *Ibid.*

78. *AJC Files*, Executive Committee Meeting, October 25–26, 1952.

79. *Divrei HaKnesset*, November 4, 1952, pp. 24–25.

80. *Ibid.*, p. 44.

81. *Ha'Aretz*, November 26, 1952, p. 2.

82. Irving Engel, "Highlights of 1952"—Report of the AJC; Morris Fine, ed., *American Jewish Year Book, 1954*, p. 506.

83. *Ibid.*, p. 117.

84. Cited in *Encyclopedia Judaica*, 10: 1486. The rule that every Jew has the right to enter Israel as an *oleh* is qualified by health and public safety considerations.

85. *AJC Files*, letter from Jacob Blaustein to Moshe Sharett, January 8, 1955.

86. *AJC Files*, letter from David Ben-Gurion to Herbert Ehrmann, April 23, 1961.

87. The material in this section, unlike that of other sections, is based almost exclusively on personal interviews. I am especially indebted to three individuals whose advice and information were of primary importance: Dr. Shlomo Sitton, of the Ministry of Finance, Yeshayahu Stoper, Director of the Government of Israel Investment Authority, and David Golan, Managing Director of the First International Bank of Israel and former Director General of the Ministry of Commerce and Industry. Other individuals who were interviewed requested that their names not be mentioned. For this reason, sources for statements derived from personal interviews are not cited. Dr.

Sitton was also kind enough to review a preliminary draft of this section.

88. *Newsweek*, January 31, 1972, p. 51.
89. *Ibid.*, February 7, 1972, p. 4.
90. *Ha'Aretz*, April 16, 1972, p. 3; February 5, 1973, p. 12.

CHAPTER FIVE

1. A. A. Ben Asher (psuedonym of a former Israeli Ambassador), *YaKhasei Khutz* (Tel Aviv: Ayanot, 1957), p. 195. An excellent analysis of the problem with the conclusion that Israel's stress on *aliya* derived from its security needs is Ernest Stock, "Immigration as a Factor in Foreign Policy in the 1950's," paper delivered at the Fifth World Congress of Jewish Studies, Jerusalem, August 1969.
2. Ben Asher, p. 115.
3. In 1951 the Jewish Restitution Successor Organizations, composed of all major Jewish organizations that had been negotiating with Germany on behalf of Jewish claims other than those of the State of Israel, awaited Israel's decision for or against reparations before it concluded its negotiations with Germany. (See the speech by Foreign Minister Moshe Sharett to the Knesset in *Divrei HaKnesset*, January 9, 1952, p. 959 and *Davar*, January 4, 1952, p. 1.) Had Israel decided against reparations, other Jewish organizations might not have pressed their claims, or, pressing them, might have found Germany less disposed to pay the sums it eventually did pay.
4. It was clear to all that regardless of how Jews viewed the acceptance of reparations, acceptance of reparations helped cleanse Germany of Nazi guilt in the eyes of the world. An excellent discussion of this and the whole reparations question is found in Aryeh Rubinstein, "German Reparations In Retrospect," *Midstream* 8 (Winter 1962): 29–49. Rubinstein quotes Chancellor Adenauer, the day after the agreement was ratified by the Bundestag, as follows:

> The government is extraordinarily pleased about the ratification of the agreement, since it will be of great significance for future relations between Germany and the rest of the world. The prestige of the German people, which suffered through the Nazi chief's crimes against the Jews, will gain much in the eyes of the free world from this agreement. (p. 31)

5. Nicholas Balabkins, *West German Reparations to Israel* (New Brunswick, N.J.: Rutgers University Press, 1971), p. 86.
6. *Ibid.*, p. 92 and Michael Brecher, "Images, Process and Feedback in Foreign Policy: Israel's Decisions on German Reparations," *American Political Science Review* 67 (March 1973): 90.
7. N. Balabkins. A more extended discussion of Goldmann's role as a spokesman for Israel, which was not yet prepared to enter direct negotiations with Germany, is found in a book by a man who

subsequently led the Israeli reparations mission in Germany, P. Eliezer Shinar, *B'Ol Korakh V'Rigashot* (Tel Aviv: Schocken Publishing House, 1967).

8. Brecher, "Images, Process and Feedback. . . ."

9. This argument, directly or indirectly, and in various nuances is found in Sharett's speech to the Knesset as early as November 1951 (*Divrei HaKnesset*, November 4, 1951, p. 278) and during the torrid violent debates that shook the country in January 1952 when the Government proposal was placed before the Knesset. See, for example, *Davar*, January 1, 1952, p. 2. and January 3, 1952, p. 1. *Hador* (then the afternoon paper of Mapai), January 6, 1952, p. 1, and *Divrei HaKnesset*, January 7, 1952, p. 903; January 8, 1952, p. 922; January 9, 1952, p. 945, including the declarations of Prime Minister Ben-Gurion, January 7, 1952, pp. 895–97 and Foreign Minister Sharett, January 9, 1952, pp. 956–59.

10. Interview with Nahum Goldmann, October 1970.

11. Quoted in Michael Brecher, *The Foreign Policy System of Israel* (London: Oxford University Press, 1972), p. 110.

12. Foreign Office. *Kinus Tzirei Yisrael, July 17, 1950–July 23, 1950* (Jerusalem: Foreign Office (mimeo), n.d.), pp. 1–2.

13. Brecher, *The Foreign Policy System . . .* , p. 41; see also p. 43; Nadav Safran, *The U.S. and Israel* (Cambridge, Mass.: Harvard University Press, 1963), pp. 215, 221; and Joshua Gilboa, "Tkufat Gromyko V'Shichtuva," *Gesher* 38 (Winter 1968): 138.

14. *Divrei HaKnesset*, November 5, 1951, pp. 326–28. Ernest Stock, *Israel On the Road to Sinai* (Ithaca, N.Y.: Cornell University Press, 1967), p. 51 quotes Sharett in a similar statement.

15. Foreign Office, p. 29.

16. N. Safran, p. 214.

17. Brecher, *The Foreign Policy System . . .* , pp. 240–41.

18. The comment was made by Avraham Harman in an interview, February 1971.

19. *Ha'Aretz*, January 8, 1960, p. 1. The swastika incident is discussed in Brecher, *The Foreign Policy System . . .* , p. 237. The Foreign Office deliberately refrained from revealing the countries involved but they certainly included most western European countries, Argentina and the U.S. This can be ascertained from newspaper reports. See *Ha'Aretz*, January 8, 1960, p. 1; January 14, 1960, p. 3; and January 27, 1960, p. 3.

20. Naomi W. Cohen, *Not Free to Desist: The American Jewish Committee 1906–1966* (Philadelphia: Jewish Publication Society, 1972), p. 314.

21. Brecher, *The Foreign Policy System . . .* , p. 240. Brecher cites Eshkol to this effect and quotes Peres as saying ". . . if we would have thought that there was a basic danger to Argentine Jewry, we would not have taken Eichmann. We discussed carefully the probable effects on them."

22. *AJC Files*, Memorandum of October 24, 1960.

23. Interview with Nahum Goldmann, October 1970.

24. Interview with Yaacov Tsur, July 1971.

25. This is to be found in statements by the Prime Minister and Foreign Minister respectively before the Knesset, *Divrei HaKnesset*, November 27, 1961, pp. 449–50 and November 13, 1962, p. 138.

26. Henry Katzew, "Jews in the Land of Apartheid," *Midstream* 8 (December 1962): 73.

27. South African Jewish Board of Deputies, *Report: September 1960–August, 1962* (Johannesburg: South African Jewish Board of Deputies, 1962), p. 11.

28. *Ibid., September 1962—June 1965*, p. 6.

29. Katzew, p. 74.

30. Interview of Dr. Shimon Herman with Gustav Saron, Secretary of the South African Jewish Board of Deputies, Oral History Division, Institute of Contemporary Jewry, Hebrew University of Jerusalem, p. 57.

31. Katzew, pp. 74–75.

32. Quoted in Brecher, *The Foreign Policy System . . .* , p. 234.

33. *Ibid.*

34. Interview with Dr. Eliezer Yapo, former Israeli consul to South Africa, January 1971.

35. Interview with Binyamin Eliav, October 1970.

36. Interview with Natanel Lorch, formerly of the Foreign Office, January 1971.

37. Interview with Gideon Shimoni, February 1972.

38. Brecher, *The Foreign Policy System . . .* , p. 235.

39. Eliezer Schweid, *Israel At the Crossroads* (Philadelphia: Jewish Publication Society, 1973), p. 220.

40. The author was present at the time the incident was related.

41. *Ha'Aretz*, February 19, 1973, p. 2.

42. Ben Asher, p. 10.

43. *Ibid.*, pp. 170–79.

44. Letter to the author, March 4, 1973.

45. Interview with Yaacov Yanai of the Israeli Foreign Ministry, September 1971. Yanai's comments were well illustrated a year later. British M.P. Andrew Faulds delivered an anti-Israel speech in Parliament claiming that Palestinians under Israeli rule were subject to systematic oppression. In a sharp exchange that followed between Faulds and a Jewish M.P., he accused the latter of dual loyalty. In defending this statement he went on to attack the campaign in Britain on behalf of Soviet Jewry "organized and orchestrated by Israel and her friends." This brought a third M.P. to his feet, condemning Faulds for "an entirely unworthy smear." He denied that the campaign was orchestrated by Israel or by Jews, claiming "it was a humanitarian campaign supported by many who could agree with several of the things Mr. Faulds had said" (*Jewish Chronicle* [December 22, 1972], p. 8). The implications are clear. Even among those who oppose Israel's policy toward the Arabs are to be found some

who sympathize with the campaign on behalf of Soviet Jewry. The further Israel fades into the background in this campaign the better it will be for Soviet Jews.

46. Brecher, *The Foreign Policy System* . . . , p. 236
47. Cited in *ibid.*, p. 236.
48. *Ibid.*
49. Safran, p. 214.
50. Interview with Binyamin Eliav, October 1970.
51. *Jerusalem Post,* January 2, 1971, p. 9.
52. World Jewish Congress, *Press Survey* no. 3508 (July 10, 1973), p. 1.
53. Interview with Yaacov Yanai, September 1971.
54. *Divrei HaKnesset,* January 8, 1952, p. 932.
55. *Ibid.*, November 13, 1962, p. 129.
56. *Ibid.*, p. 137.
57. From a speech by Ben-Gurion to the Knesset in defense of reparations and cited by Shinar, p. 103.
58. Brecher, *The Foreign Policy System* . . . , p. 232.
59. Foreign Office, p. 65.
60. Brecher, *The Foreign Policy System* . . . , p. 232.
61. *Ibid.*, pp. 232–33.
62. Not only is a strong Diaspora important to Israel in a particular sense, but even the perception of close Diaspora-Israeli relations is an important political asset to Israel. Yaacov Tsur noted that, during his service as an Israeli Ambassador in both South America and France, he experienced the sensitivity of foreign governments to Jewish public opinion in the United States, which they considered an important factor in American policymaking. Israeli's importance in their eyes was enhanced by the fact that it was considered capable of influencing Jewish opinion and thereby influencing American foreign policy. Tsur reported that there were even indirect efforts in France to have Israel influence Kennedy when the latter, as Senator, attacked France's Algerian policy. According to Tsur, the power of American Jewry, real or imagined, is one of Israel's most important political assets even in its relations with countries other than the U.S. (Interview, July 1971.)
63. See, for example, "Israel's Argument with South Africa. A Test of Jews' Dual Loyalty," *Patterns of Prejudice* 5 (July–August 1971): 15–17. In the case of Western Jewry in general (South Africa to a lesser extent, the U.S. to a greater extent), listing the problem as one of "dual loyalty" is an oversimplification. American Jews, for example, are Americans. They are likely to support their country's foreign policy not so much because they are under "pressure" to do so, not even so much out of "loyalty" to their country, but because by and large (Vietnam being a notable exception) American policymakers and the American people (Jews included) share the same sense of right and wrong. American Jews favored Israeli withdrawal from Sinai in 1956, as we shall see, not because

Eisenhower and Dulles favored it, but because, like Eisenhower and Dulles, they had serious reservations about Israel's right to be there in the first place. This is not to deny, of course, that policymakers can to some extent influence the communications media, which in turn influence public opinion, or that Jews would find it awkward to support Israel against their own government even if they agreed with Israel. It is, however, important to understand that most Jews in Western countries respond to their own sense of right and wrong more than to "pressure" from any side. Israelis do not always appreciate this fact, nor do they understand (see n 68) that the ability of Western Jewry to influence their countries' policymakers rests, in part, on this fact. If, for example, American Jews or even South African Jews responded to policy questions in a radically different manner from the rest of the effective citizenry, their influence would be lessened. It is precisely because American Jews are Americans that their efforts at influence carry legitimacy. The Israeli (n 68) who made invidious comparisons between American and Polish Jewry forgot that Polish Jewry was ineffective in influencing Polish policy despite the fact that it was proportionately far more numerous.

64. Interview with Emmanuel Neumann, August 1970. Michael Bar Zohar, *The Armed Prophet: A Biography of Ben-Gurion* (London: Arthur Barker, 1967), p. 241, reports the incident as a request from Eisenhower, through Sherman Adams, that Silver convey a "message" to Ben-Gurion. However, if only a "message" was involved, it is difficult to understand why the mediation of the former Zionist leader was required. On the other hand, to think that Silver, even had he been willing, could have influenced Ben-Gurion, would be a stupid calculation. It would be hard to think of a Zionist leader less able to influence Ben-Gurion. The fact, however, that if one accepts Neumann's version, American policymakers in 1956 appear quite ignorant does not in my opinion make Neumann's story any less credible. In fact, it tends to support it.

65. Cohen, p. 323.

66. *Ibid.*, p. 324.

67. Interview with Nahum Goldmann, October 1970. Other sources for the activity of the Presidents' Conference in that period are interviews with Emmanuel Neumann, August 1970 and Yehuda Hellman (executive director of the Presidents' Conference), June 1972.

Bar Zohar reports the pressure somewhat differently: Goldman [*sic*], the president of the Jewish World Congress [*sic*] informed Ben Gurion that American Jewry had been most happy about the Sinai victory but would not stand behind Israel if she persisted in keeping the conquered territory; and he added that collections for the national Jewish funds might be forbidden. And Germany too, under American pressure, might stop paying reparations. (p. 250)

68. American Jews, and Zionists in particular, did come under sharp attack from Israeli Zionists at the meetings of the Zionist General Council in December 1956. Small Zionist General Council, *Summary of the Proceedings, December 11–12, 1956* (Jerusalem: World Zionist Organization, 1957). According to one speaker:

When the "dual loyalties" issues was put to the test for the first time, it immediately became clear that Zionism had suffered a reverse. . . . Dr. Goldmann has assured us that the Zionist Movement will stand firm behind the State, but with one reservation: if a conflict should arise between the Zionists in the Diaspora and the countries in which they live, he does not know what the outcome will be. Is this, then, the result of decades of Zionist education? (p. 39)

Another speaker said:

We must educate the Jews of America to have the strength and courage to speak out openly against their Government, as the Jews of Poland did at a time when they lived under far worse conditions, under a semi-facist regime. (p. 56)

69. Small Zionist General Council, pp. 10, 13. See also Zvi Lurie's remarks (p. 51).

70. Interview with Yaacov Tsur, July 1971. Of course, not all French, British or American Jews support Israel. I am discussing the organized community leaders who are in a position to pressure Israel precisely because they do represent their local Jewish communities in one form or another.

71. Brecher, *The Foreign Policy System* . . . , p. 144.

CHAPTER SIX

1. *AJC Files*, Mimeo Report of the American Jewish Committee, July 29, 1954.

2. *Ibid.*, memorandum from Irving Engel, December 2, 1957.

3. It is Goldmann's analysis that is being presented here. It is therefore perhaps gratuitous to point out that whereas I agree in general with his perception of the WZO–JA problem in the 1950s and 1960s, I do not believe that the organization of the WZO along party lines had much to do with its inability to attract more members, except in an indirect way.

4. The CJFWF (Council of Jewish Federation and Welfare Funds) is the roof organization of all the local Jewish Community Federation and Welfare Funds in the U.S. Since it is the local Jewish Federations and Welfare Funds (different communities use somewhat different names) that conduct the philanthropic campaigns for Israel as well as for local and other national needs, the leaders of the CJFWF are in fact the leaders of American Jewsh philanthropy.

5. Letter to the author from Nahum Goldmann, February 18, 1973.

6. In a letter of April 2, 1959 (*AJC Files*), an AJC official wrote to the Anglo-Jewish Association complaining that they were acting in an undignified manner and embarrassing other non-Zionist organizations by accepting membership in the JA.

7. The JDC shares (on a minority basis) with the UIA the funds collected from the United Jewish Appeal. Whereas the UIA was concerned exclusively with funding WZO–JA activity in Israel, the JDC supports educational, health, and welfare institutions all over the world, including some in Israel.

8. Interview with Philip Bernstein, executive vice-president of the CJFWF, March 1973.

9. Interview with Philip Bernstein. See also Zelig Chinitz, "Reconstitution of the Jewish Agency," *Jewish Frontier* 37 (December 1970): 7.

10. This last point was suggested by Zelig Chinitz, interview of September 1972.

11. The organization actually established in 1960 was the Jewish Agency for Israel Inc., an organization distinct from the Jewish Agency–American Section, which was the American Section of the Jewish Agency executive. In 1966 the UIA was formed by a merger of the Jewish Agency for Israel Inc. and the old Keren Hayesod United Israel Appeal, which by that time had become nothing more than a paper organization.

12. The NIA is controlled by a 210-member board of trustees and a 27-member board of directors. One hundred trustees are designated by American Zionist Organizations, one hundred by local community leaders (the CJFWF) and ten are elected at large. The trustees elect 21 of the 27-member board of directors and the remainder are designated by the American section of the JA. Thus, theoretically the Zionists have a majority control of the UIA. This, however, is purely theoretical, since the big contributors and fund-raisers are the non-Zionists whose money the UIA is designating. Therefore, no one is going to antagonize the non-Zionists. They, in turn, have been continually sympathetic to Israel's needs and the UIA itself does not divide along non-Zionist lines anymore than, as we shall see, does the reconstituted JA.

13. Interview with Zelig Chinitz, present UIA representative in Israel, September 1972.

14. On Sharett's role I am indebted to Moshe Rivlin, Director General of the JA, interview, July 1971.

15. *Session of the Zionist General Council, January 8–15, 1967* (Jerusalem: Organization Department of the Zionist Executive, 1967), pp. 15–16.

16. Ernest Stock, "The Reconstitution of the Jewish Agency: A Political Analysis," Morris Fine and Milton Himmelfarb, eds., *The American Jewish Year Book 1972* (Philadelphia: Jewish Publication Society, 1972), p. 187.

17. *Ibid.*

18. Letter from Ernest Stock to the author, April 27, 1972. Stock had personal knowledge of the events he describes.

19. Primarily in the fields of welfare, health, higher education, and the housing of immigrants. Interview with Moshe Rivlin, July 1971.

20. Interview with Philip Bernstein, March 1973.

21. In the early 1950s, Edward Warburg, then head of the UJA, told Nahum Goldmann, then chairman of the Jewish Agency Executive in New York, that he would resign if UJA funds were used to encourage immigration of American youth to Israel. Goldmann promised that such activities would be funded from WZO–JA income from non-American sources. See American Jewish Committee, Library of Jewish Information, *The Jewish Agency for Palestine* (New York: American Jewish Committee (mimeo), May 1957), p. 23.

22. Interview with Philip Bernstein, March 1973. The importance of tax considerations in the division of responsibility between the WZO and the JA is evident in the official *Agreement for the Reconstitution of the Jewish Agency for Israel.* Article 1, section D stipulates that "the functions and tasks and programs administered by the Agency or to which it may contribute funds, shall be only such as may be carried on by tax-exempt organizations."

23. *Proceedings of the Founding Assembly of the Reconstituted Jewish Agency* (Jerusalem: Jewish Agency, 1971), p. 81.

24. *Ibid.*

25. *Ibid.*

26. Louis Pincus, *The Jewish Agency in Action: A Report to the Members of the Jewish Agency Assembly* (Jerusalem: Jewish Agency, 1973), p. 37.

27. The Technical Advisory Committe on Housing of the Ministry of Housing and the Jewish Agency Committee on Housing, "A Progress Report," included in the binder *Annual Assembly,* prepared by the JA for the February 1973 Assembly meetings, p. 4.

28. "Jewish Agency Committee on Housing," in *The Jewish Agency Board of Governors* (Jerusalem: Jewish Agency, 1972), p. 2.

29. The Jewish Agency for Israel. "Higher Education," in *Annual Assembly,* pp. 213.

30. References to committee deliberations are from the author's notes taken during the meetings.

31. The *Jerusalem Post,* "Special Supplement," June 21, 1971, p. 11.

32. Furthermore, he might have added, a number of JA reports suggest that one reason the Government accepted so many of the Housing Committee recommendations is that these are recommendations that professionals with the Ministry of Housing had themselves favored.

33. Interview with Zelig Chinitz, September 1972.

34. Interview with Philip Bernstein, March 1973. A report on the 1972 Board of Governors meetings also suggested that fund-

raising leaders were seeking greater authority and the right to establish program priorities (*Ha'Aretz*, February 25, 1972), p. 14.

35. Another indirect consequence has been a weakening of WZO
status. Yehuda Peleg, Secretary General of Habonim, the Labour
Zionist Youth Organization (interview January 1973) expressed himself on consequences of the reconstitution of the JA for the WZO
in general and Zionist youth work in particular. With the separation
of the JA from the WZO, the latter lost its source of income. An
unwritten agreement at the time of the reorganization provided that
ten percent of the JA income should go to the WZO. (Since WZO
activity is not entitled to tax exemption under American law, it was
also understood that no money from the U.S. would be transferred
to the WZO). According to Peleg, this agreement limits the ability
of the WZO to expand or even carry on its existing activity in a
period of rapid inflation and rising costs. The fund-raising leaders,
according to Peleg, are not sympathetic to Zionist activity abroad,
but only they have the authority to increase the WZO budget. The
fund-raisers argue that the money that Diaspora Jews contribute is
intended for use in Israel, not for expenditure on Zionist activity
abroad. Peleg, and others like him, fear that if the Jewish "establishment" in the Diaspora is uncomfortable with Zionist calls for
emigration from Western countries, they can even cut into present
programs.

Zionist leaders, according to Peleg, increasingly feel that they are
playing in the "minor leagues." For example, he noted as did many
others, that whereas Government Ministers vied with each other to
be present at meetings of the Jewish Agency Assembly, their
absence is noticeable at sessions of the WZO General Council, which
follow the Assembly meetings. When Ministers travel abroad they
meet with fund-raisers and philanthropists, but have no time for
Zionists. (Golda Meir, he noted, was an exception to this rule.) In
Israel itself the public knows the names of the millionaires prominent
in the JA, but not the names of the leading Zionists. He was not
saying, he went on, that there was a deliberate intention to silence
Zionism, but "there is a tendency to support friends of Israel rather
than the Zionist movement."

36. I am relying on my conversations and interviews with a
number of delegates, primarily UIA people.

37. Cited in Zelig Chinitz.

38. *Proceedings of the Founding Assembly* . . . , p. 105.

CHAPTER SEVEN

1. Jewish Community Relations Council of San Francisco, "The
Four Jewish Issue Publics—First Report" (Jewish Community
Relations Council of San Francisco, mimeo, August 1970). See
especially p. 9.

2. Charles S. Liebman, *The Ambivalent American Jew: Politics,*

Religion and Family in American Jewish Life (Philadelphia: Jewish Publication Society, 1973).

3. Charles S. Liebman, "Reconstructionism in American Jewish Life," *American Jewish Year Book* 1970, ed. Morris Fine and Milton Himmelfarb (Philadelphia: Jewish Publication Society, 1970), pp. 3–99. Responses of respondents to questions about Israel and additional unpublished data were presented in Yeshayahu (Charles) Liebman, "The Role of Israel in the Ideology of American Jewry,' *Unity and Dispersion* 10 (Winter 1970): 19–26.

4. Marshall Sklare and Joseph Greenblum, *Jewish Identity on the Suburban Frontier* (New York: Basic Books, 1967), pp. 231–34.

5. Bernard Lazerwitz, "Some Jewish Reactions to the Six Day War," *Reconstructionist* 34 (Nov. 8, 1966): 23.

6. Doris Bensimon-Donat, "North-Africa Jews in France: Their Attitudes to Israel," *Dispersion and Unity* 10 (Winter 1970): 124–26.

7. *Ibid.*, p. 127.

8. This section reproduces the discussion in Charles S. Liebman, *The Ambivalent American Jew*, pp. 105–6.

9. For evidence that Orthodox Jews are more "religious" than non-Orthodox, see *ibid.*, pp. 142–43.

10. For an elaboration of this point see Yeshayahu (Charles) Liebman, "The Role . . . ," pp. 19–26.

11. The story is quoted from *Judaism for the Modern Age* in Samuel Halperin, "Zionist Counterpropaganda: The Case of the American Council for Judaism," *Southwestern Social Science Quarterly* 41 (March 1961): 454–55.

12. *Ibid.*, p. 455.

13. Eliezer Whartman, "Attitudes of American Rabbis on Zionism and Israel," *Jewish Social Studies.* 17 (April 1955): 121–32.

14. See n3.

15. In December 1971, Israeli prime minister Mrs. Golda Meir visited the United States. She was greeted in New York by thousands of zealots, followers of the Satmar Rebbe, carrying signs and demonstrating against "religious persecution in Israel." Previous efforts to intercede with the Satmar Rebbe to have him cancel the demonstration were of no avail. According to his spokesman: "Today when we receive telephone calls from Jerusalem (from followers of the Satmar Rebbe in Israel) we don't hear words, only the sounds of crying. The giants of Torah, public figures, phoned us and they literally cried and beseeched us to help them. These tears are shocking and painful and bring us to the conclusion that there is no course other than demonstrations. If such demonstrations are not wanted, then more understanding must be shown to the demands of the pious (literally "fearful") in the Land of Israel. We cannot abandon this group. We represent their last support. . . ." Quoted in *Panim El Panim* (December 24, 1971), p. 7.

16. *New York Times,* Nov. 24, 1969, p. 14.

17. Interview with Gus Saron, Secretary of the South African

Board of Deputies, August 4, 1961, pp. 33–35. (Oral History Division, Institute of Contemporary Jewry, Hebrew University.)

18. *Ha'Olam*, September 2, 1948, p. 679.

19. See the *23rd World Zionist Congress, 1951 Stenographic Report* (Jerusalem: Zionist Executive, 1951).

20. *Ibid.*, pp. 166–67.

21. *Jerusalem Post Supplement*, January 17, 1969, p. 6.

22. The system whereby Israel was given double the amount of representation it would otherwise be entitled to in the selection of delegates to the World Zionist Congress.

23. *Session of the Zionist General Council*, July 21–29, 1954, p. 189.

24. *Ibid.*, p. 166.

25. *Ibid.*, p. 167.

26. *Ibid.*, p. 163.

27. *Ibid.*

CHAPTER EIGHT

1. Since *Israel* refers to a political entity established in 1948, and the literature and activity described in this chapter often precedes 1948, the country will be referred to by its traditional appelation, *Eretz Yisrael,* the Land of Israel. The term *Palestine* is eschewed because in contemporary usage it signifies a territory or refers to a people other than Israel and Israelis. In point of fact, Palestine up until 1948 was called in Hebrew *Eretz Yisrael.*

2. On Dubnow, see Simon Dubnow, *Nationalism and History* (Cleveland, Ohio: Meridian Books, The World Publishing Co., 1958), pp. 158, 162, and 168. For similar notions in Ahad Ha'am, see Ahad Ha'am, *Al Parashat Derakhim* (Tel Aviv: Dvir, 1952), 2: 9–12, 133.

3. Ahad Ha'am, *Al Parashat . . .* , p. 19.

4. *Ibid.*, p. 29.

5. *Ibid.*, p. 294.

6. This statement was published as the program of *Die Welt,* the Zionist newspaper established by Herzl. The phrase, in one form or another, is found a number of times in Herzl's writings, beginning at least as early as 1896. Binyamin Herzl, *Bifnei Am V'Olam: Zionist Speeches and Articles* (Jerusalem: The Zionist Library, 1961), 1: 10, 57, 192, and 321.

7. *Ibid.*, pp. 35, 192, 321, 341.

8. *Ibid.*, 2: 85.

9. *Ibid.*, p. 285.

10. On the influence of Brenner and Gordon, see Israel Kolatt, "Theories on Israel Nationalism," *Dispersion and Unity* 7 (Winter 1967): 13–50.

11. *Ibid.*, p. 29.

12. Quoted in selections from Brenner in Arthur Hertzberg, *The Zionist Idea* (Garden City, N.Y.: Doubleday and Co., 1959), p. 312.

13. Kolatt, p. 29.

14. *Ibid.*, p. 33.

15. *Hertzberg*, p. 375.

16. *Ibid.*, p. 377.

17. *Ibid.*

18. *Ibid.*, p. 382.

19. *Ibid.*

20. Walter Laqueur, *A History of Zionism* (London: Weidenfeld and Nicolson, 1972), p. 313.

21. *Kitvei Berl Katznelson* (Tel Aviv: The Workers Party of Israel, 1946), 2: 83.

22. *Ibid.*

23. *Ibid.*, p. 88.

24. *Ibid.*, pp. 89, 97; 3: 262.

25. *Ibid.*, 1: 317.

26. *Ibid.*, 5: 352.

27. *Ibid.*, 7: 380. See also 6: 285.

28. Raphael Patai, ed., *Encyclopedia of Zionism and Israel* (New York: Herzl Press, McGraw Hill, 1971), p. 119.

29. The speech is reprinted in *Molad* 5 (May 1950): 67–76.

30. One should add that Ben-Gurion was not always consistent. He addressed himself to many of the same problems over a period of more than sixty years. It would be remarkable indeed, and hardly to his credit, if he never changed his mind. In addition, however, his official role as chairman of the Jewish Agency Executive, but more especially as Prime Minister, exposed him to severe pressures in defining Israel-Diaspora relations that would satisfy the international community, world Jewry, and also guard Diaspora Jewry against charges of dual loyalties. One has the impression that some of Ben-Gurion's statements do not always reflect his true sentiments. Since the present concern, however, is with Ben-Gurion's influence over Israeli leaders, I will focus attention on those ideas which recur in his writings, that are addressed to an audience that includes, at least in part, Israelis, and that form a consistent part of a general philosophy or approach to Israel-Diaspora relations.

31. David Ben-Gurion, "The Call of Spirit in Israel," State of Israel, *Government Year Book 5712* (1951–52), p. ix.

32. David Ben-Gurion, *M'dinat Yisrael Ha'Mkhudeshet* (Tel Aviv: Am Oved, 1969), 1: 61. Berl Katznelson expressed himself in a similar vein in 1941. See the quotation in Yigal Ilam, *Mavo L'Historia Zionit Acheret* (Tel Aviv: Lewin-Epstein, 1972), p. 149.

33. Ben-Gurion, *M'dinat* . . . , pp. 706–7; *idem, Khazon V'Derekh* (Tel Aviv, The Workers Party of Israel, 1951), 1: 120; (1953), 3: 152; (1957), 5: 48; and *idem, BaMa'arakha* (Tel Aviv: Am Oved, 1947), 1: 281.

34. David Ben-Gurion, "Israel and the Diaspora," State of Israel, *Israel Government Year Book 1957*, pp. 31–32.

35. David Ben-Gurion, *Netzakh Yisrael* (Tel Aviv: Ayanot, 1964), p. 59.

36. *Ibid.*, p. 177.

37. *Ibid.*, p. 230. See also *Khazon V'Derekh*, 5: 60, and "Israel and the Diaspora," p. 25.

38. David Ben-Gurion, "Israel's Security and Her International Position," State of Israel, *Israel Government Year Book 5720* (1959–1960), p. 22.

39. David Ben-Gurion, "M'dinat Yisrael V'Atido shel Ha'Am," *Hazot* 4 (1958).

40. Ben-Gurion, "Israel's Security . . . Position," p. 83.

41. Ben-Gurion, "M'dinat . . . Ha'Am," p. 10, and *Netzah Israel*, p. 230.

42. Ben-Gurion, "Israel and the Diaspora," p. 35.

43. *Ibid.*

44. Maurice Samuel, "The Sundering of Israel and American Jewry," *Commentary* 16 (September 1953): 200.

45. Maurice Samuel, "Why Israel Misunderstands American Jewry," *Commentary* 16 (October 1953): 310.

46. David Ben-Gurion, *Khazvon V'Derekh*, 3: 156.

47. *Ibid.*

48. *Ibid.*, 1: 120.

49. Ben Gurion, *Netzakh Yisrael*, p. 178.

50. *Ibid.*, pp. 178–79, 180–81.

51. Ben-Gurion, *M'dinat Yisrael Ha'Mkhudeshet*, pp. 308–9.

52. David Ben-Gurion, *Khazon V'Derekh*, 1: 297.

53. Ben-Gurion, *BaMa'arakha*, 1: 296.

54. Quoted from an interview by the author with Ben-Gurion in Michael Brecher, *The Foreign Policy System of Israel* (London: Oxford University Press, 1972), p. 232.

55. David Ben-Gurion, "Israel's Security . . . Position," p. 81.

56. Moshe Sharett, "Ha'Medina Ha'Yehudit Vha'Am Ha'Yehudi," n.d., reprinted in *Am Yisrael U'Tfutzotav* 7 (pamphlet series published by the Office of Information of the World Zionist Organisation, Jerusalem, 1970): 2.

57. *Ibid.*, p. 3.

58. *Ibid.*

59. *Jewish Observer and Middle East Review* 16 (March 3, 1967): 10. The case in question involved the secret trial and sentence to one-year imprisonment of two editors of *Bul*, an Israeli weekly of a sensationalist nature. The editors were acused of violating security regulations by publishing an article that charged that Israeli officials had concealed Israeli involvement in the 1965 kidnaping of a Moroccan nationalist leader.

60. *Ibid.*, p. 3.

61. *The Times*, March 9, 1967, p. 1; March 19, 1967, p. 12; March 11, 1967, p. 1; and the *Jewish Observer and Middle East Review* 16 (March 17, 1967): 1–2, 4–6.

62. *Jewish Observer and Middle East Review* 16 (March 17, 1963): 3. Eshkol himself acknowledged this in Knesset debate. See *Divrei HaKnesset*, March 20, 1968, p. 1752.

63. Also of interest is the fact that the Zionist Federation of Britain was equally anxious to remove the stigma of charges that it had sought to influence Israeli policies.

64. *Divrei HaKnesset*.

CHAPTER NINE

1. Interview with Binyamin Eliav, October 1970.

2. Interview with Nahum Goldmann, October 1970.

3. Interview with Yoav Biran, Office of the Foreign Minister's Adviser for Diaspora Affairs, November 1970.

4. Interview with Yaacov Tsur, former foreign affairs official and ambassador, July 1971.

5. For example, Guy de Rothschild, president of the French *Fonds Social Juif Unifie*, charged that French Jewry gave too much money to Israel which reduced the local Jewish community to a "distress budget." He insisted and obtained a redistribution of income from the United Jewish Appeal campaign in France (*Jewish Chronicle*, December 15, 1972, p. 4).

Bert Gold, executive director of the American Jewish Committee, lamented that American Jews provided funds for social and education programs in Israel while the same needs are neglected in the U.S. "Who is it that determines it is more important to provide funds for higher education in Israel than funds for Jewish education in the United States?" Gold was quoted as saying (*Jewish Chronicle*, February 9, 1973, p.4).

6. An article in the *Jewish Chronicle*, February 3, 1973, p. 4, cites "many American Jews, who opposed the war [in Vietnam and] objected to Israel promoting the view that an American retreat from Vietnam would imply a renunciation by the U.S.A. of the use of power on behalf of a distant ally and might, in turn, lead to an abandonment of Israel."

In his speech to the world executive meetings of the World Jewish Congress, Dr. Joachim Prinz criticized Israeli interference or pressure on American Jews to moderate their opposition to American policy in Vietnam and their suggestion that American Jews should support Nixon in the 1972 presidential campaign (World Jewish Congress, *Record of the Evening Session*, July 1, 1973).

7. Rabbi Gerson Cohen, present head of the Jewish Theological Seminary, stressed the need for spreading cultural and spiritual life in the Diaspora, citing an "autonomous and self-sustaining Diaspora tradition on American soil" (World Jewish Congress, *Press Survey*, no. 3392, March 23, 1972). According to American Jewish Congress president Rabbi Arthur Hertzberg, himself a member of the Jewish Agency Executive, it was unfortunate that fund-raising for Israel

had come to dominate the activities of the Jewish community, to the neglect of Judaism, which assures continuation of Jewish life (World Jewish Congress, *Press Survey*, no. 3392, March 23, 1972). Rabbi Judah Nadich, president of the Conservative Rabbinical Assembly of the U.S., expressed concern that the immigration of young American Jews to Israel would remove an important element from the American scene and would endanger the future of Jewish leadership. He said that the time had come to devote more efforts to strengthening American Jewry (*The Jerusalem Post*, November 24, 1972, p. 3).

8. It is a matter of historical curiosity that Emanuel Neumann, leader of the Zionist Organization of America, also expressed concern on this point, although for reasons different from those of other critics. Neumann argued that there must be a clear political separation between Israel and the Diaspora. It is in Israel's own self-interest, he maintained, that it determine its own policies and orientation. Israel should consider, he said, "the position and welfare of Jews elsewhere," but must act "without constraint or the exercise of undue influence on the part of the Diaspora" (Emanuel Neumann, "The Turning Point," address to the Z.O.A., Pittsburgh, July 3, 1948, p. 6). Neumann assumed, as a matter of course at that time, that the World Zionist Organization would fulfill some kind of political role. He argued, therefore, that Israeli influence must be removed from that organization lest the Diaspora exercise undue influence on Israel, or, one suspects, as he really feared, that Diaspora Jews would be guilty of "dual allegiance." He argued that

the World Zionist Organization must be so reconstructed as to remove the temptation and the possibility of involving the Diaspora unduly in the affairs of Israel, or conversely of involving Israel unduly in the affairs of the Diaspora. Both should have complete autonomy and freedom of action in their respective spheres. This must lead to the conclusion that the Zionist movement should henceforth become a purely Diaspora organization. In relation to the Jewish State, it would bear the character of a world-wide association of friends of Israel, which would make its maximum contribution by being left free to organize its own affairs in the manner it deems best. ("The Turning Point," p. 9)

Two months later, at the World Zionist Organisation General Council meetings, the American Zionists demanded the resignation of Israeli Government officials from the Zionist Executive, arguing that otherwise the non-Israeli members of the Executive were susceptible to charges of dual loyalty. In addition, Neumann demanded an independent role for the New York Jewish Agency (the Zionist Executive had been divided into a New York and a Jerusalem office) in performance of such functions as information and organization, tourism, and attracting of private investment (*Ha'Olam*, September 9, 1948, p. 682).

9. *The Jerusalem Post*, November 24, 1972, p. 3. Among those

cited were Rabbi David Polish, president of the Association of
American Reform Rabbis, who said that American Jews were concerned about problems of morality in Israeli society and wanted to
express criticism of Israeli internal affairs. Rabbi Louis Bernstein,
president of the Association of Orthodox Rabbis in the U.S., said
that in order for American Jews to completely identify with Israel,
there must be mutual criticism. See also Philip Klutznick, "Beyn
Yisrael La'Tfutzot," *Gesher* 18 (December 1972): 22.

    10. Klutznick, "Beyn Yisrael . . . ," p. 22.

    11. Jacob Neusner, "American Jewry and the State of Israel:
Toward a Mature Relationship," *Jewish Advocate,* March 23, 1972.

    12. The clearest presentation of his views was his reply to Prinz
at the World Jewish Congress executive meetings in July 1973. I am
grateful to Dr. Natan Lerner for providing me with both the transcript of his statement and a corrected copy of that speech, which
could not have been made by Pincus more than a week or two before
he died.

    13. In leaping from Ben-Gurion's stress on "ingathering the
exiles" to "serving the Jewish people," there is at least a superficial
distortion of Ben-Gurion's views, but not, I believe, a basic untruth.
Ben-Gurion and his associates, who stressed the value of "ingathering
the exiles," were also defining "service to the Jewish people." In view
of their own conception of Zionism and galut, there was simply no
other possiblity for real service.

    14. *Ha'Aretz,* January 18, 1973, p. 12.

Bibliography

Archives and Organization Files
American Jewish Committee Files—New York
Beit Meir Archives—Jerusalem
Rabbinical Council of America Files—New York
Religious Zionist Archives—New York
Union of Orthodox Jewish Communities of America Files—New York
Central Zionist Archives—Jerusalem

Public Documents

COJO Report. The Plenary Session of World Conference of Jewish Organizations (mimeo), July 1971.

Din V'Khesbon Shel Vaadat Ha'Khakira B'Inyenei Ha'Khinuch B'Makhanot Ha'Olim. Jerusalem: n.p., May 9, 1950.

Divrei HaKnesset.

Ha'Merkaz Ha'Olami Shel Mizrachi. *Din V'Kheshbon 1949–1955.* Jerusalem: Ha'Merkaz Ha'Olami, 1955.

The Jewish Agency for Israel. *Annual Assembly* (1973). The Technical Advisory Committee on Housing of the Ministry of Housing and the Jewish Agency Committee on Housing, "A Progress Report." "Higher Education."

The Jewish Agency Board of Governors (August 1972). "Jewish

Agency Committee on Housing." Jerusalem: Jewish Agency, 1972.

The Jewish Agency. *Proceedings of the Founding Assembly of the Reconstituted Jewish Agency.* Jerusalem: Jewish Agency, 1971.

Rabbinical Assembly of America. *Proceedings of the Rabbinical Assembly, 1964.* New York: Rabbinical Assembly of America, 1964.

Royal Commission on Alien Immigration. *Minutes of Evidence taken before the Royal Commission on Alien Immigration.* London: Wyman and Sons, 1903.

Sessions of the Zionist General Council, April 19–25, 1950. Jerusalem: The Zionist Executive, 1950.

Sessions of the Zionist General Council, May 7–15, 1952. Jerusalem: Jewish Agency, n.d.

Session of the Zionist General Council, July 21–29, 1954. Jerusalem: Organization Department of the Zionist Executive, n.d.

Session of the Zionist General Council, August 23–31, 1955. Jerusalem: Organization Department of the Zionist Executive, n.d.

Session of the Zionist General Council, January 8–15, 1967. Jerusalem: Organization Department of the Zionist Executive, 1967.

Small Zionist General Council. *Summary of the Proceedings, December 11–12, 1956.* Jerusalem: World Zionist Organization, 1957.

South African Jewish Board of Deputies. *Report: September, 1960–August, 1962.* Johannesburg: South African Jewish Board of Deputies, 1962.

Twenty-Third World Zionist Congress (1951). Stenographic Report (Hebrew). Jerusalem: Zionist Executive, 1951.

The Twenty-Fourth Zionist Congress April 24–May 7, 1956. Jerusalem: The World Zionist Organization, 1957.

World Jewish Congress. *Record of the Evening Session, July 1, 1973.*

Newspapers and Magazines
The following newspapers and magazines were utilized selectively:

Davar

Der Tog-Morgan Journal

The Economist

Forward

Ha'Aretz

Hador

Ha'Olam

Ha'Tzofe

Herald Tribune

Jerusalem Post

Jewish Chronicle

Jewish Observer and Middle East Review

Jewish Press

Maariv

Molad

Newsweek

New York Times

Panim El Panim

Press Survey, published by the World Jewish Congress

Books and Articles

Ahad Ha'am, *Al Parashat Derakhim*, vol. II. Tel-Aviv: Dvir, 1952.

American Jewish Committee. *In Vigilant Brotherhood*. New York: Institute of Human Relations, n.d.

American Jewish Committee Library of Jewish Information. *The Jewish Agency for Palestine*. New York: American Jewish Committee (mimeo), 1957.

Avni, Chaim. *Yahadut Argentina*. Jerusalem: Hebrew University, Institute of Contemporary Jewry, 1972.

Balabkins, Nicholas. *West German Reparations to Israel.* New Brunswick, N.J.: Rutgers University Press, 1971.

Barkai, Avraham. "Ha'Mashkia Mi'Khul." *Al Ha'Mishmar* (weekly supplement), August 8, 1972.

Bar Zohar, Michael. *The Armed Prophet: A Biography of Ben-Gurion.* London: Arthus Barker, 1967.

Bein, Alex. *Theodore Herzl.* Translated by Maurice Samuel. Philadelphia: Jewish Publication Society, 1941.

Ben Asher, A. A. *Yachasei Khutz.* Tel-Aviv: Ayanot, 1957.

Ben-Gurion, David. *Ba'Marakha,* vol. I. Tel-Aviv: Am Oved, 1947.

————. "The Call of Spirit in Israel." State of Israel, *Government Year Book 5712* (1951–1952).

————. *Khazon V'Derekh,* vol. I. Tel-Aviv: The Workers Party of Israel, 1951.

————. "Israel and the Diaspora." State of Israel, *Israel Government Year Book 1957.*

————. "Israel's Security and Her International Position." State of Israel, *Israel Government Year Book 5720* (1959–1960).

————. *M'dinat Yisrael Ha'Mkhudeshet.* Tel-Aviv: Am Oved, 1969.

————. "M'dinat Yisrael V'Atido shel Ha'am." *Khazot* 4 (1958).

————. *Netzakh Yisrael.* Tel–Aviv: Ayanot, 1964.

Bensimon-Donat, Doris. "North-African Jews in France: Their Attitudes to Israel." *Dispersion and Unity* 10 (Winter 1970).

Brecher, Michael. *The Foreign Policy System of Israel.* London: Oxford University Press, 1972.

Brecher, Michael. "Images, Process and Feedback in Foreign Policy: Israel's Decisions on German Reparations." *American Political Science Review* 67 (March 1973).

Castro, S. "Current Status of European Jewry." Address to the International Conference of Jewish Communal Services, Amsterdam, August 17, 1972. Paris: European Council of Jewish Community Services, 1972.

Chinitz, Zelig. "Reconstitution of the Jewish Agency." *Jewish Frontier* 37 (December 1970).

Cohen, Naomi W. *Not Free to Desist: The American Jewish Committee 1906–1960.* Philadelphia: Jewish Publication Society, 1972.

Dubb, Allie. "The South African Jewish Student and His Jewishness." *Jewish Affairs* 25 (July 1970).

Dubnow, Simon. *Nationalism and History.* Cleveland: Meridian Books, The World Publishing Co., 1958.

Easton, David. *The Political System.* New York: Alfred A. Knopf, 1953.

Engel, Irving. "Report of the Executive Committee: Highlights of 1949." *American Jewish Year Book 1951,* edited by Morris Fine. Philadelphia: Jewish Publication Society, 1951.

Eytan, David. *The First Ten Years: Diplomatic History of Israel.* New York: Simon and Schuster, 1958.

Ferber, Pinchas, ed. *L'Parashat Ha'Kashrut B'Oniyat Ha'Degel Ha'Yisraelit Shalom.* Tel-Aviv: Information Department of the NRP, 1964.

Fine, Morris, ed. *American Jewish Year Book 1952.* Philadelphia: Jewish Publication Society, 1952.

Fine, Morris, and Himmelfarb, Milton, eds. *American Jewish Year Book 1971.* Philadelphia: Jewish Publication Society, 1971.

Foreign Office. *Kinus Tzirey Yisrael, July 17–23, 1950.* Jerusalem: Foreign Office (mimeo), 1950.

Frankel, William. "The State of World Jewry." Address to the Annual Meeting of the American Jewish Committee, Waldorf Astoria, New York, May 16, 1971.

Gilboa, Joshua. "Tkufat Gromyko V'Shikhtuva." *Gesher* 38 (Winter 1968).

Gold, Bertram. "Who Speaks for the Jews?" Text of an address delivered to the 1972 annual American Jewish Committee meeting in New York City.

Gottlieb, Moshe. "The Anti-Nazi Boycott Movement in the American Jewish Community, 1933-1941." Brandeis University, doctoral dissertation, 1967.

Halevi, Nadav, and Klinov-Malul, Ruth. *The Economic Development of Israel.* New York: Praeger, 1968.

Halperin, Samuel. "Zionist Counterpropaganda: The Case of the American Council for Judaism." *Southwestern Social Science Quarterly* 41 (March 1961).

Halpern, Ben. *The Idea of the Jewish State.* Cambridge, Mass.: Harvard University Press, 1961.

Hertzberg, Arthur. *The Zionist Idea.* Garden City, N.Y.: Doubleday and Co., 1959.

Herzl, Binyamin, *Bifnei Am V'olam: Zionist Speeches and Articles.* Jerusalem: The Zionist Library, 1961.

Himmelfarb, Milton. "McGovern and the Jews." *Commentary* 54 (September 1972).

Hirsch, Richard G. "Ordination address delivered at the Hebrew Union College-Jewish Institute of Religion." Cincinnati, Ohio (mimeo), June 3, 1972.

Ilam, Yigal. *Mavo L'Historia Tzionit Akheret.* Tel-Aviv: Lewin-Epstein, 1972.

Israel Government Tourist Corporation. *Tourist Survey.* Annual Report published by the Israel Government Tourist Corporation.

Israel Information Services. *Background Note,* "Post Mortem Examinations in Israel." Consulate General of Israel, New York City, June 1969.

Jewish Community Relations Council of San Francisco. "The Four Jewish Issue Publics—First Report." Jewish Community Relations Council of San Francisco (mimeo), August 1970.

Katzew, Henry. "Jews in the Land of Apartheid." *Midstream* 8 (December 1962).

Kitvei Berl Katznelson. Tel-Aviv: The Workers Party of Israel, 1946.

Klutznick, Philip. "Beyn Yisrael La'Tfutzot." *Gesher* 18 (December 1972).

Kolatt, Israel. "Changing Relations Between Israel and the Diaspora." *Study Circle on Diaspora Jewry,* Series 6-7. Jerusalem: The Institute of Contemporary Jewry, The Hebrew University, 1968–69.

Kolatt, Israel. "Theories on Israel Nationalism." *Dispersion and Unity* 7 (Winter 1967).

Kreitman, Benjamin. "Who Is A Jew?" *Conservative Judaism* 24 (Summer 1970).

Krivine, David. "The Jewish Partnership in Israel's Industry." *The Jerusalem Post* "Weekend Magazine" (October 24, 1969).

Laquer, Walter. *A History of Zionism.* London: Weidenfeld and Nicolson, 1972.

Liebman, Charles S. *The Ambivalent American Jew: Politics, Religion and Family in American Jewish Life.* Philadelphia: Jewish Publication Society, 1973.

———. "American Students in Israel and Israel-Diaspora Relations." *Unity and Dispersion* 12 (1971).

———. "Orthodoxy in American Jewish Life." *American Jewish Year Book 1965,* Morris Fine and Milton Himmelfarb, eds. Philadelphia: Jewish Publication Society, 1965.

———. "Reconstructionism in American Jewish Life." *American Jewish Year Book 1970,* Morris Fine and Milton Himmelfarb, eds. Philadelphia: Jewish Publication Society, 1970.

———. "Who is Jewish in Israel?" *The American Zionist* 61 (December 1970).

Liebman, Yeshayahu (Charles). "The Role of Israel in the Ideology of American Jewry." *Unity and Dispersion* 10 (Winter 1970).

Lorch, Natanel. *Ha'Nahar Halokhesh: Al Peru V'Yisrael.* Tel-Aviv: Ministry of Defense, 1969.

Mandel, Arnold. "The Jews in Western Europe Today." *American Jewish Year Book 1967,* Morris Fine and Milton Himmelfarb, eds. Philadelphia: Jewish Publication Society, 1967.

Ministry of Finance. "Pirut Ha'Hachnasot MiMosdot V'Irgunim" (mimeo).

Neumann, Emanuel. "The Turning Point." Address to the Z.O.A., Pittsburgh, July 3, 1948.

Neusner, Jacob. "American Jewry and the State of Israel: Toward a Mature Relationship." *Jewish Advocate,* March 23, 1972.

Patai, Raphael, ed. *The Complete Diaries of Theodor Herzl.* Translated by Harry Zohn, vol. 4. New York: The Herzl Press, 1960.

Pincus, Louis. *The Jewish Agency in Action: A Report to the Members of the Jewish Agency Assembly.* Jerusalem: Jewish Agency, 1973.

Rafael, Yitzchak. "Baayat Nitukhei Metim." *Givilin* 25 (September 1966).

Rubinstein, Aryeh. "German Reparations In Retrospect." *Midstream* 8 (Winter 1962).

Safran, Nadav. *The U.S. and Israel.* Cambridge, Mass.: Harvard University Press, 1963.

Samuel, Maurice. "The Sundering of Israel and American Jewry." *Commentary* 16 (September 1953).

Samuel, Maurice. "Why Israel Misunderstands American Jewry." *Commentary* 16 (October 1953).

Schechtman, Joseph B. "The Frozen Stampede." *Midstream* (Summer 1960).

Schweid, Eliezer. *Israel At the Crossroads.* Philadelphia: Jewish Publication Society, 1973.

Sharett, Moshe. "Ha'Medina Ha'Yehudit Vha'Am Ha'Yehudi," n.d., reprinted in *Am Yisrael U'Tfutzotav* 7. Pamphlet series published by the Office of Information of the World Zionist Organization, Jerusalem, 1970.

Shinar, P. Eliezer. *B'Ol Korakh V'Rigashot.* Tel-Aviv: Schocken Publishing House, 1967.

Shub, Louis. "The Diaspora Factor in Israel's Foreign Policy." *Judaism* 15 (Summer 1966).

Sklare, Marshall, and Greenblum, Joseph. *Jewish Identity on the Suburban Frontier*. New York: Basic Books, 1967.

Stock, Ernest. *Israel On the Road to Sinai*. Ithaca, N.Y.: Cornell University Press, 1967.

Stock, Ernest. "The Reconstitution of the Jewish Agency: A Political Analysis." *American Jewish Year Book 1972*, Morris Fine and Milton Himmelfarb, eds. Philadelphia: Jewish Publication Society, 1972.

Tsur, Yaacov. *Yoman Paris*. Tel-Aviv: Am Oved, 1968.

Wasserstein, Bernard. "Jewish Identification Among Students at Oxford." *The Jewish Journal of Sociology* 13 (December 1971).

Weizman, Chaim. *Trial and Error*. New York: Harper and Brothers, 1949.

Whartman, Eliezer. "Attitudes of American Rabbis on Zionism and Israel." *Jewish Social Studies* 19 (April 1955).

World Jewish Congress. *The Jewish Communities of the World*. 3d rev. ed, London: Institute of Jewish Affairs, World Jewish Congress, 1971.

World Jewish Congress. *Unity in Dispersion: A History of the World Jewish Congress*. New York: World Jewish Congress, 1948.

Yisraeli, David. "The Third Reich and the Transfer Agreement." *Journal of Contemporary History* 6, no. 2 (1971).

Index

Abramov, Zalman, 103
Adenauer, Konrad, 158, 272 n. 4
Adut, Ha', 223
Agudath Israel (Israeli); autopsy controversy, 75–82; education in immigrant camps controversy, 65, 69, 73; national service law controversy, 75–82; "Who is a Jew?" controversy, 100, 103, 265 n. 121. *See also* Religious Front
Agudath Israel of America (Agudah), 107; education in immigrant camps controversy, 63, 74; national service law controversy, 77–79, 256 n. 28, 257 n. 34
Agudath Israel of England, 77
Agudath Israel school system, 65
Agudath Israel Youth, 92, 262 n. 108
Ahad Ha'am, 33–34, 217–18
Algeria, 161
Aliyat Ha'Noar, 105
Allon, Yigal, 190
American Committee for Safeguarding Human Dignity, 91–94. *See also* Public Committee for Safeguarding Human Dignity
American Council for Judaism, 120–21, 204, 211
American Israel Public Affairs Committee, 214
American Jewish Committee, 43, 203, 206–11; Ben-Gurion-Blaustein exchange, 118–31; as critic of Israel, 93, 147–48, 160, 172–73, 237–38; status of WZO-JA, 132–47, 177–78
American Jewish Congress, 93, 111, 121, 206
American Joint Distribution Committee, 24–25
Anatomy and Pathology Law of 1953, 89–91, 96
Anglo-Jewish Association of England, 178
Anglo-Transjordan Treaty, 215
Anti-Semitism, 25, 119, 218
Apartheid. See South Africa, Union of
Aranne, Zalman, 127
L'Arche, 47
Argentina, 160, 273 n. 21
Association of Orthodox Jewish Scientists, 91–92